Song of the Stubborn One Thousand

SONG
OF THE
STUBBORN
ONE THOUSAND

The Watsonville Canning Strike, 1985–87

Peter Shapiro

Haymarket Books
Chicago, Illinois

In memory of my parents,
Sophie Mirviss and Phil Shapiro,
American-born children of immigrant families,
who passed along their passion for social justice

Published in 2016 by
Haymarket Books
P.O. Box 180165
Chicago, IL 60618
773-583-7884
www.haymarketbooks.org
info@haymarketbooks.org

ISBN: 978-1-60846-680-1

Trade distribution:
In the US, Consortium Book Sales and Distribution, www.cbsd.com
In Canada, Publishers Group Canada, www.pgcbooks.ca
In the UK, Turnaround Publisher Services, www.turnaround-uk.com
All other countries, Publishers Group Worldwide, www.pgw.com

This book was published with the generous support of Lannan Foundation
and Wallace Action Fund.

Cover design by John Yates. Cover image courtesy of *Unity*.

Printed in Canada by union labor.

Library of Congress Cataloging-in-Publication data is available.

10 8 6 5 4 2 1 3 5 7 9

Contents

Preface   ix

Introduction   1

Chapter 1: The Frozen Food Capital of the World   15

Chapter 2: The Biggest Union in the Country   27

Chapter 3: The Teamsters in Watsonville   41

Chapter 4: Local 912 at Bay   53

Chapter 5: The Strikers' Committee   71

Chapter 6: Exit the King   91

Chapter 7: The Shaw Settlement   107

Chapter 8: Enter the Teamsters   129

Chapter 9: Mort Console at Bay   151

Chapter 10: The Final Days   167

Epilogue   191

Bibliography   201

Notes   209

Index   229

Preface

I n May of 2007 I took a day off from my job delivering mail in Hillsboro, Oregon, to attend a plenary session of the Pacific Northwest Labor History Conference in Portland. The featured speaker was Joseph McCartin, who was at the time still working on *Collision Course*, his seminal book on the air traffic controllers' strike of 1981. The subject of McCartin's talk was a grim one: the virtual disappearance of the strike as an effective weapon in the arsenal of the US working class since the 1980s, when organized labor suffered a succession of catastrophic setbacks.

McCartin noted that an entire generation of workers has grown up with little or no conception of what it means to walk a picket line. He rattled off a litany of Reagan-era walkouts that ended not just in the union's defeat but in its outright decertification: strikers had either returned to work without union representation or had not returned to work at all, having been "permanently replaced" by strikebreakers.

After his presentation I approached him and told him I knew of one strike during that period that had the opposite outcome. I pointed out that it had been waged against an employer who tried the same strategy McCartin had spoken of in his talk—provoking a walkout and prolonging it until it was legally possible to decertify the union. I mentioned that the union itself was largely dysfunctional at the start of the strike but was revitalized in the course of it. I spoke of the strikers themselves, largely Mexican women with little or no prior strike experience, who showed an extraordinary capacity for self-organization. I told him how in the end the owner of the struck plant was forced to sell it in order to stay out of bankruptcy court, and a thousand strikers —not one of whom had crossed the picket line—signed a collective bargaining agreement with the new owner and returned triumphantly to work after eighteen months.

McCartin heard me out. When I was done he said simply, "You should write about it."

A year later, having retired from the Postal Service, I decided to take his advice. It took a little longer than I expected. The first two chapters came quickly enough, but not until I returned to the Bay Area after a twenty-year absence was I able to give the Watsonville Canning strike the attention it required and deserved. I was able to track down new interviewees and follow up on interviews I had done earlier. I spent long uninterrupted hours at the Labor Archives and Research Center at San Francisco State University, which houses not only Frank Bardacke's papers on the strike but also the voluminous and as yet uncatalogued archives of Teamsters Local 70. The latter includes an entire box of material on Watsonville that proved extraordinarily valuable, since the Teamsters' role in the strike was as complicated as it was critical.

I hope the results justify the effort. For all its drama, there has been remarkably little written about the Watsonville Canning strike, and no comprehensive account of it. Kim Moody's influential book *An Injury to All* is dedicated in part to the Watsonville strikers but devotes only a few pages to the strike itself. A handful of monographs have focused on one or another aspect of the strike that reflect the authors' particular scholarly concerns, but none has attempted a full overview.

Several months after the strike ended, Frank Bardacke, a longtime left activist deeply involved in the Watsonville strike support work, published a thoughtful discussion of the struggle in the Trotskyist journal *Against the Current*. His essay is worth reading, but it is a work of political analysis rather than narrative history. Jon Silver's documentary film *Watsonville on Strike*, which has been broadcast several times on public television and is therefore probably the most widely circulated account of the strike, provides a vivid visual record. I watched it repeatedly in researching this book and found it more than helpful. But an hour-long film, however skillfully made, cannot do full justice to such a complex story, and I have some interpretive differences with Silver (and a few factual ones as well) that will be apparent to anyone who has seen the movie and reads this book.

Before going further, I should disclose my own personal connection to the material. Frank Bardacke's essay includes a discussion of the left activists who were involved with the strike; he describes them as belonging to "two distinct camps." As it happens, Frank was in one camp and I was in the other. Throughout the 1980s I served as labor editor of *Unity*, published by the now-defunct League of Revolutionary Struggle. The paper sought to persuade its readers that an effective movement for working-class political power was not only necessary but also possible. As the person responsible for its labor coverage, I often found myself hard-pressed to find encouraging things to say about what sometimes seemed like a continuing series of disasters.

The Watsonville strike was another story. *Unity* was in good position to cover it, since the League had a history of work in the California canneries, played an active role in the strike, and was able to develop strong relationships with many strikers. More fundamentally, the strike was a badly needed antidote to the confusion and despair that threatened to overwhelm so many union activists in that difficult time. It showed that working people were still capable of winning major victories in the face of the most daunting odds; it held out the hope of better outcomes for a besieged labor movement. The struggle left me both moved and inspired.

I was in Watsonville for one of the big support rallies when Frank Bardacke came up to me on the picket line and struck up a conversation. He began by telling me that a certain League activist who had become prominent in the strike was "one of the best organizers I've ever seen"; he then proceeded to explain to me everything he thought the League was doing wrong.

Frank and I continued this conversation when I interviewed him for this book, and, while I found it enjoyable and often thought-provoking, I have not attempted to use the book to settle our differences. To do so at this late date would be counterproductive, since we have no way of knowing for sure how the course of events would have been altered if certain people had done certain things differently.

Counterfactual accounts of historical events can make for good fiction: both Philip Roth and Philip K. Dick have written absorbing novels that try to imagine what life would be like if the United States had succumbed to fascism instead of resisting it successfully on the battlefield.

But theirs are works of the imagination, not history, and as Eric Hobsbawm has written, "It is not the historian's task to speculate on what might have been. His duty is to show what happened and why."[1] Mindful of Hobsbawm's words, I have tried to keep my editorializing to a minimum, and have resisted the temptation to second-guess those who lived through the events under discussion. Not only would it be presumptuous of me to second-guess them, it would also make it that much harder for me to comprehend their motivations and actions.

At one point I was interviewing Manuel Díaz, a League activist who did important work developing rank-and-file leadership early in the strike. Manuel still talks about the experience with insight and eloquence. When I mentioned the political differences referred to in Frank Bardacke's essay, he gave me a steady look and said quietly, "We all should have done better."

Joe Fahey, who also figures prominently in this story, made essentially the same point in a different way. More than once, he stressed that everybody who participated in the strike or the support work brought something positive to the table and that the strike's success was a happy confluence of contributions on the part of different forces, often at odds with one another but objectively working toward the same end. He hoped that my work would bring this out in a way that was not always obvious while the strike was happening. I am grateful to both him and Manuel for reminding me of my responsibilities.

I have many other people to thank.

No one who undertakes a project of this kind can avoid incurring a huge debt to research librarians. I am grateful to Catherine Powell at the San Francisco State archives, Lillian Castillo-Speed at the Chicano Studies Library at University of California–Berkeley, Terrence Huwe at UC Berkeley's Institute for Labor and Economic Research, and Pat Johns, curator of the Agricultural History Project at the Santa Cruz County fairgrounds outside Watsonville.

I was also fortunate to be given access to papers that are not available to the general public. Chuck Mack and Alex Ybarrolaza made sure I saw the relevant material in the files of Teamsters Joint Council 7; it proved indispensible to my research. Duane Beeson, attorney for Joint Council 7, retrieved the strike-related documents from his firm's files and arranged for them to be copied and mailed to me. Michael Johnston,

Manuel Díaz, and especially Steve Morozumi all shared their personal files. Eddie Wong shot some riveting video footage for a documentary film that was never completed; he gave me the opportunity to watch it, and it gave my account of the strike's dramatic last days a degree of immediacy and vividness that would not otherwise have been possible.

The national media may have ignored the Watsonville Canning strike, but there was some excellent coverage by local reporters, including Elizabeth Schilling of the *Watsonville Register-Pajaronian*, Donald Miller of the *Santa Cruz Sentinel*, and especially Bob Johnson, a free-lancer whose articles frequently appeared in the *San Jose Mercury News*. I have made extensive use of their work.

I owe a special debt to two of my oldest and closest friends, Tom Ryan and Fay Wong. I met them both one warm summer evening in 1973, in a railroad flat in San Francisco's Mission District, where the Liberation School Collective (to which I belonged) was getting acquainted with its newest recruits. Tom and I wound up teaching a course on labor history together; Fay taught a class on the Chinese revolution. Three years later Fay and I were married, and if I have done anything worthwhile with my life since then, she gets a lion's share of the credit. Like me, she was trained as a historian but forsook academia for revolutionary politics; unlike me, she eventually returned to school and finished her degree. When I edited my union paper in Portland, I made a point of not submitting any of my articles for publication until I had run them by her. I have followed the same practice here. One blessing of being married to Fay is having been rescued more than once from making a horse's ass of myself in print.

As for Tom, he was responsible for overseeing the League's labor work at the same time I was working as *Unity*'s labor editor. During the Watsonville Canning strike he and I spent a lot of time talking about the strike, trying to make some sense out of what was happening. We are still at it today, but with the greater humility and wisdom that only hindsight can bring. Tom encouraged me to write this book and was my go-to guy whenever the challenge of getting a handle on the material threatened to overwhelm me.

Among the friends, colleagues, and fellow activists who read the manuscript and offered criticisms, suggestions, and encouragement were Anatole Anton, David Bacon, Steve Early, Larry Hendel,

Barbara Jaquish, Pam Tau Lee, Mark Prudowsky, and Susan Weiss. I did not always take their advice, so they cannot be held responsible for my mistakes. I do believe the manuscript is better for their input, and for that I am deeply grateful. Caroline Luft and Rachel Cohen of Haymarket Books deserve a shout-out as well. Rachel skillfully proofread the manuscript. Caroline was a careful, conscientious, and supportive editor who, besides teaching me the difference between "which" and "that" (something I should have learned long ago), had a true feeling for what I was trying to say, and made sure I said it as clearly and accurately as possible.

Of all those I interviewed for this book, I am most indebted to Gloria Betancourt. Not only did she speak to me at length, she also took me around town on my trips to Watsonville, introducing me to her fellow strikers and translating patiently and skillfully through some long and complicated interviews. Like most people who heard her speak during the strike, I was impressed at that time by her charisma and her uncanny combination of humility and toughness. Since undertaking this project I have come to appreciate even more her remarkable intelligence and political acuity. I wish the Teamsters had made more use of her talents.

Telling the story of people who don't leave much of a paper trail means relying more on their spoken recollections. Scholars call it oral history. In the right hands—those of Studs Terkel, say, or Isabel Wilkerson, whose *Warmth of Other Suns* shows how much can be done with told material—it can be both powerful and illuminating. But it can be problematic, too. With some justice, it has been called a gift horse that should be looked in the mouth.

Memory is by its very nature self-serving. This is not just because people want to be treated kindly by posterity. On a deeper level, their memories reflect what matters to them emotionally. This can be helpful in understanding the deeper meanings of an individual life. It can be frustrating when trying to piece together a coherent narrative involving hundreds of lives. Often people's stories conflicted, and I had to reconcile them as best I could.

However, multiple accounts of the same event allow for more than simple fact-checking. They can provide insight into the different ways the event can be interpreted, depending on who your sources are and which aspects of the story touched them most deeply. More important, you come to know and better understand them as individuals, something that is often far more valuable than any specific facts they are able to recall. The folks I talked to were coming from different places, but I always came away with a better sense of who they were and why they had acted the way they did. Invariably, the experience was enriching and enjoyable as well as enlightening.

Some gave me detailed recollections. Others were able to speak only in the most general terms. Some were eager to share their memories and took obvious pleasure in talking about what was, after all, a major event in their lives. Others found it hard even to think about the strike, let alone discuss it. "I'm trying to put that period of my life behind me," one striker told me. Hearing such things reminded me that, however strong the temptation to view the Watsonville Canning strike in heroic terms, it was a difficult and painful experience for many who lived it.

To all those who did share what they remembered, I owe a debt that goes beyond simple gratitude. They trusted me to get it right. I hope I have not let them down.

Introduction

Pinto Lake sits on the northeast edge of Watsonville, California, in one of the nation's most fertile and productive farming regions. At one end of the lake is a public park, with a paved footpath leading past soccer fields and a children's playground down to the water's edge. Here a plank walkway has been constructed for observing waterfowl. As night approaches, a shroud of mist rises from the water.

Just before the footpath reaches the shoreline is a forested glen at the bottom of a slope. It has been converted into a small amphitheater, with a fenced-off tree where one would expect to find the stage. The area around the fence has been decorated with votive candles, red-green-and-white banners, and a large Mexican flag. The fence itself is adorned with photos—studio portraits, pictures of babies and children, handwritten notes giving thanks for the recovery of an ailing infant or praying for the soul of a departed loved one.

A nearby plaque explains: "This is a place of prayer and pilgrimage. It is reported that the Virgin Mary appeared here on June 17, 1992, to Anita Contreras, a mother seeking divine help. Some see an image of the Virgin of Guadalupe on the tree opposite you." And, indeed, the tree behind the fence does have a section of discolored bark, and, with a little imagination, it is not hard to divine in its outline a shadowy impression of the protector of Mexico's toiling masses, whose image inspired Zapata's army.

Five years before the Virgin Mary appeared to her at Pinto Lake, Anita Contreras herself appeared in a front-page photograph in the March 11, 1987, edition of the *Watsonville Register-Pajaronian*. With her in the photograph are a group of women, one of whom holds aloft a picture of the Virgin of Guadalupe. The women are marching on

1

their knees, painstakingly making their way to St. Patrick's Church in downtown Watsonville from the gates of the frozen food plant, half a mile away, where they have been on strike for the past eighteen months.

In Mexico the faithful commonly use such processions to appeal for divine intervention. With the fate of a strike hanging in the balance, Anita Contreras persuaded her *compañeras* to join her in asking God for a just settlement.

Their prayers were answered. Within twenty-four hours, one thousand strikers at the largest employer in a town known as "the frozen food capital of the world" voted triumphantly to accept a new contract and return to work. Over the past year and a half they had weathered draconian court injunctions, police violence, hunger, evictions, and broken marriages. They had transformed their moribund local union, driven the plant's owner to the brink of bankruptcy, and held firm when the plant was bought out by a local grower, telling him, "You buy the plant, you buy the strike." Throughout the struggle, not one striker crossed the picket line.

The Watsonville Canning strikers sometimes referred to themselves as "stubborn Mexican women." (Actually, about 15 percent of them were men.) In many ways Anita Contreras was typical of the strikers. Born and raised in a village in the state of Michoacan in southwest Mexico, she had migrated to Watsonville in the early 1970s, the first of many in her family to do so. She picked apples and grapes and worked the strawberry fields in the nearby Salinas Valley before hiring on at Watsonville Canning. During the strike, unable to get by on her $55-a-week strike benefits from the Teamsters union, she would return to the fields, but she disliked farm labor and preferred factory work. Like many strikers, she was a single mother, opting to raise her children alone rather than remain with an abusive husband.[1]

If there was one thing that set her apart from her fellow strikers, it was the intensity of her religious conviction. Her life had never been easy; she saw the privations of the strike as merely the latest in a series of hardships that could be endured if one had enough faith. Wherever she had worked, overbearing supervisors quickly learned that she did not hesitate to speak truth to power. In meetings where strike strategy was discussed and some particularly difficult or risky course of action was under consideration, she would remind her fellow strikers that God was just and would stand behind them.[2]

When the Watsonville Canning strikers first walked off the job in September 1985, a cynic might have concluded that they had little else going for them. Almost everywhere one looked, unions were in headlong retreat. Union membership in the United States had fallen off by 2.2 million in the span of just four years. Strikes by workers at Phelps-Dodge, International Paper, and Greyhound, to name just a few, ended not simply in defeat but in outright decertification of the union. A wave of plant closings hit the industrial Midwest and decimated unions like the United Steelworkers and United Auto Workers, which had served for nearly a generation as major power centers for organized labor.

Even before Ronald Reagan earned notoriety by breaking the air traffic controllers' strike and busting their union in 1981, the Carter administration had presided over the deregulation of the trucking industry, gutting the national Master Freight Agreement, which had made the Teamsters the largest and most powerful union in the country. "In industry after industry," wrote a contemporary analyst,

> the hard-won wage "patterns" that guaranteed contractual uniformity and preserved effective solidarity . . . are being destroyed, their place taken by a savage new wage-cutting competition. Within firms, multi-tier wage concessions, which allow employers to pay up to fifty percent less to new hires, are eroding inter-generational solidarity, ensuring . . . that older workers are vulnerable to replacement to exactly the extent that younger workers are made more exploitable. Meanwhile, on picket lines, workers . . . are confronted, for the first time since the 1930s, with scabs, billy clubs, and the National Guard . . .
>
> Corporations are now breaking unions and "turning back the clock" on a scale not witnessed since the [employer] offensive of the early 1920s.[3]

Labor activists and sympathetic scholars struggled to understand what was happening and to craft a strategic response. No attempt was more influential than *The Deindustrialization of America*, a pioneering study by Barry Bluestone and Bennett Harrison that became required reading for activists battling plant shutdowns across the country. Bluestone and Harrison believed that increased capital mobility, made possible by sophisticated new technology, had "shifted the fulcrum of bargaining power in favor of capital to an unprecedented degree." They painted a chilling picture of unrestrained corporate power with global reach:

> The textile conglomerate that moved to North Carolina could now also operate in South Korea or Latin America, its managers able to control the looms in all these locations by buttons on a computer console at its central headquarters in New York. At their beck and call . . . computers could keep instantaneous track of every spindle, every loom, every worker. From its world headquarters in Dearborn, Michigan, a manager at Ford could adjust the speed of the assembly line in Australia or change the shape of a hood ornament in Germany.[4]

The Bluestone-Harrison study was originally commissioned by the Progressive Alliance, a labor–community coalition spearheaded by the United Auto Workers (UAW). As such, it tended to focus on the big manufacturing industries, and its programmatic suggestions emphasized public policy measures that would restrain the flight of US capital overseas, make employers bear at least some of the cost of plant closures, and help redress the growing power imbalance between labor and management.[5] Responding to union activists who sometimes spoke as if the crisis could be mitigated if only union leaders would fight harder, Bluestone remarked that "the union, no matter how militant its stance, has little power to tame the global marketplace or for that matter rein in the multinational firm that moves its operation abroad or outsources its production to avoid the union."[6]

A widespread assumption, implicit in the analysis advanced by Bluestone and Harrison, is that global migration of capital and an increasingly competitive world market in the 1970s marked the end of a quarter-century modus vivendi between labor and capital that dated from the conclusion of World War II. Labor historian Nelson Lichtenstein has challenged this assumption, calling the notion of a postwar labor–management accord "suspect" and maintaining that it was precisely during that period that the seeds of future union decline were sown.

His analysis is buttressed by several arguments. First, he points out that while "real wages doubled in the twenty years after 1947 . . . strikes were also ten times more prevalent than in the years after 1980." While they may have "disappeared from our social imagination . . . such work stoppages demonstrated the extent to which both capital and labor felt aggrieved by the postwar labor-relations settlement. There was a continual testing of boundaries, a repeated probing for weaknesses in the adversary's organizational armor."[7] Second, he suggests that the menace posed to unions by capital flight, which figures so prominently in *The Deindustrialization of America*, did not begin with the heightened international competition of the 1970s. Lichtenstein traces it back to Operation Dixie, organized labor's unsuccessful attempt to penetrate the nonunion South in 1947. Its failure paved the way for large corporations like General Electric to move production below the Mason–Dixon line to get away from union contracts. It also fostered a bunker mentality in union leaders, who found it easier to hold on to what they had than to incur the considerable risks of organizing new constituencies.

Lichtenstein characterizes the postwar accord as having been imposed upon organized labor "in an era of its political retreat and internal division. At best it was a limited and unstable truce, largely confined to a well-defined set of regions and industries." Over time, it served to make unions insular and politically isolated. They relied on inadequate (and increasingly restrictive) federal labor laws, rather than strong shop-floor organization, to assure their legitimacy. As for the gains they did win, "White male workers in stable firms were the main beneficiaries."[8] The consequences would haunt the labor movement as the postwar boom began winding down and the US economy grew increasingly unstable.

However one views the postwar accord, there can be little dispute that unions—and working people generally—faced a much harsher economic and political climate once it was over. The air traffic controllers' strike is usually cited as a watershed; it put organized labor on notice that the federal government could no longer be expected to uphold the collective bargaining rights enshrined in the National Labor Relations Act (NLRA). But the real turning point probably came sooner, in 1973, when the Nixon administration abandoned the World War II–era policy of allowing the US dollar to serve as the medium of international exchange. Henceforth, the dollar's value would be allowed to "float" on the world currency market. Nixon's decision was forced on him by double-digit inflation, exacerbated by soaring oil prices and the runaway cost of the Vietnam War, but its long-term implications were clear. The United States had lost its predominant position in the global economy and would have a much harder time using the rest of the world as a safety valve for domestic class tensions. In the political arena, the new reality could be seen in the abandonment by government policy makers of the longstanding practice of stimulating the economy through government spending and an expanded social wage. In 1933 Franklin Roosevelt had vowed to pull the country out of the Great Depression by "restor[ing] our rich domestic market [and] raising its vast consuming capacity."[9] Usually referred to as "Keynesian," after the British prophet of demand-side economics, John Maynard Keynes, this approach eventually gave millions of Americans a chance to escape poverty through federal programs like the GI Bill and, later, Medicare. It also sanctioned unionism, since union contracts were expected to increase workers' purchasing power.

Keynesian policies were now denounced as wasteful and inefficient. They were said to inhibit business investment and undermine worker productivity, rendering the United States incapable of prospering in an increasingly competitive world market. Government safety net programs were cut back or dismantled, and federal statutes protecting unions were gutted or ignored.[10]

Changes in the economic environment were even more pervasive and far-reaching. In the early 1960s US manufacturing firms were profitable enough to finance most of their investments internally. But their rate of return on investment soon began a steady decline, and by 1980 even the biggest of them were largely dependent on bank loans for needed capital. Financial interests came to dominate their boards of directors, and their plants were increasingly used as cash cows to pay for speculative ventures and relentless diversification.[11]

US Steel provides a stark example. The nation's largest steelmaker had also been the first to sign a union contract in 1937, giving thousands of blue-collar workers a chance to earn a middle-class standard of living. By 1987, the same corporation had rechristened itself USX and become a poster child for the devastating impact of deindustrialization on workers and communities. It drastically reduced its domestic steelmaking operations, threw thousands onto the unemployment lines, and was now relying on a subsidiary, Marathon Oil, for the bulk of its income. "We're in business to make profits, not steel," its CEO said blandly.

Pundits called it "paper entrepreneurship." They noted that it was now a preferred business model in an economy whose biggest profits were generated through activity that did not actually produce anything and was, in fact, crippling the nation's industrial base.[12]

Its destructive impact did not stop at US borders. Industrializing countries desperate for investment capital found that Wall Street financiers were happy to provide it, at what proved to be usurious interest rates. Mexico was a case in point: the discovery of oil in the Gulf of Campeche induced the country's political leaders to embark on an ambitious program of state-funded industrialization, financed with huge loans from US banks that used anticipated oil earnings as collateral. But world oil prices tanked in the early 1980s, and the Mexican economy was thrown into chaos. The value of the peso dropped 80 percent in a single year. Prices doubled, real wages fell by more than 20 percent, and by the end of the decade a majority of Mexico's families were living in poverty. The bulk of the nation's wealth was being siphoned off to pay interest on its debts.[13]

Between 1982 and 1990, Kim Moody writes, Mexico had to reorient itself along "free market" lines to satisfy the demands of its creditors: "The transformation . . . amounted to a basic redesign of the Mexican economy. . . . Prices of many necessities were raised, wages frozen, the reprivatization of banks began, wholesale privatization of productive enterprises carried out . . . longstanding tariff and investment restrictions lifted or drastically reduced, and some 25 industries deregulated in the American manner."[14]

The resultant hardships imposed upon Mexico's working people helped provoke a new wave of immigration to the United States. It reinforced a growing trend whereby much essential work in the United States would be carried out by what was, in effect, a transnational labor force, uprooted by the convulsions of an increasingly globalized economy.

The wrenching changes faced by the US working class in the 1980s were the result of sweeping economic forces and long-term historical trends. But they were played out on a daily basis in the lives of ordinary working people, and ordinary working people bore the burden of responding to them. In the fall of 1985, the decade's travails came to a town of twenty-five thousand on the central California coast whose claim to be "frozen food capital of the world" was something more than mere civic boosterism.

Watsonville's eight frozen food plants and their five thousand workers produced the bulk of the industry's overall output. Watsonville Canning was the largest. Its owner, a thirty-seven-year-old law school dropout named Mort Console, had inherited the business from his father. His one thousand workers were members of Teamsters Local 912, which had negotiated collective bargaining agreements with the company for more than thirty years.

The workers of Watsonville Canning, overwhelmingly women, could be said to represent the advance guard of the immigration wave that would come on the heels of Mexico's 1982 debt crisis. Most of them were natives of Mexico who had migrated north in the previous two decades. Though many maintained close ties to their native land, they had been in Watsonville long enough to sink down roots in the community. But they remained politically powerless and largely invisible to the town's anglo political leadership.

They had a similar relationship with Local 912. Its longtime leader, Richard King, ran the local as a personal fiefdom. The contracts he negotiated on behalf of his members provided them with a living wage and modicum of economic security. Beyond that, they had no role to play in the life of their union. King collected their dues and largely ignored them.

It was, in a sense, Watsonville's version of the postwar accord, and it ended accordingly. Mort Console joined the growing ranks of private employers across the country who had concluded that unions were no longer something they had to tolerate, much less work with. He retained the services of a prominent San Francisco law firm that specialized in fostering "union-free environments" by exploiting the loopholes in federal labor law. Apparently following their advice, Console embraced a strategy of provoking a strike, hiring "permanent replacements," and operating with scab labor for twelve months, after which he could legally move to decertify the union.[15]

When his contract with Local 912 expired in July 1985, he demanded a 40 percent pay cut and drastically reduced health benefits. When the workers predictably rejected his terms and voted to walk out, he advertised for strikebreakers. He was confident that within a few weeks the strikers would be "begging for their jobs back"; if not, he believed he had the resources to run the plant without them for a year, at which point a decertification vote could be held. If they accepted his terms, he would still enjoy an enormous advantage over his competitors in an increasingly crowded frozen food market.

Console had every reason to be confident, and not just because so many other employers had implemented the strategy successfully.[16] He had secured an $18 million line of credit from Wells Fargo Bank, enough to sustain him through a protracted strike. In contrast, Local 912 was woefully unprepared. Richard King had always relied on good relations with the employers to deliver decent contracts; he was at a loss for a response to Console's sudden intransigence. Nor was he prepared to rally his troops for the battle ahead. Speaking no Spanish, he could not even communicate with most of them, and Local 912 members generally regarded him with mistrust.

The Watsonville Canning workers thus entered the fight of their lives in September 1985 with virtually no organization and no leadership. Across the country, unions with far more resources at their disposal were suffering disastrous defeats. Yet in the end, it was Console who would find himself in foreclosure, as the business his father had spent thirty years building was taken over by one of its creditors.

Years later, shortly before his death, Console was heard to complain that his lawyers had given him bad advice.[17] He was speaking with the benefit of hindsight: there was no way to predict that the strike would end the way it did. Even today, the workers' victory resists easy explanations. One cannot consider the struggle at Watsonville Canning for long without being struck by its complexity, by the wide range of forces involved and the often conflicting roles they played. There were contradictions among the competing frozen food companies, among the contending factions in the Teamsters union and at the different levels of the union hierarchy, and among the left forces that rallied to support the strikers. Watsonville's anglo political leadership faced an emerging challenge from the town's Latino majority. Local growers supplied Watsonville Canning with produce but had serious issues with its owner. Finally, there was Wells Fargo Bank, which bankrolled Console through the first year of the strike only to abandon him later.

What made the critical difference, however, were the strikers themselves—not just their tenacity and determination but their readiness, at crucial points, to take the initiative, assume responsibility, and make and carry out key strategic decisions.

Sympathetic left activists were a continuing presence during the strike, bringing contacts, material support, and the perspective that comes with an analysis of the broader social and class forces driving the struggle. The strikers were often receptive and appreciative of what these activists contributed but only so long as they respected the strikers' desire to make their own decisions and run their own strike.

Some fifty years earlier, John Steinbeck used a fictionalized version of Watsonville and the surrounding Pajaro Valley as the setting for his novel *In Dubious Battle*. The novel, a remarkably bleak account of a fruit pickers' strike, found a ready audience in a Depression-era reading public eager for gritty, "realistic" stories of class struggle. More than anything else, however, it expressed Steinbeck's highly personal view of human social behavior as driven by blind natural forces, in a world where the strong prey upon the weak and the weak fend for themselves as best they can.[18]

The predators in Steinbeck's story are the handful of large growers who dominate the local economy and have the civil authorities under their firm control. With a combination of superior organization and simple ruthlessness, they set about crushing their adversaries and imposing their will. Steinbeck's striking "fruit tramps" are portrayed sympathetically but without respect: though given to sporadic outbursts of violence, they are basically passive, inarticulate, driven by forces they only dimly understand. The Communist Party organizers who assume leadership of the strike are the sort of twisted idealists who, acting from the highest motives, resort to methods both brutal and highly manipulative, presumably because the realities of class warfare leave them with no alternative.

Steinbeck's anger at the social injustices he describes is apparent, and it occasionally gives *In Dubious Battle* a melodramatic tone. But it is a melodrama without heroes. Conscious human agency plays a very small role in his strike narrative.

To hear the Watsonville Canning workers tell it, theirs was likewise a story without heroes. Shortly after the strike ended, Gloria

Betancourt, their most prominent public spokesperson, remarked, "People have said what we have done is heroic. I don't know. We did what we had to do."[19] But people acting out of necessity still make choices, and the strikers had some remarkably tough ones to make.

Some of these involved simple survival: how to support their families, themselves, and each other on $55-a-week strike benefits. Others were a matter of strategy: determining their next moves, correcting their mistakes, deciding how to relate to the different forces involved in the strike.

Had they left such decisions to others, or done no more than react to the attacks of a predatory employer, they probably would not have won. That they did win, after eighteen grueling months, is a testament to their initiative as well as their endurance.

Again and again, they asserted to the authorities, to the media, to union officials, and to well-meaning supporters that the strike was theirs to win or lose, that they bore ultimate responsibility for its conduct.

At one point they were joined on their picket line by striking meat-packers from United Food and Commercial Workers (UFCW) Local P-9 in Austin, Minnesota. Local P-9's strike against Hormel had already attracted national attention for its tactical innovations and aggressive strategy. The strike issues in Austin and Watsonville had enough in common that the two groups of workers felt a natural affinity.

Yet their strikes ended very differently. P-9's battle against Hormel was overshadowed, and finally compromised, by an increasingly acrimonious dispute with its national union, which began as a difference of opinion over bargaining strategy and quickly spiraled out of control. In the end, the Hormel strike went down in flames.[20]

Given the initial estrangement Watsonville Canning workers felt from their own union, it would have been easy for their strike to meet a similar fate. Their relationship with the Teamsters was problematic and at times contentious. But they still managed to win significant support from the union without surrendering their own initiative. It was a remarkable achievement, and it confounded expectations of many who had come to see organized labor as an institution caught in a downward spiral of impotence and irrelevance.

For anyone who cares about the future of the labor movement, it is tempting to look to every successful strike for answers to strategic and organizational problems that other strikes face. The temptation is perhaps best resisted. There are lessons to be learned from the struggle at Watsonville Canning, but reducing it to neat formulas risks losing sight of the particularities, the nuances, the complexities that are essential to any real understanding of what took place.

Yet there is an aspect of the strike that does invite more general conclusions. When it began, there was a near-total leadership vacuum in Local 912. Over the next eighteen months, different forces would attempt to fill it. Among them were union functionaries, union reformers, community activists, self-conscious revolutionaries, and rank-and-file strikers compelled to take on new and unaccustomed responsibilities.

Each of these forces had specific ideas about the proper direction of the struggle. Each had specific ideas about what it meant to lead, what the proper relationship was between those who would assert leadership and those who would be led.

At times these forces came into serious conflict. Some of those conflicts were never resolved. Yet hindsight allows us to see how, in important ways, their efforts complemented each other as well.

In a society in which democratic ideals coexist with great disparities of wealth and power, the notion of leadership inspires ambivalence and not a little confusion. Politicians preach accountability but rarely practice it. Corporations hire high-priced consultants to instill "leadership skills" in their managers. Nonprofits pore over the works of Saul Alinsky, looking for the key to effective organizing. Unions that exist to empower the powerless find themselves going to great lengths to enforce a level of internal discipline presumed necessary to prevail over formidable enemies.

The Watsonville Canning strike served, among other things, as a kind of laboratory for different styles of leadership, the strengths and weaknesses of each, and the complicated interplay between the demands of a long and complex struggle and its most basic imperative: the desire of people to shape their own destiny.

If there are larger meanings to be gleaned from this story, they ultimately come back to a story that has been told before but bears retelling: one of ordinary people caught in an extraordinary situation and transformed by it. In the beginning they act out of pure necessity; as the situation develops, they discover both their own strengths and the weaknesses of their adversaries, and learn how to use each to their advantage. In the process, they find their voice—not simply to speak truth to power but to assert a power of their own.

In retelling their story, we may deepen our own understanding of the society we live in—and what will ultimately be required of us if we hope to change it for the better.

Chapter 1

The Frozen Food Capital of the World

Watsonville is located on the northern bank of the Pajaro River, ten miles from its mouth. San Jose is about thirty miles due north as the crow flies; the Salinas Valley, setting for much of John Steinbeck's fiction, is roughly twenty miles south.

The river flows out of central California's Coast Ranges, skirting the southern end of the Santa Cruz Mountains and meandering another twenty-five miles west through a lush valley before it empties into Monterey Bay and the Pacific Ocean. The valley is ideal for farming, with rich soil, abundant groundwater, and an unusually long growing season.

In 1868, believing that Pajaro Valley soil gave its apples a unique taste, the Martinelli family began bottling cider in Watsonville. The business still thrives today, operating out of a plant across the street from the local high school. Martinelli's was arguably the first food processing concern in a town whose economy would eventually come to be defined by the conversion of fresh produce into something that could be shipped great distances and stored for long periods of time.

Pajaro Valley farmers traditionally relied on Watsonville's network of packing sheds to buy and market what they could not sell themselves. Much of it wound up in San Jose's canneries, only thirty miles away but a world apart socially. Commercial canning involves metal fabrication as well as agricultural processing, and it requires plenty of capital. California's canneries thus tended to concentrate near industrial centers and were owned, for the most part, by large corporations rather than local entrepreneurs.

With the outbreak of World War II, food processing was transformed. Feeding the troops required a huge expansion of output, but wartime metal shortages made it difficult for canneries to meet the increased demand. Some thirty years earlier, frozen food technology had been developed and patented by Clarence Birdseye. But because it required a serious investment on the consumer's part—namely, an icebox—the idea was slow to catch on. Now the special needs of a war economy had made it suddenly profitable.[1]

Nor did it require the kind of capital that a traditional cannery did. The technology involved in packing vegetables in wax-dipped containers and freezing them was well within the means of a small investor like Edward Console, who in 1941 converted a packing shed on Ford Street into the first of Watsonville's frozen food plants.[2]

Console hailed originally from San Jose, and his new company, Watsonville Canning, began as an attempt to can produce closer to the source. But the sudden growth in demand for "quick-freeze products"— and their lower overhead—were too good to pass up, and Console took advantage of the opportunity before anyone else in Watsonville thought to do so.

Watsonville Canning was soon doing far more freezing than canning. Fresh vegetables, often hand-cut in the fields, were brought in by truck or rail car. The produce was washed outside the plant, then placed on a conveyor and trimmed by hand to uniform length, after which it was steam-treated at 190 degrees Fahrenheit for three minutes to neutralize the enzymes that hastened spoilage. Finally it was packaged, labeled, frozen, and stored until it could be sold.[3]

"The military," one industry insider observes, "is nothing but a giant food-service industry."[4] As often happens, the ready market it offered in wartime expanded into the civilian economy once the fighting ended. With the postwar boom, freezers became affordable for ordinary families, and the advent of frozen food enabled consumers to buy fruits and vegetables out of season in a form that was easy to prepare and retained more flavor and nutrition than canned goods. The newly built supermarkets soon boasted large frozen food sections with an array of new products to tempt shoppers.

David Moore, a Watsonville packer who began in the industry out of high school and gradually worked his way up, recalled that "frozen was growing more rapidly than fresh—not because it was better, but because it was new."[5] As demand soared, frozen food plants began proliferating in Watsonville. The majority did not last, but by 1952 the town had thirteen, with a combined annual output of 40 million pounds. By the end of the decade frozen food had become a billion-dollar industry, with Watsonville accounting for the lion's share of production.[6]

For Pajaro Valley growers it was a godsend. The business gave them a measure of relief from the financial pressures of unpredictable crop yields and an uncertain market. They could now put surplus inventory in cold storage, where it could serve as collateral if they needed bank loans. "The more broccoli they had," said Moore, "the more they could borrow."[7]

And borrow they did, increasingly tailoring their crops to the frozen food market. At one point 60 percent of the broccoli grown in the region was sold frozen. The coastline along Monterey Bay became "an ocean of brussels sprouts" as the rise of frozen food allowed area farmers to take full advantage of the local growing conditions uniquely suited for that crop. The Pajaro Valley soon accounted for roughly 90 percent of the brussels sprouts grown in the United States. The area also produced lima beans, cauliflower, and spinach in abundance.[8] Watsonville Canning handled the whole range—or, more accurately, its workers did.

The greater variety of crops encouraged by the frozen food industry meant a longer harvest season. When the spinach left off at the end of May, cauliflower began. When the fruit harvest ended around Labor Day weekend, brussels sprouts kicked in. Broccoli kept coming out of the fields nine months a year.[9]

The local labor market changed accordingly. Watsonville stopped being a farming village that "rolled up its sidewalks during the winter" and became, increasingly, a factory town that required a year-round work force.[10]

Initially the frozen food plants had drawn their employees from the same temporary labor pool that staffed the packing sheds. It was the sort of work force that characterized many farming communities: housewives augmenting the family income, students in need of summer jobs, the occasional Japanese or Filipino worker whom discrimination had excluded from the primary job market. There was, by and large, no significant cultural divide between the early frozen food workers and the rest of the community.[11]

But as frozen food expanded, the work force was transformed, and with it the town's demographic. The plants grew increasingly desperate for workers. A common refrain among those who got jobs was, "All you had to do was show up." Gloria Betancourt was just fifteen years old when she was hired by Watsonville Canning in 1962. No one thought to ask her age. Years later, she recalled how easy it was: "You put on a little makeup, it makes you look older." (Still, she was careful to keep a low profile when plant manager Kathryn Console, the owner's wife, appeared on the shop floor. Mrs. Console, she assumed, knew something about makeup.)[12]

Two developments—one technological, one political—made the transformation possible. The widespread introduction of the forklift in the late 1950s relieved some of the pressure on employers by eliminating much of the heavy lifting involved in frozen food work. This encouraged plants to tap into the local reserves of female labor, and frozen food quickly evolved into "women's work." But it was the continuing disintegration of the bracero program, culminating in its abolition in 1964, that truly changed the face of the industry.

The bracero program plays a defining role in the standard history of the California farmworkers' movement. According to this narrative, it was created as a temporary expedient during World War II to deal with wartime labor shortages, allowing a set number of Mexican harvest hands to migrate north as guest workers under strict federal supervision, to be sent back to Mexico once the crops were in. But California's agribusiness lobby had sufficient clout in Washington to keep the program going after the war ended, thus assuring themselves of a supply of compliant, cheap labor as protection against possible union organizing. Once the bracero program ended in 1964, the story goes, the way was cleared for Cesar Chavez to launch his historic campaign to bring union protection to California farmworkers.

In truth, the bracero program is only one chapter in a much longer story, that of the complex interplay between Mexican labor and US capital since the annexation of northern Mexico by the United States in 1848. Before World War I, Mae Ngai writes, "labor flowed more or less freely from Mexico into the United States." Traditional trade routes across the sparsely populated desert of what is now northern Mexico linked the southern part of that country with the southwestern

United States, and patterns of circular migration had existed long before English-speaking settlers arrived in the area.[13]

But Mexican settlements in Texas, California, Arizona, and New Mexico, which had begun as isolated outposts of Spanish colonialism, proved impossible for the Mexican government to defend. Aggressive anglo settlement was soon followed by military conquest. Under the Treaty of Guadalupe Hidalgo, which brought the US–Mexican war to an end, Mexican residents of the disputed territory were to become US citizens by default.

In practice it was largely citizenship in name only. Nor did the newly redrawn border have much effect on population movements: it could be crossed almost at will in either direction. The real changes occurred in the 1880s, when the policies of Porfirio Díaz effectively opened northern Mexico to capitalist development, and large numbers of Mexicans began migrating to the borderlands and across the frontier:

> Construction of the Mexican Central and Mexican National railroads, as well as the opening of new mines and agricultural enterprises, created a great demand for labor in the sparsely-settled north. Once attracted from the villages of southern and central Mexico, men were willing to move even further north, even across the border, in search of higher wages. By 1907 northern Mexican railroads were having difficulty keeping section gangs at full strength. The Mexican National claimed that virtually an entire work crew of 1,500 men had moved into Texas during the year.[14]

US railroads like Santa Fe and Southern Pacific hired private contractors to station themselves in El Paso, northern terminus for the Mexican Central, to recruit Mexican workers who had just crossed the border. It was rarely necessary to recruit in Mexico proper.

Nor was the workers' immigration status much of a concern. With the exception of the Chinese Exclusion Act of 1882, the federal government made no serious attempt to impose a systematic immigration policy before 1920, and in any case the frontier conditions that persisted along much of the nation's southwestern border meant that the few existing laws frequently went unenforced.[15] The labor market in the region was free to make its own rules.

This is not to say that it was a free market. Particularly in Texas, with its legacy of plantation slavery, Mexicans were treated by anglos as a conquered people, with all that implies. But the problematic relationship between the two peoples had little to do with immigration and everything to do with political power.

In his classic work *North from Mexico*, Carey McWilliams considered what distinguished Mexicans from the other immigrant groups who streamed into the United States in the decades before 1920. "Coming to America" from Mexico was not a typical immigrant experience, as, strictly speaking, the migrants were already American. They did not spend long weeks crossing the Atlantic in a filthy, overcrowded ship's hold. They were not compelled to run a gauntlet of official functionaries checking them for diseases at Ellis Island. They did not need to pull up stakes and turn their backs on their homeland in order to migrate; often little more was required than the price of a train ticket to El Paso.[16]

If labor market conditions or the particular circumstances of their lives changed, they could repatriate, and often they did. "For them," Francisco Balderrama and Raymond Rodriguez have written, "the border was merely an inconvenience." Acquiring US citizenship was rarely a priority—understandably, as, for the most part, second-class citizenship was the best they could expect. Census figures for 1910, 1920, and 1930 indicate that while nearly half of all immigrants from Europe became citizens, the naturalization rate for Mexicans ranged in the single digits or close to it.[17]

Between 1900 and 1930 more than one million Mexican nationals—roughly ten percent of the country's population—migrated to the United States.[18] Much of the impetus was homegrown. The Díaz regime had pursued a strategy of economic growth that encouraged aggressive foreign investment and the consolidation of small landholdings into large haciendas, most with absentee owners. The national economy grew, but the vast majority of Mexicans derived no benefit. Prices rose without a corresponding increase in wages, and thousands of peasants were driven off the land. These conditions, which helped spark the Mexican revolution in 1910, also drove unprecedented numbers of Mexicans to cross the border looking for work.

There was plenty of work to be had. In California, Texas, and Arizona, a system of large-scale commercial agriculture had emerged, requiring a steady supply of seasonal workers. It began with the passage of the Reclamation Act in 1902. The law opened up vast tracts of formerly arid land to irrigated farming, something Mexican peasants had been doing for generations and Mexican migrants understood, often better than the people who hired them. President Woodrow Wilson, speaking in 1916, was candid about their role: "This was once part of their country, and they can and will do the work."[19]

Meanwhile the extension of rail service to the region and the introduction of refrigerated railroad cars created a huge new market for fresh produce in the cities of the Northeast and Midwest. Cotton boomed as well: the old "cotton kingdom" of the Deep South, saddled with the inefficiencies of a socially entrenched tenant farming system, was hard pressed to compete with the new factory farms of the Southwest and their armies of transient wage laborers.

Employers in the Southwest appreciated the value of a labor force willing "to work hard and return to their homeland when the need for them [had] passed." They were valuable precisely because their homeland was so close by, and many retained close ties to it even when they remained in the United States. Their labor could be exploited without having to deal with the troublesome issues of social and political integration that made hiring other immigrant groups problematic. As long as they did not sink down roots, employers figured they could be kept segregated, isolated, and controlled.[20]

In 1924, riding a wave of nativist hysteria that swept the nation after World War I, Congress passed the Johnson-Reed Act and effectively slammed the door on immigration from Asia and much of Europe. Significantly, Mexicans were exempted from the bill's noxious racial quotas and allowed to enter the country largely unimpeded. Indeed, the exclusion of other immigrant groups only served to increase the demand for Mexican labor.

Unfortunately, passage of the bill put in place an enforcement infrastructure that could be readily used against Mexicans, and eventually it was. Prior to 1924, the US Bureau of Immigration (BOI) had a negligible presence on the Mexican border; after the law took effect border patrol agents were increasingly visible. According to Mae Ngai, "almost all were young, many had military experience and not a few were associated with the Ku Klux Klan." Though charged with enforcing civil rather than criminal statutes, they behaved as if they were chasing criminals, and their methods often skirted the bounds of legality.[21]

In 1931, with the country sinking deeper into Depression, the BOI swung into action. Anxious to deflect charges that the Hoover administration was doing nothing to help the jobless, Labor Secretary William Doak ordered the Border Patrol to round up all Mexican "illegals" and deport them.

In the past, little attention had been paid by anyone to legal formalities where Mexican immigration was concerned, so even those who were in the United States legally were often hard-pressed to prove it. In any case the distinction was largely lost on the authorities. Local relief officials anxious to rid their rolls of Mexicans made no allowance for either citizenship or legal residency when turning names over to the Border Patrol. When massive farmworker strikes swept through California's Imperial and San Joaquin valleys, the Border Patrol tried to break them with mass deportations. In one incident armed immigration agents surrounded a Los Angeles park where several hundred people were gathered and arrested them all; only a handful were later released.

Hauled into deportation proceedings without the resources to defend themselves, many opted to repatriate "voluntarily"; this course of action at least held out the possibility of legal reentry at some future time, which deportation ruled out. In the space of five months an estimated one-third of the Mexican population of Los Angeles repatriated. For long-term residents with children born in the United States, or people who were too old and infirm to relocate, the situation posed cruel dilemmas. It also placed an impossible burden on the Mexican government, which was never consulted about the matter and was helpless to deal with the flood of desperate people coming south.[22]

Balderrama and Rodriguez describe the impact of the raids within the United States: "Small barrios virtually disappeared. Once-bustling colonias took on the eerie look of abandoned ghost towns. Rows of houses stood empty. . . . Discarded furniture littered the yards as grass and weeds asserted their domain. No one was sure where all the residents had gone."[23]

By the end of the decade, they estimate, roughly one million people had left the country. Other scholars place the figure at four hundred thousand. There is no way to determine the precise number, but in any case with the exception of the slave trade it was the largest forced transfer of population in US history, dwarfing both the internment of

Japanese during World War II and Andrew Jackson's expulsion of the Cherokees to Oklahoma on the Trail of Tears.

Then World War II broke out. Thousands of former harvest hands were absorbed into the military or the defense industries, and the factory farms of the Southwest were left with no one to work their crops. It was time for the Mexicans to come back.

Bringing them back required a more sophisticated kind of social engineering than the crudely racist policies of the previous decade. The bracero program, instituted in 1942, was negotiated by the US and Mexican governments as an alternative to Mexican participation in the Allied armed forces. It was supposed to bring a measure of order and rationality to the transborder labor market: while US negotiators sought to address an acute wartime labor shortage, the Mexican government no doubt hoped the agreement would provide a modicum of protection for Mexican nationals working for US employers.

During the war the US government directly contracted for the importation of two hundred thousand field hands and seventy-five thousand railroad workers. The Mexican government did the recruiting, drawing workers from the country's interior rather than the border regions, where periodic waves of migration north had strained the local economy. The bracero program continued uninterrupted after World War II ended, as a measure designed to deal with a wartime emergency was seamlessly incorporated into peacetime economic policy. Passage of Public Law 78 in 1951 formally established it as an ongoing program, which it remained for the next thirteen years before collapsing under the weight of its own internal contradictions.

The Truman administration maintained that the bracero program would stabilize the farm labor market, stop illegal immigration, and prevent the abuse of migrant workers. It did none of these things. It certainly did not prevent abuse. Though under the program braceros were supposed to be paid the "prevailing wage," it was left to employers to determine what the prevailing wage was. Public Law 78 also required employers to furnish braceros with housing, food, transportation, and repatriation to Mexico after the harvest. But rarely if ever were there real consequences if they failed to do so.[24]

Braceros had two recourses: they could complain to the Mexican consul, or they could "skip." In some areas as many as 30 percent of them skipped, walking out on contracts either to return to Mexico or to look for better jobs. If you could get it, manufacturing work (and this included frozen food plants) might pay as much per hour as you could make for a full day's work in the fields. Mae Ngai notes that "in the border areas many braceros simply went home after they had earned what they wanted," whether or not their contracts were up.[25]

The program also exposed the conflicting interests of large and small farmers. Big corporate operations employed most of the braceros, since they had the resources to make most effective use of their labor. With ready access to a government-supplied work force, these operations could take full advantage of economies of scale and flood the market at prices that smaller competitors were hard-pressed to match. Not surprisingly, many small farmers resented the program and preferred to hire undocumented workers, whose employment did not require dealing with government bureaucrats.

Whatever its failures, the bracero program did succeed in pumping dollars into the Mexican economy: in the 1950s, Justin Akers Chacón writes, braceros sent home $30 million a year, contributing more to the national income than all but two of Mexico's domestic industries.

But the program, far from stopping illegal immigration, actively encouraged it. For every Mexican worker recruited into the program there were perhaps five to seven others who applied but were not selected. Knowing that work was available in *el Norte*, many of them simply crossed the border on their own, without papers.

Braceros who were in the United States legally were often joined by family members who weren't. By 1960, according to Akers Chacón, roughly three-quarters of California's agricultural workforce consisted of "mixed crews" made up of both braceros and undocumented workers, often members of the same family.[26]

In Watsonville, the bracero program established patterns of migration that persisted long after it was abolished. Workers in the frozen food plants were increasingly likely to have migrated north from Mexico to join family members who already lived in the area. Patricia Zavella, a scholar who spent years studying the town's changing demographics, found that 80 percent of the villagers of Gómez Farias, in the Mexican state of Jalisco, had relatives in Watsonville.[27]

Gloria Betancourt's father was a bracero working in the Imperial

Valley, supporting his family in Mexico but rarely seeing them. In 1962 a sympathetic employer made it possible for him to get citizenship papers, allowing his wife and children to join him in California. Soon after their arrival, he settled the family in Watsonville, where he had saved enough to buy a house.

Concerned that years of hard labor in the fields were destroying their father's health, Gloria and her older brother Armando tried to lighten his burden, augmenting the family income with jobs at Watsonville Canning. They considered themselves lucky to get the work. Farm labor rarely paid enough to support a family, and it was not unusual for young people to take jobs while still in their teens and living with their parents. But frozen food plants were another story: the work was more stable and it paid better, since the plants were under a Teamsters contract.[28]

Cuca Lomeli was also the daughter of a bracero who had settled in Watsonville; her aunt lived there as well. All through her childhood, she spent her summer vacations with her father, returning to Jalisco when school started. When she reached her teens she decided to live with her father year-round, and her aunt arranged for her to get citizenship papers. But Watsonville High School, she found, was too rough for her, and at sixteen she dropped out because "I didn't want to be a gangster." Like Gloria Betancourt, she lied about her age and got a job at Watsonville Canning.[29]

Chavelo Moreno first came to the United States as a bracero in 1958. After several years of seasonal work in the strawberry fields, he managed to obtain a green card and settled permanently in Watsonville, where his brother worked on the cleanup crew at Watsonville Canning. His brother was able to get him hired on as well, but Chavelo—serious, hard-working, and ambitious—eventually concluded that the cleanup crew was a dead end. As soon as he had enough seniority, he requested and got a job on the day shift so that he could attend night school, learn English, and get his GED. His newly acquired language skills earned him a promotion from the maintenance foreman on his operation, who could not communicate with the English-speaking USDA inspectors who came to the plant.[30]

Esperanza Torres hailed originally from Michoacán. In 1975, when she was twenty-eight, she "walked across the border" to join her husband, Enrique, who had arrived in Watsonville five months earlier. Her mother was already working in the Watsonville Canning plant, and Esperanza had "a lot of friends" living in town as well. She hired on at Watsonville Canning two years later, attracted by the pay, benefits, and seniority protections.[31]

These stories were typical. Watsonville Canning's workforce came to consist largely of workers who had been born in Mexico and retained strong ties to their native land. By 1980 the population of the town itself was rapidly approaching 50 percent Mexican, and the majority of its wealth came from the labor of five to seven thousand frozen food workers, most of whom had migrated north from Mexico or were related to people who had.

But their numbers were not reflected in the town's major institutions of power. Watsonville's influential citizens in many cases traced their roots back to early settlers who had migrated in the nineteenth century from Italy, Portugal, or the Balkan region. Thanks in part to an at-large election system that would later be the target of a successful voting rights lawsuit, the city government was controlled by an entrenched elite of anglo farmers and local business owners who did their best to tighten their grip when the United Farm Workers (UFW) began organizing in the Pajaro Valley in the early 1970s. In short, Watsonville was a community dominated by white ethnics who treated the fast-growing Mexican population as outsiders, even though they had emerged as the backbone of the local economy.

Because so many were undocumented (roughly 35 percent, according to a 1989 estimate), frozen food workers were less likely to cast ballots in city elections than they were to participate in their union's contract ratification votes, in which citizenship was not an issue.[32] But the local Teamsters union, like the rest of the town, was under anglo control. Significantly, when it came time for Watsonville's Mexicanos to make their bid for power, they would begin with the union.

Chapter 2

The Biggest Union in the Country

In the 1950s the International Brotherhood of Teamsters (IBT) emerged as the most powerful, and probably the least understood, labor organization in the United States. In the popular imagination it came to be associated with corruption, racketeering, and the infiltration of unions by organized crime. It was the target of media exposes, congressional investigations, and propaganda broadsides from conservative ideologues who cited it as evidence of the danger unions posed to a free society. In 1957 it was expelled from the AFL-CIO, which hoped to avert antilabor legislation from Congress by distancing itself from the bad publicity the Teamsters had attracted.

The bad publicity stuck because at least some of it was true. Jimmy Hoffa, who assumed the top leadership position in the union in 1958, was indeed autocratic. He did have underworld ties. There were mobrun Teamster locals. But none of these things by themselves can explain the ferocity of the attacks on Hoffa, or the obsessive pursuit of him by liberal icon Robert Kennedy, first as legal counsel to the McClellan Committee on labor racketeering and later as US attorney general.

What made the Teamsters particularly threatening was the leverage they had gained over the US economy by the late 1950s. With the construction of the interstate highway system, trucking replaced railroads as the nation's principal means of commercial shipping. Over-the-road trucking was traditionally a fragmented, decentralized, highly competitive industry whose workers labored in isolation.[1] All of these conditions usually make union organization difficult to achieve. The success of the IBT in bringing the nation's long-distance drivers under a single, strong collective-bargaining agreement in the 1960s remains one of the more remarkable achievements of the US labor movement, and Jimmy Hoffa played no small part in it.

Founded in 1899, the IBT in its early years was made up of small craft locals whose members operated in local markets and were organized according to the goods they hauled. In the winter of 1934, a small group of seasoned activists from the Trotskyist Socialist Workers Party (SWP) launched an organizing drive in the Minneapolis coal yards. It soon mushroomed into a general strike, which paralyzed the city and won union recognition for Minneapolis Teamsters. Farrell Dobbs, a coal hauler who had been recruited into the SWP in the course the struggle, emerged as a union leader. He was able to win over key Teamster officials in the Midwest to the notion that organizing long-distance drivers was a realizable objective, one that would transform the IBT.[2]

Dobbs's organizing strategy centered on a tactic that would eventually be outlawed: the secondary boycott. Shippers in one city who did not deal with the union were dependent for their business on shippers in other cities who did. The Teamsters were able to bring these employers to terms by disrupting the shipments they got from employers who were already under union contract. Passage of the Taft-Hartley Act in 1947 made this "leapfrog" strategy illegal, but by that time Teamster organizing efforts had progressed far enough, and given them sufficient bargaining leverage, that they were effectively able to get around it.[3]

The point was not simply to organize truck drivers but to impose uniform conditions on an anarchic industry. This would discourage individual employers, for whom labor costs were the bulk of expenses and profit margins were typically small, from trying to gain a leg up on the competition by paying their drivers less. Eventually, it would bring to the industry a measure of stability that employers could not have achieved on their own.[4]

At the start of his union career Jimmy Hoffa was mentored by Dobbs. He proved a brilliant student of Dobbs's methods and continued his work in the Midwest after Dobbs abruptly left the Teamsters in 1940 to work full time for the SWP. With the signing of the Master Freight Agreement in 1964, Hoffa in effect completed a job that Dobbs had begun in the late 1930s.[5]

Hoffa did not share Dobbs's revolutionary politics. No larger social vision informed his brand of unionism. It was, however, informed by one belief that Dobbs shared: a conviction that, as Hoffa biographers Ralph and Estelle James characterize it, "Law is not something to respect, but rather a set of principles designed to perpetuate those already in power."[6] He also believed, according to the Jameses, "that capitalism is doomed. He is in the incongruous position of one who likes the present system, but does not believe it can work." In private conversations he would spell out his own version of the Marxist theory that overproduction and stagnation are built into the structure of a market economy.[7]

Hoffa had little patience with the social-democratic unionism of fellow Detroiter Walter Reuther, president of the United Auto Workers. Reuther helped forge organized labor's alliance with the liberal wing of the Democratic Party and looked to government intervention to achieve what could not be won at the bargaining table. For Hoffa, the government was a treacherous ally; legislation that was supposed to legitimize unions and protect workers' rights had too many strings attached. It was at best a nuisance, depriving the Teamsters of the flexibility they needed to pursue their objectives in an essentially hostile environment. Generally, he felt that the less of a role the government played in the labor-management conflict, the better.

Believing that workers could never count on a fair shake from the existing system but lacking any faith in political solutions, revolutionary or otherwise, Hoffa poured his considerable talent and energies into extending the power of his own organization and making sure that power within that organization stayed firmly in his own hands. He did not like to delegate authority. He dealt ruthlessly with adversaries and was constantly fending off charges from federal prosecutors that he used underworld figures as muscle and rewarded them with access to union pension funds.

In keeping with the union's origins, Teamster local and regional bodies have traditionally enjoyed a good deal of autonomy. Hoffa skillfully embraced the tradition while simultaneously using it to consolidate his control, especially when bargaining with the trucking companies. The Master Freight Agreement permitted strikes over local agreements; this gave many rank-and-file drivers a sense of empowerment or at least a belief that the national union respected their issues. But it also served as an extra weapon in Hoffa's arsenal: by skillfully manipulating local grievances, he could employ the leapfrog strategy without resorting to illegal secondary boycotts.[8]

Hoffa's command of market conditions in the industry was formidable; he knew how to play employers off one another, and he knew just how far to push them in negotiations. Over-the-road drivers, once a particularly vulnerable sector of the US working class, did well on his watch. As Dan LaBotz writes, "Teamsters in the freight industry could expect job security, high wages, and good benefits, and came to feel entitled to them."[9]

Teamster power extended itself well beyond the freight industry, with mixed results. The leapfrog strategy that worked so well in organizing long-distance trucking proved equally effective in other highly competitive industries where employment was low-paying and uncertain. A small manufacturer or food processor whose business was sensitive to the fluctuations of a seasonal market was particularly vulnerable to a sudden interruption of deliveries. Because of their strategic position in the movement of goods, Teamsters could give valuable support to striking workers in other unions, and often did. More than one intransigent employer was brought to terms when Teamster drivers refused to cross a picket line in front of his plant.

The downside was that nonunion employers, anxious to avoid trouble, often signed collective bargaining agreements with the Teamsters without bothering to consult the workers involved.[10] There was also a powerful temptation for the IBT to raid other unions. Teamster history is replete with nasty jurisdictional disputes—from the IBT's battles with the International Longshore and Warehouse Union during the organizing drives of the 1930s to its dust-up with Cesar Chavez and the UFW in the California lettuce fields some forty years later.

Most relevant to the Watsonville Canning story is the struggle between the Teamsters and the Food, Tobacco and Agricultural Workers (FTA) in the Northern California canneries immediately after World War II.[11] The FTA was affiliated with the Congress of Industrial Organizations (CIO), which broke away from the American Federation of Labor (AFL) in 1935 and launched a dramatic and largely successful drive to organize auto, steel, and other basic industries. Among the

FTA officers and organizers were veteran activists who had cut their teeth in the communist-led farmworkers' strikes of the mid-1930s.

The FTA (under its former name, the United Cannery, Agricultural, Packinghouse and Allied Workers) had made significant headway in the California fields and built a highly effective organization in the Southern California canneries during World War II. It seemed poised to organize the Northern California canneries after the war, and actually won a major National Labor Relations Board (NLRB) election in October 1945.

Then the Teamsters moved in, backed by the AFL. The union announced that its drivers would not haul goods to or from canneries covered by FTA contracts. As a result, one FTA plant in Oakland was forced to lay off 150 workers. Aided by charges that the FTA was "communist-dominated," the IBT succeeded in pressuring the labor board to throw out the earlier election and hold new ones. New federal legislation withheld NLRB protection from unions that failed to demonstrate that none of their officers were members of the Communist Party.

California Processors and Growers, which represented the industry's employers, did not even bother to wait for the vote. It signed with the Teamsters. Management locked out workers in a Sacramento plant who remained loyal to the FTA. In other plants, FTA members who refused to hand over dues to the Teamsters were fired. FTA pickets were attacked by goons and FTA leaders were red-baited in the press.

The new vote, when it finally came, was remarkably close, but the Teamsters prevailed. The FTA never recovered. In 1950 it was one of ten unions purged from the CIO in a move to rid the federation of communist influence. California's canneries would remain a Teamster stronghold until the 1980s, when plant shutdowns left the industry a shadow of its former self.

The IBT–FTA conflict was the product of a particular historical period, when anticommunist hysteria was gaining force in both the labor movement and the country as a whole. But it represents an extreme version of a tendency that surfaced at other times and left an enduring mark on the Teamsters, especially as the IBT expanded outside its traditional jurisdiction. "Organizing the employer" instead of the workers and carrying out successful raids on shops that were already organized brought more dues money into the Teamster treasury and frequently gave the IBT added leverage in enforcing the Master Freight Agreement. For previously nonunion workers brought into the Teamster fold, it meant at least rudimentary protections of a union contract, which they might not otherwise have enjoyed.

Yet it also created what has been termed a "two-tier union." Dan LaBotz summarizes it this way:

> The members . . . fell into two separate social groups. The first group included freight, car haul, rock-sand-and-gravel, and beverage drivers, almost all white men who earned the highest salaries and enjoyed the best health and pension benefits. These workers . . . dominated local unions and sent delegates to International conventions. Under them was a second group, composed of lower-paid truck drivers and dock workers, as well as food processing and manufacturing workers, many of them African American and Latino. These members of the union had less power, sometimes even in their own local unions, and were politically less significant in the International union.[12]

The divisions within the union power structure were even more apparent on the shop floor. A longtime cannery activist recalled:

> My local, like most cannery locals, had the majority of its members in seasonal jobs, working three to five months out of the year, while 10–30 percent had year-round warehouse and maintenance jobs. Seasonal workers were overwhelmingly Chicana and Mexicana women. Off-season elections and English-only union meetings were used to rob them of any voice in the local. Employers gave relatively good contracts to the smaller number of year-round workers, helping the union to buy their loyalty, in return for the union keeping the seasonals in line.[13]

Local cannery agreements often contained flagrantly discriminatory wage scales and were the object of a flurry of civil rights lawsuits in the 1970s.

IBT members in both groups, it turned out, had issues with the Teamster leadership, which began to surface once the long arm of the law finally caught up with Jimmy Hoffa in March 1967. When Hoffa went to prison, he was replaced by Frank Fitzsimmons, who did not come close to matching his predecessor's extraordinary bargaining skills. Nor was he strong enough to control the Mafia elements that

Hoffa had occasionally used to maintain his authority.

The trucking industry itself was changing. New technology had a lot to do with it: forklifts and pallets replaced hand-loaded cargo, and giant containers that could be loaded onto ships and rail cars as well as trucks replaced the old trailer-trucks. The new technology raised the cost of doing business, enabling big corporations to buy out many cash-strapped smaller operators and, in so doing, extend their control over the industry. Since the Teamsters had traditionally thrived by playing employers off one another, the growing monopolization of trucking posed a new challenge, which Frank Fitzsimmons was ill-equipped to meet.[14]

It also made things tougher on the drivers, who were accustomed to good contracts and a fair amount of autonomy on the job. Heavily capitalized employers demanded new levels of efficiency and higher productivity from their workers. Mechanization eliminated jobs and required more output from those workers who remained. Their hours were longer and supervision more onerous. Meanwhile, runaway inflation, touched off by the Vietnam War, cut deeply into their paychecks.

The 1970s saw growing unrest among Teamster drivers. It began with a series of wildcat strikes by steel haulers, who felt the union had failed to pursue their particular issues. It soon broadened to include local officers, some of them old Hoffa supporters, who did not like the direction in which Fitzsimmons was taking the union. Rank-and-file publications began springing up, with names like *Fifth Wheel* and *From the Horse's Mouth*. Consumer advocate Ralph Nader got into the act, launching a campaign for safer road conditions, which soon trained its sights on the IBT leadership, particularly the lack of accountability to its members and the misuse of union funds. Nader had little interest in the economic issues facing Teamster drivers, but union reformers made ready use of his muckraking exposés of how the IBT was run.[15]

In 1974, activists from International Socialists (IS) succeeded in pulling together dissidents in the union around the forthcoming negotiations for the National Master Freight Agreement, laying the groundwork for what was to become Teamsters for a Democratic Union (TDU). IS was one of a number of left-wing groups that had emerged on the nation's college campuses during the 1960s and now sought to establish a base in the working class through involvement in union politics. Its focus on the IBT had a certain logic: IS came out of the Trotskyist movement, and the emergence of the Teamsters as a powerful national union a generation earlier is perhaps the biggest success story of American Trotskyism.

But aspects of the IS brand of revolutionary socialism also lent themselves well to the organizational culture of the Teamsters and its increasingly restive drivers. Like the Industrial Workers of the World (IWW) and its European syndicalist counterparts of an earlier generation, IS saw autonomous action by workers at the point of production as both a wellspring of democratic values and a critical component of revolutionary strategy. Since rank-and-file workers acting on their own initiative are apt to come into conflict with those running their unions, union leaders invariably became the targets against which IS directed its fire. When labor leaders stood in the way of workers' efforts to assert themselves, IS saw it as the inevitable result of "business unionism"—referring not just to the social outlook of union officials who identified with employers but also to their tendency to run their unions like business organizations, hierarchically structured and functioning to enrich their officers.

Other left groups attempting to build rank-and-file caucuses in different unions embraced this analysis or some variation of it. But it was particularly well-suited to the IBT under Frank Fitzsimmons, a "business union" in both senses of the term. Teamster pension funds, which reputedly "built Las Vegas," were a lucrative source of investment capital; top Teamster officials were notorious for holding multiple offices and drawing extravagant salaries for each. As for the truck drivers who chafed under Fitzsimmons's rule, they had a long tradition of taking things into their own hands, especially since their strategic role in the movement of goods gave them an economic leverage that other workers could only dream about.[16]

Thus, TDU—unlike rank-and-file caucuses organized by other left groups—attracted an immediate following, and not just inside the Teamsters. Campus radicals who disdained organized labor as part of "the establishment" saw in TDU prospects for a labor movement they could believe in. Mainstream liberals who might have been appalled at the idea of an opposition group in a liberal union like the UAW embraced it enthusiastically in the Teamsters. A public treated to years of media stories about corrupt and brutal Teamster officials saw TDU organizers as taking on a badly needed, long overdue task, one that required physical courage on top of everything else. (Pete Camarata, the lone TDU delegate to the IBT's 1976 convention, was beaten up by goons after he challenged Frank Fitzsimmons from the convention floor.)

IS never did parlay its work in TDU into lasting political gains. TDU's very success touched off furious debate within IS about how to conduct socialist agitation in a political milieu that had been organized around a more modest agenda. The organization was unable to resolve these differences and ended up splitting into three factions.[17] But TDU grew into an enduring force in the Teamsters and by the 1990s was contending for power in the national union.

As TDU was getting off the ground, another center of opposition within the union was developing in California's canneries. This one, too, was largely spontaneous at first, and drew much of its inspiration from the example of Cesar Chavez and the UFW. The predominantly female seasonal workers in the canneries included many nationalities and shared many grievances, but the issue of language equality was of foremost importance to the Chicanas and Mexicanas and embodied the frustration most cannery workers felt with their jobs and their union. Spanish-speaking workers not only could not participate in union meetings, they could not even read the union contract that laid out the terms under which they worked. The situation was especially galling because the contract language typically consigned seasonal workers, particularly the women, to lower-paying jobs with fewer benefits and fewer opportunities.

Strong social, cultural, and family ties bound cannery workers with field laborers. The gospel of workers' rights and Chicana/o empowerment that captured the imagination of California's farmworkers in the late 1960s and early 1970s made an immediate impact in the canneries. As early as 1969, rank-and-file cannery workers had organized in San Jose, Stockton, and Hayward to demand more opportunities for Latinos on the job and more say in their Teamster cannery locals. These groups sprung up independently; several years would go by before they became aware of each other's existence and began looking for ways to work together. Eventually local groupings also formed in Oakland, Sacramento, and smaller towns in the Salinas area like King City, Gilroy, and Hollister.[18]

The regional network that emerged out of these efforts was initially an ad hoc affair. When the Teamsters' master agreement with the cannery owners was up for renewal, local groups would reach out to each other to discuss ways to improve it. A more concerted effort at cooperation emerged in the wake of a 1973 class action lawsuit, *Alaniz v. California Processors, Inc.*, which targeted race and sex discrimination in the canneries. Cannery workers' committees (CWCs) around the state signed on to the lawsuit, which concluded in 1976 with a federal court ruling mandating affirmative action in the plants, establishing seniority rights for seasonal workers, and requiring Spanish translation on the job and in union meetings.

Maintaining an ongoing network of cannery workers was not easy. Functioning CWCs were scattered across Northern California. Cannery workers toiled seven days a week during the season and then were laid off and often dispersed when it ended. Most of them earned less than $10,000 a year and could not afford the membership dues required to sustain a far-flung organization.

Hoping to bring a measure of continuity and cohesion to their organizing efforts, they took a page from the farmworkers' book. Michael Johnston, a San Jose activist who had taken a cannery job in 1974 and immediately become active in the local CWC, had worked for the UFW after graduating from high school. He noted how the farmworkers' union set up service centers to stay in continuing contact with a highly mobile membership of seasonal workers.

Using his contacts with Catholic social service agencies that supported the work of the UFW, Johnston succeeded in getting funding for cannery worker service centers in San Jose and Sacramento, home to two of the strongest and most established of the local CWCs. The centers were intended to "help us communicate during the season [while] at the same time providing a place where seasonal workers could come in in the off season for help around their benefits, grievances, immigration problems, etc."[19]

The centers were almost too successful. Johnston would recall that, while they "helped to stimulate more sustained local organizing than we had ever had before," they also "ended up spending more and more time doing work which we should have been pushing the union to do." Worse, workers came to regard the centers as service agencies that were there to help them with their problems rather than as organizations through which workers could assert their own initiative and build their political power.[20]

Like many young white activists, Johnston admired TDU and looked to it for a possible solution. He attended his first TDU convention in 1979 as a representative of the CWC and was struck by the fact that, of the over three hundred delegates present, only three were Latino. He concluded that TDU had much to gain by aligning itself with the cannery workers' movement, while cannery workers had compelling reasons to be part of the fight to make the Teamsters more democratic. He began pushing for a serious TDU presence in the canneries.

Johnston was also concerned about the long-term financial stability of the CWC. One of its main funding sources, a five-year grant from the Campaign for Human Development, was due to run out in 1982 and could not be renewed. Johnston realized the funding could continue through a new grant if administered by TDU, and he persuaded TDU to launch a Cannery Workers Organizing Project (CWOP) to continue the work of the CWC. Johnston was hired to run it while simultaneously serving as TDU's West Coast organizer. Manuel Díaz, another activist from the San Jose CWC, got a paid organizer's position and a seat on TDU's national steering committee.

Both sides seemed to benefit from the arrangement. As Manuel Díaz would recall, "TDU didn't have much of a foothold in Northern California, and this was the first time they'd gone into an industry that was mainly Latinos. We gave them thirteen locals, and they got bragging rights about working with minority workers. We got a clearing house for our funding."

But the alliance proved problematic. Most cannery workers had little interest in the issues that preoccupied TDU, and TDU's national leadership lacked a deeper understanding of where cannery workers were coming from. Nor was there a common understanding of how much autonomy the CWOP should have within TDU. The majority of the project's funding came from the same church groups and foundations that had funded the service centers. Johnston complained to Ken Paff, TDU's national organizer, that the money was being siphoned off for purposes other than that for which it was intended.[21]

Left politics as well as bureaucratic turf wars figured in the dispute. TDU's national leadership reflected the influence of IS and its strategic approach to union work. Johnston and Díaz were members of the League of Revolutionary Struggle. Like IS, the League was a revolutionary socialist organization, but the two groups had very different approaches to organizing and long-term strategy. The League represented a coming together of several left-wing organizations in the Asian, Chicano, and African American movements whose initial inspiration came from the Black Panther Party. The Panthers had wielded considerable influence on the American left in the late 1960s, and the activists who founded the League appreciated their efforts to meld Marxist theory with the revolutionary nationalism of Malcolm X and earlier generations of Black activists.

Mao Zedong's writings were a serious influence on the Panthers, and they found a receptive audience among League activists as well. They were particularly interested in Mao's analysis of the national united front, developed when the Chinese Communists were struggling to provide leadership to a broad popular movement in opposition to the Japanese occupation of China. It seemed remarkably germane to the difficult strategic questions posed by the interplay of race and class in the United States.

The League believed that socialist revolution would come about in the United States not through a simple seizure of power by the working class but by a "strategic alliance of the working class and the oppressed nationality movements."[22] It advocated for the right of self-determination for Black people, as had the Panthers, but it also advanced the same demand for the "Chicano Nation" residing in the territory annexed by the United States following the Mexican War.[23] (The League never argued that either African Americans or Chicanos should secede from the United States, only that they had a right to do so.)

However abstract they might seem, the doctrinal differences between IS and the League had real practical consequences. IS had focused its organizing on industries with a strategic role in the economy, where organized labor had a strong presence. It emphasized struggle within the union movement, hoping to win workers away from "business unionism" and restore the labor movement to its historic mission of class struggle. League activists placed more emphasis on community organizing, and their labor work focused on the "lower stratum of the working class . . . low-paid, unskilled production workers in manufacturing, service, and agriculture," who were "relatively more oppressed and in many instances suffer[ed] national and women's oppression."[24] In some respects their differences reflected a long-standing debate on the left between those who engaged in what some have termed "identity politics" and those who rejected this approach as divisive and a deviation from "pure" class struggle.[25]

At the heart of the matter is a question that has dogged the US working class since its earliest days: how to achieve unity in the face of persistent divisions along ethnic lines. As early as 1844, immigrant Irish Catholic and native-born Protestant workers fought violent battles in the streets of Philadelphia over the content of school textbooks. Fifteen years later, working people who flocked to the banner of Abraham Lincoln and Free Soil Republicanism were driven by a hatred of the "slave power," which often translated into fear and contempt for slaves. In California of the 1870s, the rise of the Workingmen's Party was fueled by the same violent xenophobia that eventually led Congress to pass the Chinese Exclusion Act in 1882. Southern Populism in the 1890s began as an interracial movement, and a deeply class-conscious one at that; however, unable to reconcile the agendas of the Black and white tenant farmers it sought to represent, it eventually degenerated into virulent white racism.[26]

From time to time in the history of the United States, appeals to class solidarity have found a receptive audience, but sustaining them over the long term has proved difficult. Jay Gould, the nineteenth-century railroad baron, was being both hyperbolic and cynical when he famously declared that he could "always hire one-half of the working class to kill the other half." But he put his finger on a problem, and the problem has often manifested itself in debates over organized labor's role in speaking for the working class as a whole.

Both IS and the League recognized that in "the biggest union in the country," a significant group of members lacked a meaningful voice. Both were determined that they should have it. But without a common analysis of why the workers in question were disempowered, differences were bound to emerge over how best to empower them.

Because the IS approach remained influential on the left even after

IS as an organization had ceased to exist, these differences persisted. They would emerge into the open during the Watsonville Canning strike, especially as the higher levels of the Teamster hierarchy became involved. The union's often contradictory role in the strike posed complex strategic questions. There were hard choices to be made. In the end, it would be up to the strikers to make them.

Chapter 3

The Teamsters in Watsonville

Teamsters Local 679 represented San Jose cannery workers, but in 1949 it established a beachhead in Watsonville, negotiating contracts with Ed Console and two other local frozen food employers. A militant strike the following year, involving mass demonstrations and the blocking of railroad tracks, succeeded in winning a pay hike and quickly persuaded other local frozen food plants to sign contracts as well.[1]

By 1952 the union had enough members in Watsonville for the Western Conference of Teamsters to grant them their own charter. Local 912, a general local encompassing not just frozen food workers but truck drivers and others, was formed with Con Hansen holding the top position of secretary-treasurer. President and second in command was Richard King, a former merchant seaman who had hired on at Meadowgold Dairy. (In many Teamster locals, the president ran meetings, but secretary-treasurer was the top leadership post.) Hyperactive, hard-drinking, and physically imposing, the red-headed King had gotten his initial exposure to militant unionism as a member of the Seafarers International Union during his stint in the merchant marine. He would take over Local 912 when Con Hanson retired in 1967 and run it for eighteen years. As early as 1956, his name appeared as Local 912's representative on the Teamster collective bargaining agreements with the frozen food companies.[2]

Frozen food was emerging as a big business, but Watsonville was still a small town. The firms that came to dominate its economy were for the most part locally owned, and their owners and managers traveled in the same social circles as the union officials they bargained with. Richard King owned the Waterfront Bar, a popular watering hole two doors down from the Local 912 hall on Lake Street; Ed Console was as likely to be seen drinking there as the people who worked for him. At contract time, recalled Watsonville Canning worker Chavelo Moreno, "Ed Console and Richard King would get together, have a few drinks, and come to an agreement right there. They'd make deals without any input from us." King was so close to the Console family that he regarded himself as a kind of surrogate father to Console's son Mort, who dropped out of law school and took over the family business at age twenty-four when his father passed away.[3]

Because of his personal ties to the owners, and because frozen food plants were often desperate for workers, Richard King was able to negotiate good contracts as long as the industry continued to thrive. In 1959, recognizing that he had more bargaining leverage than the heads of other food processing locals, he succeeded in getting a separate master agreement with the frozen food employers instead of bargaining through the Teamsters' California Cannery Union Council. The separate contract paid off handsomely in 1971, when Local 912 became the first Teamster local to provide health benefits for its seasonal workers. King "had the facts," the head of the Frozen Food Employers Association recalled. "He had talked to the health insurance companies and showed us that we could afford to do it."[4]

According to John Bubich, longtime vice president of Local 912, "Richard dominated the union, and he ran it with a heavy hand. He got things done, but there are drawbacks to doing things that way. We should have had more open discussion with the membership." King was as aloof from the rest of the union as he was from his own members. Joint Council 7 leader Chuck Mack, who oversaw Teamster locals throughout Northern California, remembered King as "kind of a bizarre guy" who "kept his own counsel," at least where union business was concerned. Local 912 was King's personal bailiwick and he needed no help from the Teamsters in running it—at least, not until the summer of 1985, when his world would abruptly collapse.[5]

When King assumed leadership of Local 912, its membership was already changing. By 1972 the workforce in the frozen food plants was increasingly female and Mexican. Typically, they had plenty of experience working in the fields, and many knew about the efforts of Cesar Chavez's UFW to organize lettuce pickers in the Salinas Valley. Some had been involved with unions and working-class politics in Mexico.

Yet all of this counted for little in Watsonville. Where Local 912 was concerned, Margarita Paramo recalled wryly, there seemed to be little workers could do besides "pay our dues and be happy."[6] Anglo men ran the union. Childcare issues, as well as the perception that the union was a male domain, discouraged rank-and-file participation.

Potential activists like Esther Gonzalez quickly became frustrated: "People would get up and argue. They'd talk about the same things over and over. I wanted changes but they never happened." Guillermina Ramírez made a point of attending union meetings regularly, but "we always came out tired and fed up."[7]

Inside the plant, the work could be brutal and the hours long, but the pay was good and there were health benefits—especially important for Esther Gonzalez, whose daughter had a congenital heart condition. The way the union was run left much to be desired, but the benefits of a union contract were undeniable—particularly when the plants provided enough work to assure something approaching year-round employment.

For many, factory work was a welcome escape from the drudgeries of field labor—"no hot sun, no dirt," as one worker put it. Others found the pace and the constant discipline of the production line oppressive. Even those who liked the work complained that "some of the floor ladies yell at us because we're Mexican."[8]

The long hours could be a particular problem for single mothers, who by some estimates made up nearly half of Local 912's membership. To avoid paying for childcare, Reina Lagusman told a reporter, "I work 5 p.m. to 3 in the morning . . . I've slept four hours a night for the last five years." She added, "If one of your kids gets sick, you have to go home but sometimes they don't let you till the end of the shift."

"I did everything," Emma Jiménez remembered. "We had to trim, sort, run machinery—everything." The work required manual dexterity and could be dangerous when the line ran too fast. "We stand in one place for eight hours or more," Gloria Betancourt told a reporter who asked about the job. "Many women have arthritis. People come close to losing fingers every day. They go to the hospital, get it sewn up, and come back to work using one hand."[9]

Fidelia Carrisoza had known hard physical labor growing up on her family farm in Mexico, but she was unprepared for the production line at Watsonville Canning. "They wanted machines," she recalled. "I worked nine hours my first day, and I never worked so hard in my life. I had pains in my back, and vomiting. The floor lady kept saying, 'Pick it up, pick it up, the boss is coming.' Every day I said, 'I don't want to go back.' It took me two hours to fall asleep every night because of the back pain, and I dreamed about brussels sprouts."[10]

A worker in another plant was more blunt. "It's like slavery," she said. "All the foremen need is whips." She gladly left the plant for the fields as soon as strawberry season opened.[11]

Among those who remained, the rigors of the job forged a close bond. "We were like a family," said Emma Jiménez of her fellow workers at Watsonville Canning.[12] But the culture of solidarity and mutual support that developed on the shop floor did not carry over into the union, where workers still felt like outsiders.

Richard King did not speak a word of Spanish. When he presided over meetings, Gloria Betancourt's main recollection was that he "looked kind of mean," and frequently appeared to be drunk. Esther Gonzalez remembered being stood up when she made appointments with local officers. The union health plan may have been a blessing, but Guillermina Ramírez complained that copies of it were not available in Spanish. Nor was the contract translated. Union meetings, conducted in English, were often canceled for lack of a quorum, something that did not appear to trouble King.[13]

To his credit, King recognized the need for someone in local leadership who could represent the union to its Spanish-speaking members. He turned to Sergio López, a shop steward at Meadowgold Dairy, who had once worked at King's Lake Street tavern.

López was born in Mexico and came to the United States when he was fifteen. The stepson of a Puerto Rican GI, he was fluent in both English and Spanish. At eighteen, he was married and supporting his family with a succession of odd jobs. Upon turning twenty-one, he hired on as a bartender at the Waterfront Bar and met Richard King.

The red-headed union officer made a tremendous impression on López, for whom he became something of a father figure. "I could see how he would eat with the owners, would eat with the workers right at the bar," López recalled. "He was a dynamo when I first met him. He was loved and revered by people, he was full of vim and vigor, he was very eloquent, he was very compassionate." Watching King, Sergio López "caught the fever and fell in love with unionism." He followed in King's footsteps and took a job at Meadowgold Dairy; there he became a shop steward, mastered the union contract, and began translating at union meetings.[14]

With King's encouragement, López earned his GED and obtained his US citizenship. King put him on the union payroll in 1972. As a Local 912 business agent, López distinguished himself as a hard worker who was unflaggingly loyal to his boss. According to Frank Bardacke, who ran against King in 1982, "Sergio's job was to make King look good."[15] If Spanish-speaking rank and filers had problems, questions about their rights under the contract, or needed be sold on the terms of a new contract King had just negotiated, Sergio López was the one they talked to.

Bardacke himself arrived in Watsonville in 1979, a seasoned radical activist from Berkeley. A veteran of the Free Speech Movement, he was subsequently a defendant in a celebrated conspiracy trial that grew out of Stop the Draft Week, a series of massive antiwar demonstrations that effectively shut down the Oakland Induction Center for several hours in October of 1967. Later he emerged as a leader of the fight over People's Park, a vacant lot belonging to the University of California that had been expropriated by local squatters and turned into a community garden. That struggle saw one protester killed by a police bullet and prompted then governor Ronald Reagan to call in the National Guard to put down the protests.

Bardacke eventually left Berkeley and settled in Seaside, on the Monterey peninsula, where he was involved in an unsuccessful attempt to set up a coffeehouse catering to antiwar GIs at nearby Fort Ord. He got a job teaching physical education at a local elementary school, then lost it when the school board found out about his Berkeley arrest record. He worked in the fields, got active in the UFW, and found he had issues with the leadership style of Cesar Chavez. Years later he would publish a scathing critique of the way Chavez ran the UFW.[16]

Idled by the UFW's massive lettuce strike in the Salinas Valley in 1978, Bardacke decided to look for a job in Watsonville's frozen food industry. A trucking firm that supplied the local plants hired him with no questions asked as a "lumper," working on the dock loading and unloading cargo. Thanks to a Teamster contract, the job paid well and took him from plant to plant, providing an overview of conditions in the industry. It also brought him into contact with a wide range of workers, and his Spanish was good enough for him to talk to them. Observing the disconnect between Richard King and the people he represented, Bardacke decided Local 912 was ripe for rank-and-file organization.

A self-described anarchist and believer in "radical democracy," Bardacke had never been a member of IS, but there were veterans of the organization from Berkeley whom he knew and respected. They put him in touch with TDU's national organizer, Ken Paff. With Paff's help, he launched a TDU chapter in Watsonville, raising the boilerplate issues TDU used to demand a greater rank-and-file voice in Teamster locals: rank-and-file committees, lower salaries for union officials, elected shop stewards.[17]

An early recruit was Joe Fahey, a young UPS driver who had dropped out of the teaching credential program at University of California–Santa Cruz. "I'll never forget the first time I met him," Bardacke recalled. "He came into a meeting wearing his UPS uniform—and barefoot." Fahey was the product of a working-class Irish family from Los Angeles. He had an emotionally difficult childhood: when he was still quite young, his mother was institutionalized, ending his parents' marriage and leaving his father with responsibility for the children. His mother fell in love with and married another patient from the mental hospital, who happened to be African American. This did not sit well with her ex-husband.

"I loved my stepfather," Fahey said years later, "and I wanted my family to be all right again." A teaching career seemed like a good, socially useful way to resolve the personal issues that had dogged his childhood. But he felt out of place in the rarefied atmosphere of the Santa Cruz campus, and the credential program, while long on theory about education and social change, was less than helpful on more mundane topics such as classroom management.

Fahey happened to read Steven Brill's popular exposé of the Teamsters, with its glowing descriptions of TDU, and decided that, instead of teaching, he wanted to involve himself in the union reform movement. So he went to work for UPS, where he quickly impressed his supervisor as a hard worker.

One day he noticed a problem with his paycheck and went down to the Local 912 hall to try to get it straightened out. He did not get a sympathetic reception. Returning to work the next day, his supervisor told him he'd received a call from the union characterizing Fahey as a "troublemaker" and suggesting that he be fired. He wasn't, but when he saw a TDU leaflet at a local supermarket—it featured a crude drawing of a Cadillac in front of the union hall—he decided to attend the next meeting. Within a few years he would be running the Watsonville chapter of TDU along with José López, a militant Watsonville Canning worker with a background in Mexico's anarchist movement.[18]

At the outset, the TDU chapter was less concerned with shop floor issues than with how Local 912 was run. Frank Bardacke noted that Richard King did little or nothing to encourage members to attend union meetings. He suspected that it was deliberate: since regular attendance was required of anyone who ran for union office, the practical effect when meetings were repeatedly canceled for lack of a quorum was to protect the incumbent officers from challenge. Much of Bardacke's energy thus went into getting enough people to the meetings to make sure they were held. To encourage more women to attend, TDU also demanded, successfully, that childcare be provided.

The meetings, when they did happen, were apt to be stormy. King was not popular with the members; some of them—men, chiefly—used the opportunity to tell him just what they thought of him. Women, a majority of the local, were seriously underrepresented. Though she eventually became one of Local 912's most active members, Gloria Betancourt, during the early part of her career at Watsonville Canning, went down to the union hall "only to pay my dues." Of the union officers, her coworker Emma Jiménez recalled, "We let them get away with murder."

TDU's big problem, according to Frank Bardacke, was that "the leader of it was me, a white man with barely adequate Spanish." But he was an experienced agitator who projected an aura of confidence and self-assurance, and he was able to get outside help when needed, drawing upon both TDU's national reputation and his own network of contacts on the left. Unfortunately, he lost his job as a lumper after he set up a local meeting with Ken Paff and made the mistake of opening it to the public. He managed to land another job in a Hansen's bottling plant and thus kept his Local 912 membership, but he no longer had direct access to workers inside the frozen food plants.[19]

"Then," Bardacke recalled, "we got a tremendous break." One day in October 1981, Juan Parra, a gentle, unassuming dockworker at Watsonville Canning, was verbally abused by his anglo foreman. According to Anita Contreras, who witnessed the incident, the foreman's behavior was typical: "He was always cursing at everybody." Like many other workers in the plant, she was a devout Catholic and found the foreman offensive. So did Parra, who uncharacteristically lost his temper and hit his tormenter over the head with a broomstick. The company promptly had Parra arrested for assault with a deadly weapon and fired him.[20]

Local 912 officers said there was nothing they could do. When Parra raised his problem at a union meeting, TDU offered to help. Bardacke contacted Dan Siegel, a Bay Area attorney who had been active in the People's Park struggle as a Berkeley student. Bardacke even wrote an agitprop sketch about the incident and prevailed upon R. G. Davis, champion of Brechtian political theater and founder of the San Francisco Mime Troupe, to stage it. (The actor who represented Sergio López had his face painted half white and half brown; Davis liked to make his points with over-the-top ethnic stereotypes.)

Dan Siegel vowed to "put Watsonville Canning on trial," and there was no shortage of potential witnesses. Juan Parra had friends and relatives inside the plant. The foreman was universally despised: workers regarded him as incompetent as well as abusive, and rumor had it that he held onto his job only because his wife was sleeping with Mort Console. On the day of the preliminary hearing a number of workers showed up to testify for the defense. They never got the chance. Apparently at Console's request, the Border Patrol (enforcement arm of the Immigration and Naturalization Service [INS], popularly known as *la Migra*) arrived at the courthouse and arrested everyone who could not prove legal residency.

The INS action provoked a storm of outrage in the community. Undocumented workers made up a huge part of Watsonville's labor force, and local businesses no less than workers were threatened by the prospect of more immigration raids. A crowd of 250 people showed up to protest at a city council meeting. Congressman Leon Panetta, the future CIA director, got involved, arguing that it was inappropriate for the INS to intervene in what was essentially a labor dispute. He set up a task force to monitor the agency's conduct in his district. TDU's José López, who happened to be undocumented, was one of those appointed to the task force.[21]

Juan Parra never did get his job back. The Teamsters eventually challenged his dismissal, but the grievance was lost in arbitration. However, the assault charges were thrown out, and Siegel filed a racial discrimination suit on Parra's behalf that won a $135,000 settlement. For all the legal repression that would be directed at Watsonville Canning workers after they went on strike in 1985, their immigration status would rarely be an issue. For that, Frank Bardacke credits the Parra case, which clearly did force the INS to lower its profile in Watsonville.

In fall of 1982, with union elections looming, Richard King sensed that his administration might be in trouble. Watsonville TDU was still a relatively small organization, with perhaps fifty-five active supporters, but it fielded a slate headed by Frank Bardacke, running against King for secretary-treasurer, that was getting surprising traction. Earlier King had loaned Sergio López out to the Western Conference of Teamsters to help with a strike in the San Joaquin Valley; now he called López back to Watsonville, pointing out that if the election went badly they would both be out of a job.[22]

By this time King was drinking heavily, but more was at issue than his personal deportment. After more than three decades of unchecked expansion, the frozen food industry was showing the first signs of over-capacity. Competition for market share had become more intense. Watsonville's Green Giant plant, owned by an outside corporation rather than local entrepreneurs, was experimenting with production south of the border, hoping to save on labor costs. And since 1976 Watsonville Canning had faced a new locally owned competitor. Richard Shaw, a longtime manager at Watsonville Canning, had had a bitter falling out with the Console family after Ed Console's death, and left the firm to start his own company. He knew the business inside out, and within a few years had coaxed enough money out of investors to launch a new, state-of-the-art plant several blocks from his old employer.

Unlike Mort Console, who played his cards close to the vest, Richard Shaw was not shy about publicity. He sought Teamster help in launching an aggressive "Buy American" campaign that entreated consumers and US trade officials alike to "save American jobs" by shunning frozen food imported from Mexico.[23] He made sure the media knew about the efficiencies of his new high-tech plant. If Console had any particular advantage over Shaw, it was his workforce. Shaw had to recruit many of his workers from outside of Watsonville; Console's were experienced, highly skilled, and rooted in the community.

Gratitude for their skill and service does not appear to have entered into Console's calculations when his collective bargaining agreement with Local 912 expired in summer of 1982. He demanded that line workers' pay be reduced from $7.05 to $6.66 an hour. Plant manager Smiley Verduzco, a third generation Mexican American who spoke fluent Spanish, circulated through the plant, warning workers that Watsonville Canning was in dire financial straits and might close if they did not agree to the cut. He implied that the pay cut was only temporary and the old wage would be restored once the company was back on firmer footing.[24]

This was not just an attack on the workers: Console's move directly threatened other frozen food manufacturers and undermined the union's standing in the industry, where competition had always been stiff and was becoming more so. The employers had long counted on the Teamsters to enforce uniform wage standards, making labor costs a predictable, fixed expense and "taking wages out of competition." Should the process break down, the battle for market share would turn into a free-for-all, and employers would lose a major incentive for dealing with the union.

The longtime leader of Local 912 did nothing to stop it. Years later Frank Bardacke still professed amazement that Richard King—"who was not stupid"—had let Console get away with it. Sergio López, who knew King well, took a stab at explaining:

> Richard King got to believe that Mort Console, who was like a son to him, would never betray him or jeopardize his political career in any way. . . . His dad was a really close friend, and King was in awe of the kid. King forgot the rule: employers want to make a profit. They never like a union. They will tolerate you, but they will never become your friend. He actually came to think that he was special, that employers liked him and adored him for all he had done for them over the years . . . And

Mort Console got to believe that King was weak. He thought, well, as long as I've got the leadership in my pocket, or at least thinking my way, I can do whatever I want to the people.[25]

Under a Teamster rule that would later be abolished, it took a two-thirds vote of the rank and file to reject an agreement accepted by union negotiators. TDU argued against it but did not have enough influence in the plant to swing the necessary votes. Console got his pay cut. Richard Shaw, who assumed Console was trying to put him out of business, was furious; his heavily capitalized firm could ill afford the labor-cost advantage that Local 912 had just handed his competitor. Had they been watching the situation more closely, higher-level Teamster officials might have been equally disturbed, since the deal undercut the pattern bargaining arrangement that was central to Teamster power in the industry. Many workers in other frozen food plants were angry as well; they feared, not unreasonably, that their own paychecks would be next.

When the Local 912 election ballots were tallied in November, the TDU slate got 44 percent of the vote. Frank Bardacke, who had been a Teamster for barely three years, came within two hundred votes of assuming responsibility for running a local with eight thousand members.[26] It might have been an auspicious start to a union career, but Bardacke did not remain a Teamster much longer. He disliked his job at Hansen's and decided to leave it in favor of work teaching English as a Second Language (ESL) at Watsonville Adult School, where many of his students were farmworkers.

Leadership of Watsonville TDU was passed along to José López and Joe Fahey. The former was well-known to his coworkers at Watsonville Canning for his in-your-face approach to union politics; well before the local TDU chapter had formed, he had served as the CWC point man in Watsonville. An articulate and brilliant agitator, López was also a highly volatile personality. The twenty-five-year-old Fahey, though relatively inexperienced and unfamiliar with frozen food work, was no doubt meant to be a steadying influence. In the end, Fahey would take on most of the responsibility.

He was not entirely comfortable in his new role. Though he agreed that it would not be appropriate for Bardacke to remain active in TDU, he continued to consult with him whenever he was unsure of something. "Frank was my first mentor," he would recall. "He had huge gobs of confidence. . . . He was good at being a magnet for the angry Mexican guys," who would "go to union meetings and call the leaders names," something José López did with gusto. But it seemed to Fahey that there should be more constructive ways of directing that anger. He eventually came to believe that "the real power was the women. They didn't say a lot, they didn't strut the same way, but there was a cohesion among them."[27]

TDU remained active after Bardacke stepped down; among other things, it succeeded in building local community support for Juan Parra's discrimination lawsuit. As far as Local 912 politics was concerned, however, it never really consolidated the gains it had made in the 1982 election. Fahey believed that the organization went into something of a lull without the force of Bardacke's personality to drive it. Part of the problem, though, may have the extent to which TDU's program was centered on reform of the local, something that had not yet become a burning issue for workers in the plants.

Richard King may not have been popular with the members. His leadership style may have been autocratic and out of touch. But he did bring home the bacon. Until the early 1980s, Local 912 enjoyed an unusually strong bargaining position vis-à-vis the frozen food companies. A working mother whose likely alternative was casual labor in the fields for a fraction of the pay could appreciate the value of the Teamsters' frozen food contract: a union wage, health benefits, and steady work nine months out of a year. It was enough to outweigh any immediate concerns about how the union was run.

This is not to say that frozen food workers did not have serious grievances, only that they were apt to lie elsewhere—on the shop floor or in the community at large. Those of them who were already interested in union politics found an outlet in TDU. For the rest, the state of Local 912 would not become a pressing concern until their living standards came under attack and the union failed to defend them.

Chapter 4

Local 912 at Bay

Gloria Betancourt was a teenager working on the production line at Watsonville Canning the first time she saw Mort Console. Roughly the same age as herself, he was accompanying his mother, the plant manager, on rounds across the shop floor. "He was very handsome," she would recall wryly.[1]

Once he had left law school to take over the family business, young Mort developed into something of a playboy. He eventually acquired several expensive cars, a pair of private jets, and two hundred thousand dollars' worth of furniture in his nearby Aptos home. His workers gossiped about his alleged fondness for cocaine. He had claimed Watsonville Canning needed a wage cut to stay profitable in 1982; once he had it, he built a new headquarters for the company on Green Valley Road, so well-appointed that Sergio López took to referring to it as "the Taj Mahal."[2]

He maintained his close relationship with Richard King, a frequent passenger on his Lear jet. King, whose fondness for alcohol provided similar fodder for local gossip, does not appear to have been bothered by Console's free-spending ways. He was given to extravagant gestures himself: Teamsters attorney Duane Beeson recalled the elaborate clambakes King threw at a nearby beach and the used fire engine he bought and liked to drive around town.[3]

Had he been paying closer attention, King might have realized that Console's propensity for throwing money around had come to involve more than his lifestyle. Having significantly lowered his labor costs in the 1982 contract talks, Console was now positioned to drive his competitors—particularly Richard Shaw—out of business.

He invested $750,000 in upgrades to his plant, significantly increasing its productivity. He hired time-study men to help him get more out of his workers. He began flooding the frozen food market, driving prices down. His intent, it would appear, was to precipitate a shakedown in the industry, with the expectation that Watsonville Canning would survive it and feed off the remains of the competition.[4] Wells Fargo Bank must have found the scenario plausible, because in August 1985 it extended Console an $18 million line of credit.[5]

Ominously, earlier that spring Console had availed himself of the services of the nation's leading union-busting law firm. Littler, Mendelson, Fastiff, and Tichy was based in San Francisco, but by the 1980s it had expanded across the country and spawned a host of imitators. The firm had a long history of representing management in routine negotiations with unions; after Wesley Fastiff joined in the early 1970s, it began aggressively courting clients who, rather than accepting collective bargaining as a normal part of doing business, had come to see it as a burden they were no longer willing to bear.

Duane Beeson knew all about Fastiff. He had supervised Fastiff when they worked together at the NLRB a quarter century earlier and observed his subsequent career with growing unease. He regarded Fastiff as a mediocre litigator who had learned how to make the most of his modest skills. Fastiff's time on the labor board had taught him that federal labor law was full of loopholes, and there was plenty of money to be made showing employers how to exploit them. Whereas Beeson moved on from the NLRB to become chief counsel for Teamsters Joint Council 7, Fastiff had gone to work for the other side. At his urging, Littler, Mendelson adopted a business model that paid off so handsomely that by the mid-1980s the firm had grown to include nearly three hundred partners.[6]

Central to the firm's new modus operandi was an unresolved contradiction in the National Labor Relations Act (NLRA). The law, passed in 1935, guaranteed workers' right to strike, but a Supreme Court ruling three years later held that, while workers could not be fired for striking, they could be "permanently replaced." The high court reasoned that if workers could not be forcibly prevented from withholding their labor, neither could employers be forced to suspend operations during a strike. Realistically, a strike-bound company that wished to keep operating in the face of a union picket line would be hard-pressed to recruit strikebreakers if all it could offer them was temporary employment, so a "level playing field" required that it reserve the right to hire permanent replacements.[7]

Logically, this ruling cut the ground out from under the law's protection of striking workers. In practical terms, it made settling strikes more problematic, since any back-to-work agreement would have to be reconciled with the company's commitment to keep strikebreakers on the payroll. Even if both strikers and scabs could somehow be accommodated, putting them to work side by side after a labor dispute made for a toxic work environment and threatened to undermine productivity at a time when management could ill afford it.

Employers also had the political climate to consider. Precisely because the law was so ambiguous, they could not count on federal protection if they hired permanent replacements during a strike, particularly if the strikers enjoyed public sympathy. Furthermore, strikebreakers had no union to advocate for them, so an employer risked little by reneging on a promise to keep them on once a strike was settled.

For all these reasons, permanently replacing strikers was considered a "nuclear option" that employers were reluctant to use prior to 1981. Despite the ambiguities in the law, union members could still walk off the job without feeling that they were putting their livelihoods at risk, and the three decades before 1980 saw an average of three hundred major strikes a year in the United States. During that period only two other countries saw more workdays lost annually to labor disputes.[8]

Then, in August 1981, twelve thousand air traffic controllers walked out on strike. They were highly skilled workers whose grievances involved public safety no less than their own working conditions. President Ronald Reagan declared that, inasmuch as they were federal employees, their strike was illegal, and he gave them forty-eight hours to return to work. When they failed to do so, he fired them all and permanently barred them from federal employment.

Reagan not only destroyed the air traffic controllers' union, he also put employers on notice that it was possible to exercise their "nuclear option" after all, and to emerge, relatively unscathed, with a nonunion workforce. For those with sufficient resources, it was simply a matter of forcing a strike, hiring permanent replacements, and stonewalling in negotiations until twelve months had passed, at which point the union lost its standing as a bargaining agent. A union's only legal recourse in such situations was to convince the NLRB—an increasingly politicized body—that management had refused to bargain in good faith and was therefore guilty of unfair labor practices. This outcome was far from assured.

Increasingly, going on strike was no longer simply a matter of fighting for better wages and working conditions. For unions it was a life-and-death struggle, involving huge risks and limited chance of success. Large corporations like Greyhound, Phelps-Dodge, and International Paper successfully drove unions out of their plants by provoking strikes and permanently replacing striking workers. Other employers hastened to follow their example. To provide the legal muscle needed to implement this strategy, union-busting law firms began cropping up across the country.

Arguably, none of these firms was more proficient, or more ruthless, than Littler, Mendelson, Fastiff, and Tichy. Mort Console had initially availed himself of their services in defending the company against Juan Parra's ultimately successful discrimination suit. But his decision to retain them on the eve of the 1985 contract talks should have alerted Local 912's leaders to the very real possibility that he was playing for keeps.

Since the 1950s, Local 912 had negotiated a master agreement with Watsonville's frozen food processors, Watsonville Canning among them. Richard King typically handled the negotiations himself. According to Sergio López, King indulged Mort Console's ego by meeting with him separately, usually making some minor concessions that persuaded Console that he was getting special treatment from the union.[9]

This practice must have irritated other plant owners, but prior to 1982 it was not enough of an issue to disrupt contract talks. Now it was: with the frozen food market becoming ever more competitive, the labor cost advantage that Console had gotten from Local 912 three years before posed a serious threat to the master agreement.

The old contract expired on June 30, 1985. Early in the bargaining Richard Shaw indicated that, inasmuch as Watsonville Canning was no longer bound by the master agreement, he would not be either. He insisted on negotiating separately with Local 912.

Typically, an expired contract would be extended by mutual consent until a new one could be hammered out. But on July 5, Shaw announced he was unilaterally imposing new terms on his workers. Line workers' pay would be reduced to the same level as that of Watsonville Canning workers. New hires would make $2 an hour less. There would be fewer paid holidays and weaker seniority rules. Shaw justified his actions to the press by claiming that Local 912 was not seriously negotiating with Watsonville Canning. He cited King's decision to cancel a scheduled July 3 meeting with Console. "Every day the union allows [him] to operate under a disparate wage," Shaw declared, "we have been losing money."[10]

King denounced Shaw's move as "shocking" and "sneaky." On Sunday morning, July 7, Shaw workers, accompanied by family members and several hundred sympathizers from other plants, jammed the Veterans Hall and voted 475 to 15 to reject Shaw's "final offer" and authorize union officials to call a strike. It was an open meeting, and the militant mood was buttressed by calls for solidarity from workers at other plants. José López was applauded when he warned Shaw workers not to let themselves to be isolated as López and his fellow Watsonville Canning workers had been three years ago.

"The members are damned mad," King told the media before the vote. "They aren't going to let Shaw roll things back to the 1950s." He suggested that the union could walk out as early as Monday.[11]

The threat was enough to bring Shaw back to the bargaining table, but it is doubtful that King meant to carry it out—at least not yet. If nothing else, he needed to secure sanctions from the international union before the workers could get strike benefits.

But King also appears to have been operating under the assumption that he would be able to negotiate an acceptable contract from Mort Console—presumably one that restored wages at Watsonville Canning to pre-1982 levels. The 1982 pay cut was, after all, supposed to be temporary. Sergio López recalls King acknowledging that Console was playing hardball in negotiations, but "he swore up and down that it was all a big bluff, that he [Console] just wanted to make sure Shaw did not get a better deal." Console had managed to undercut his competitors three years earlier; in King's assessment, the owner of Watsonville Canning was afraid that King and Shaw would try to turn the tables in the new contract to "teach Console a lesson." Once it became clear that the union would not accept Shaw's concessionary demands, King reasoned, Console would come to terms. And if Console settled, Richard Shaw was sure to follow.[12]

Workers on the shop floor at Watsonville Canning could have told him a different story. It was obvious to them that the company was doing everything it could to build up inventory. Summer was supposed to be slack season, but the plant was running three shifts, with workers coming in at 6 a.m., 2:30 p.m., and 10:30 p.m. "Vegetables were coming in like crazy the whole summer," Esther Gonzalez would recall. "We couldn't keep up."[13]

Workers knew little or nothing about the progress of negotiations, but the stepped-up pressure inside the plant was enough to set the rumor mill working overtime. The changes had, in fact, begun well in advance of contract talks. One day in April, plant managers had assembled the employees in the big trailer where they took their lunch breaks and told them their production quotas were being raised. Their work was to be monitored closely. Esperanza Contreras recalled that "the floor ladies started walking around with timers"; even trips to the bathroom were timed. She remembered the two anglo time-study men who were constantly seen walking around the plant. She and her co-workers referred to one of them as Porky Pig; she never did learn his actual name.[14]

The job had never been easy; now it was brutal. Emma Jiménez was pregnant and in her third trimester. "They'd switch me from one line to the next, hot to cold," she recalled. "They were on people the whole time. People tried to keep up, because they needed to keep their jobs."[15]

"They were pushing us," said Chavelo Moreno. "After working there for so many years, they started telling people they were too slow. They started firing people—senior people—for no reason."[16] Elva Álvarez complained that her boss had grabbed her hand and held it against a moving conveyor belt to impress upon her that she needed to work faster.[17]

Margarita Martínez was a "floor lady," paid an extra $2.50 an hour to get more production out of the line workers: "Some people thought I was mean, but I would tell them, 'Hey, it's my job.'" But the increasingly toxic atmosphere in the plant appalled her: "The women had been trimming about fourteen broccoli a minute and suddenly they were supposed to do seventeen to twenty. It was not reasonable." Some of the older women were falling behind; for the first time in her career, she began fudging her production reports to protect them.[18]

In the past, workers routinely took home leftover produce from the packing line; now Margarita Paramo was fired for "stealing company property" when she tried to leave the plant with a head of cauliflower for her children.[19] Hers was not an isolated case. Sergio López remembers filing ninety to a hundred grievances at the plant that summer, and roughly one-third of them involved the company's attempting to fire someone.[20]

Armed with his Wells Fargo credit line and his crack legal team from San Francisco, Mort Console clearly had no intention of giving up what he had gained in 1982. In early August he made his own "last, best offer." Company spokesperson Larry Vawter told the press, "We're after the same thing Shaw is after." But Console's contract proposal actually went farther: it contained disturbing language eliminating the dues checkoff and the "union security" clause in the old agreement that required new hires to join the union after thirty days.[21]

Richard King appears to have been stunned by this turn of events. If he had regarded himself as a father figure to the thirty-nine-year-old plant owner, he now resembled King Lear, turned out in the storm by his ungrateful offspring. Though regularly quoted in the media, he was rarely seen around the union hall, and Sergio López, for one, guessed that he was off drowning his sorrows. For the press, King insisted that bargaining was not at an impasse and a settlement was still possible. Privately, he put through a call to Chuck Mack at Joint Council 7 and warned him that a walkout at both plants seemed unavoidable.[22]

As in fact it was. Watsonville Canning workers met at the Veterans Hall on August 11 and rejected Console's terms by a near-unanimous vote. At the end of the meeting they marched, six hundred strong, to Callaghan Park to "show our resolve." Three days later, Watsonville Canning began running bilingual advertisements for strikebreakers on local radio stations. Full-page ads appeared daily in the *Register-Pajaronian* as well.[23]

On August 19 Watsonville Canning began implementing its final offer. Plant manager Smiley Verduzco claimed the company had received six hundred job applications and expected to have a full crew of strikebreakers by the end of the month; Mort Console himself predicted that, if his union workers walked out, "They'll be begging for their jobs back in two weeks." Sergio López and fellow union business agent Leon Ellis entered the plant on routine union business and were arrested for trespassing. Meanwhile, Richard Shaw announced he would no longer deduct union dues from his workers' paychecks.[24]

TDU, which had been engaged mainly with Juan Parra's civil suit, became feverishly active in the contract struggle. Joe Fahey had been working nights at UPS; he wangled a day shift assignment so he could attend Local 912's regular monthly meetings. To make sure the meetings were not simply unproductive shouting matches between officers and angry rank and filers, Fahey and José López arranged for local members to gather on the Sunday beforehand to agree on what they wanted to accomplish and how. Fahey had proposed the August 11 march at the July union meeting; it had passed over the objections of president Fred Heim, who chaired the meeting and had his hands full keeping it under control.[25]

Among workers at Shaw and Watsonville Canning, sentiment was building for an immediate strike. Sergio López felt compelled to warn them that they could not expect unemployment benefits and advised them to hold off until the international union authorized payment of $55-a-week strike benefits—enough to "at least buy a few beans," as Richard King gracelessly put it.[26]

The strike benefits came through in mid-August, but King remained evasive when asked when and if a strike would occur. "We know what's best for our members and they'll follow what their union officers tell them," he told the *Register-Pajaronian*. "The workers are mad, but they aren't foolish, and we won't strike until it will hurt."[27]

Local 912 had no strike fund, so a special meeting had to be called on August 18 to set one up. More than 1,200 people jammed the Veterans Hall and voted to assess every frozen food worker in the local five dollars a week for that purpose. An eighteen-member committee, representing nine frozen food plants, was set up to handle the assessment and disburse funds as needed; Watsonville Canning was represented on the committee by Guillermina Ramírez, who had worked with TDU, and by Armando Morales. A notification to the members that went out under Richard King's signature on August 27 advised, "You will have to come to the Teamsters office, 163 West Lake Avenue . . . to pay this assessment."[28]

Local 912's monthly meeting took place on August 28. The members voted overwhelmingly in favor of a strike at both Shaw and Watsonville Canning the following week. But the final decision still rested with King, who said, "We can't strike until we've reached the end of the line."[29]

Console made another offer on Monday: he would agree to keep the union security clause and the dues checkoff if the union would grant a 30 percent pay cut, bringing production line wages down to $4.65 an hour. Watsonville Canning was, of course, already paying its workers 40 cents an hour less than its competitors; the new proposal was probably the last straw for Local 912's officers, one of whom remarked that Mort Console was "begging for it." Six frozen food companies continued to bargain with Local 912 for a new master agreement while the old one remained in effect, but a few days later Green Giant announced that it intended to follow Richard Shaw and Watsonville Canning and negotiate separately.[30] The union was in deep trouble.

On Friday, September 6, about two hundred Local 912 members gathered at the union hall, hoping to get the latest on negotiations. At last, the word came: a strike could not be put off any longer. Elizabeth Schilling of the *Register-Pajaronian* observed the gathering. The next day she told her readers that, although the workers were clearly ready to strike, "Union officials did not seem anxious to call them out." Little or no preparations had been made, so an informal group agreed to meet in the hall on Saturday morning to do some rudimentary planning, while a general call went out for people to show up at the hall on Sunday to make picket signs. Shaw and Watsonville Canning were served with strike notices on Saturday.[31]

At 5 a.m. on Monday, September 9, workers reported to the union hall, were given picket signs, and dispatched to the gates of the two struck plants. Several hundred gathered in front of Watsonville Canning and formed a picket line eight blocks long. The picket line in front of Shaw extended a third of a mile. The mood of the pickets was upbeat, even exuberant, despite steady rain that fell for much of the day. Very little appeared to be going on inside the struck plants.[32]

It did not take long for things to turn ugly. At eight o'clock that night, Superior Court Judge William Kelsay, responding to a request from the district attorney's office and Mort Console's claim that he "feared for [his] personal safety," issued a temporary restraining order that effectively outlawed mass picketing. The union was allowed no more than four pickets within twenty feet of each of the plant's eight gates, and the pickets had to be at least ten feet from each other. Apart from these, no one was allowed to congregate within one hundred yards of Watsonville Canning unless they were entering the premises to go to work.[33]

The order had the effect of restraining not just the pickets but residents and businesses across from the struck plant along Ford and Walker streets. In an effort to make it even more restrictive, Watsonville Canning replaced several gates to the plant with chain-link fencing, effectively reducing the number of legal pickets. The company also announced that striking workers would not be allowed on the premises to pick up their last paychecks but would have to wait for them to come in the mail. Union attempts to provide the company with updated addresses were ignored.[34]

To enforce the restraining order, local police chief Ray Belgard immediately put his entire force on twelve-hour shifts, insuring that at least a dozen officers would be on the scene at all times. By one o'clock in the morning on September 10, police had cleared the area around the plant, and at least one striker had been cited for hitting a delivery truck with a picket sign—the first of many citations to come. By the time the strike was three days old, the workers were feeling the full force of the police presence.

The situation would have challenged even a strong union. Local 912 was barely functioning. TDU attempted to fill the leadership vacuum—"acting as if we were the union," as Frank Bardacke put it years later.[35] But what happened over the next two weeks was largely spontaneous. According to Esperanza Contreras, after four months of working under increasingly onerous conditions inside the plant, the strikers were "ready for anything" and more than willing to defy the injunction—especially as it became apparent to them that "the police were on the side of the company."[36]

Watsonville Canning had begun bringing in strikebreakers from out of town, but few made it into the plant unchallenged. A Santa

Cruz contractor who supplied Watsonville plants with brussels sprouts, worried about losing business, arranged to have fifty scabs bussed in daily from Salinas to work a shift at Shaw so that at least some of the produce could be processed. To avoid detection, the route and arrival time of the bus were changed regularly. But strikers invariably found it and frightened the passengers enough to dissuade them from returning, causing Richard Shaw to complain that constant turnover was crippling production in his plant.[37]

Gloria Betancourt summed up the mood of many of the striking women when she remarked, "Just because you're Catholic doesn't mean you can't throw rocks at scabs." Esperanza Contreras recalled filling socks with sand to use on bus windows. "We were so mad, so angry, so desperate," she said. "But we weren't using our heads." She managed to avoid arrest, but according to Chief Belgard anywhere from one hundred to three hundred others were either cited or taken into custody in the first weeks of the strike.[38]

Though the restraining order was supposed to prevent violence, strikers quickly learned that they could expect no help from the police. "The court order is aimed at the picketers," Belgard said. In one particularly galling incident, a delivery truck driver tried to run down a picket. When she complained to an officer, he consulted briefly with Watsonville Canning personnel manager Larry Vawter, who was on the scene, then cited her for violating the restraining order. Picket captain Henry Celis asked why she was being cited and was cited himself. He called the union hall for help; when Sergio López showed up to investigate, he too was cited.

To the strikers, the police were not simply partial to the company. Thanks in part to the breadth of the restraining order, they were indiscriminate. Aurora Trujillo, a Shaw striker whose misfortune it was to live across the street from Watsonville Canning, was arrested for standing on her front porch. Richard Baca, who owned the neighboring El Rinconcito restaurant, complained that enforcement of the order had all but wiped out his business, since customers could not patronize it without risking arrest. "The police won't let anyone come here to eat, use the restroom, or buy a cup of coffee," he said.[39]

The crackdown on picketing often went well beyond the judge's mandate. Four strikers were cited when they followed a busload of strikebreakers returning to Salinas after their shift ended. Four others were cited for writing down the license numbers of scab vehicles. As the restraining order did not bar such activity, Chief Belgard conceded that his officers "may have erred," but added, "I agree wholeheartedly with people's right to strike, but how far should they be allowed to go? Should they be allowed to commit acts of violence? . . . I'm not going to have any problem holding my head up and knowing that we enforced this court order the best and fairest way we could." Local 912 business agent Leon Ellis retorted that Watsonville Canning "seems . . . to have a pipeline into Belgard's office."[40]

When they were able to talk to them, pickets sometimes succeeded in dissuading potential strikebreakers, one of whom commented, "I'd be striking, too, if I were making $4.25 an hour." Richard Shaw found that he had to go to some lengths to get produce delivered to his plant. Posse Freight, which normally shipped cauliflower to Shaw from the San Joaquin Valley, simply shut down its operations rather than cross a picket line and "risk getting something poured into the engine of one of my trucks," as owner Phil King put it. "Besides," he added pointedly, "I was a union member for twenty-five years." A laid-off Posse driver was hired by Shaw to take his rig to a deserted dirt lot a mile out of town, where he made a rendezvous with drivers from another trucking firm, which also did not want its employees crossing the line. Union drivers for the firm made a point of trying to get assignments that did not take them anywhere near Watsonville.[41]

At Watsonville Canning, things were hardly normal. Strikers and the media got a glimpse of what was going on inside the plant when a group of strikebreakers walked off the job and showed up at the union hall. One of them, hired off the street in Salinas, described a chaotic scene: "There's too much work and not enough workers . . . The work builds up and the vegetables spill because we can't handle it. Then the floor supervisor yells at us. . . . People are shouting and bins of vegetables [are] being spilled on the floor." He said many of the strikebreakers didn't seem to know what they were doing; he had been put on a forklift even though he had never driven one in his life. Another worker had crossed the picket line reluctantly: "I felt bad going against my people, but I needed the money." When his first paycheck came, however, he realized his take-home came to only $3.30 an hour, and concluded that it wasn't worth it. A third, furious over the constant verbal abuse, told her supervisor, "We're people, not dogs," and walked out with the others.[42]

Termicold, a nonunion storage facility on Riverside Drive that contracted with Watsonville Canning, had to drastically cut its employee hours; the owner made no secret of his disgust with Mort Console, whom he held responsible for the situation. North of town, growers in the village of Davenport on Monterey Bay had no place to go with their newly harvested brussels sprouts. Their anticipated losses ran into the millions of dollars, and one of them described their situation as "desperate." A San Joaquin Valley lima bean grower discovered that his contract with Watsonville Canning released the company from responsibility to buy his produce in the event of a labor dispute. He had not known about the strike, and Watsonville Canning would not tell him anything; he had to go to the union hall to get the facts. He was bitter because the company "did not make their intentions clear. If I'd known they were going to hold out I wouldn't have planted like I did."[43]

Delia Mendez, a social studies teacher at Watsonville High School, had a different concern: a number of her students were children of strikers, and if an acceptable settlement was not forthcoming soon, there was a real possibility that at least some of them would have to drop out of school and go to work to help support their families. Mendez was the daughter of Fresno farmworkers and had worked in the fields herself as a child; her sympathies ran naturally with the strikers, and from the strike's first days she had made a point of driving by the pickets after work and honking her horn in support. Sometimes she would have several students over to her house, where they would prepare sweetbreads and menudo and bring it to the pickets.

One of her students, senior class president Maribel Medina, had both her parents on strike at Watsonville Canning. She organized her fellow students to go down to the line after school on September 20 to show their solidarity. Their teacher offered to accompany them and record their action with a borrowed video camera.

The young people had barely arrived at the corner of Ford and Walker when the paddy wagons showed up. Seventeen students were placed in custody, and Maribel Medina was roughed up by a cop who grabbed her by the neck. Her father, on picket duty half a block away, saw what was going on; furious, he rushed over and tried to intervene. Curiously, he was not arrested, but Delia Mendez was. She would speculate later that the police knew who she was and wanted to make an example of her.

Since most of her students were underage, they were booked and released, but Delia Mendez spent the night in jail, charged not simply with violating the restraining order but with contributing to the delinquency of a minor. The latter charge, had it stuck, would have meant the loss of her credential and the end of her teaching career. When she reported for work on Monday morning, principal Tony Calvo called her into his office and told her that a member of the school board had contacted him over the weekend and demanded that she never be allowed into the classroom again. Fortunately, Calvo was sympathetic to the young teacher. He told her not to worry and stood behind her until the charges against her were eventually dismissed.[44]

News of the students' arrests spread quickly. The reaction was predictable: it took a squadron of police in full riot gear to disperse the angry crowd that gathered at the plant gate Friday night. The city council meeting Monday night was attended by two hundred strikers and supporters loudly protesting the restraining order, which had just been upgraded by Judge Kelsay to a formal injunction. (Mort Console had tried unsuccessfully to make it even more restrictive.) Aurora Trujillo gave the council an account of her own arrest. Also speaking were José López, community activist Cruz Gómez, and Maribel Medina, who said the police "treated us as if we were animals." The council took no action.[45]

At the monthly meeting of Local 912 two nights later, the membership overwhelmingly approved a TDU motion, seconded by Gloria Betancourt, to call for a "Solidarity Day" demonstration on October 6. The motion called on outside supporters to converge on the town that day to demand an end to "martial law in Watsonville." During the discussion, several members demanded to know why Richard King had failed yet again to show up for a monthly meeting.

Fred Heim could do little to alter the tenor of the meeting, but his lack of enthusiasm made it obvious to the workers that whatever happened on October 6 would have to be done without the help of Local 912 officials. At one point Guillermina Ramírez moved that local meetings be held weekly rather than monthly while the strike was in progress. Heim called the idea impractical and ruled her out of order.[46]

By now the situation in the local had the attention of Joint Council 7 in San Francisco. President Chuck Mack had realized something was amiss when Richard King called him three weeks earlier, since in the past King had never had much use for the Joint Council. But King had made no specific requests, and the Joint Council 7 president was reluctant to intervene in a local situation without the local leaders' approval—especially since Mack, as he himself readily acknowledged, knew little about the frozen food industry.[47]

Chuck Mack was a remarkably adroit union politician. Over the years he had endeared himself to the Bay Area left by repeatedly lending his name, and Joint Council 7's prestige, to a host of progressive causes. At the same time, he invariably maintained good relations with the top leaders of the international union, whoever they might be at any given time, and was careful not to identify himself with Teamster dissidents.

Once the decision was made to call for the Solidarity Day event, Joe Fahey sent Mack a formal request for Joint Council 7's participation. The request could easily be characterized as an appropriate courtesy toward Northern California's top Teamster official, but it served a political purpose as well. If Mack signed on to the event, it would further isolate Richard King. If he did not, it would reinforce TDU's arguments that Teamster higher-ups could not be trusted and the entire union was due for an overhaul.

Chuck Mack had his own agenda: he wanted to help the strikers without exacerbating tensions within the local and the IBT generally. Joint Council 7 did not endorse the rally. Instead, Mack dispatched two members of Local 70, his home local, to Watsonville. Their assignment was twofold: to set up ongoing material support for the strikers, and to make a strategic assessment of the strike itself.

The first task fell to Bill Walsh, who drove into town on Solidarity Day in a truck bearing the Joint Council's logo and musicians from the Joint Council 7 Band. A dedicated union man, Walsh was also a recovering alcoholic. When his drinking problem cost him his job in a Teamster shop, he had checked into a twelve-step program in East Oakland where, as Mack put it, "he was the only white guy in the room."[48]

Now that Walsh was on the wagon, Mack was happy to put him on the union payroll. He was to remain in Watsonville for the duration of the strike. It proved a life-changing experience for him. He helped strikers run the food bank that kept their families from going hungry and made sure the donations kept coming in. He went out of his way to talk to strikers, bringing coffee to the pickets on cold or rainy mornings. His obvious emotional connection with their struggles earned him the trust and affection of the strikers, who quickly realized that he was there to help, not give orders. Even those who maintained a jaundiced view of the union had only good things to say about him.

Alex Ybarrolaza, the second emissary from the Joint Council, had been entrusted with strategy. He arrived in Watsonville on October 2 and "immediately got into a confrontation with Dick King . . . [who] had a strong resentment of my presence there." To avoid inflaming things further, he set up an office for himself in Santa Cruz and tried to avoid being too conspicuous when in Watsonville.[49]

Unlike King, who had never led a strike, Ybarrolaza had a wealth of experience with walkouts and was regarded by Mack as a shrewd and resourceful strategist. His first task was to assess the strike's chances: "Was it winnable or were we just pissing in the wind?" A few days of talking with the strikers—Ybarrolaza was of Basque descent and spoke fluent Spanish—convinced him that it was indeed winnable; he was deeply impressed with the strikers' unity and resolve. But he also concluded that active intervention from the higher levels of the union was critical to its strike's chance of success.

His confidential report to Mack was blunt and in many respects astute.[50] He noted that "the morale of the strikers is high and none of the Teamster employees have crossed the picket line," adding that the strikers enjoyed broad local support despite a judiciary and police "seriously slanted in favor of the employers." Local people were reluctant to act as strikebreakers, forcing Watsonville Canning and Richard Shaw to try, with limited success, to recruit scabs from Salinas and Seaside. In short, "the strike should be a winning effort."

The big problem was what Ybarrolaza would later call "a complete lack of control" on the part of the union. His report did not spare Local 912's leadership. He praised the hard work and loyalty of the two business agents, Sergio López and Leon Ellis, but went on to say that Richard King was "despised by most of his membership":

He has not been present at a single monthly membership meeting this year, and from most all accounts last year either. He has a most serious drinking problem, and hardly ever reports to work at all. However, he still functions as the direct authority . . .

The Local Union contends that it is in serious financial straits, but has provided no financial reading or treasurer's report for quite some time now. . . . It does not fund any aspect of the strike, and a separate voluntary assessment . . . had to be established [to pay for] portable toilets, fuel for roving pickets, subsistence food programs, and coffee and refreshments for participating pickets. This situation has caused the membership of Local 912, 80% of whom are of Hispanic descent, to become very distrustful of their Local Union and Teamsters in general.[51]

The report cited the emergence of "rank-and-file leaders" who "recognize that they need the Teamsters to provide a winning effort," and were instrumental in keeping strikers' morale high despite widespread mistrust in the union. This mistrust, however, had "opened the door for outside influences," including not only left groups but also the UFW, whose regional director had shared the platform with Ybarrolaza at a meeting at Local 912 conducted entirely in Spanish.

The UFW representative, Ybarrolaza noted, "spoke in support of 912 and the Teamsters," and, despite the history of conflict between the two unions, the UFW did not appear an immediate threat. TDU was another story. It could be counted on to contend for power in Local 912, and presumably to use it to strengthen its hand in the IBT generally. Ybarrolaza reported that it was "constantly present, at 912's offices and on the picket lines." Of Joe Fahey ("of Irish descent, but he has learned to speak Spanish"), Ybarrolaza noted, "Our paths crossed repeatedly." (In fact, Chuck Mack had urged Fahey to "get to know" Ybarrolaza, but the young TDU activist found the older man remote and unforthcoming.[522])

The report concluded that the strike's rank-and-file leaders would welcome intervention by the international union: "A winning effort, together with a good showing on the part of the Teamsters leadership, would very solidly entrench us with this group of members."[523]

Chuck Mack promptly forwarded the report to International vice president Arnie Weinmeister, head of the Western Conference of Teamsters. Historically, IBT leaders had tended to neglect the union's cannery locals, and Mack had to get their attention if he hoped to involve them in the Watsonville strike. His cover letter to Weinmeister made a point of playing the TDU card: "We need to re-establish credibility with the people employed at Richard Shaw and Watsonville Canning . . . it's imperative that we provide leadership to the striking workers, not only to 'win' the strike but to blunt the efforts of TDU, who threaten to gain a real foothold in Local 912's election later this year." He urged that the International make an immediate donation of $5,000 to Local 912's strike fund, "take an active role" in negotiations, and make a point of assigning Spanish-speaking representatives to work on the strike.[544]

In fact, it would be some months before the IBT formally involved itself in the Watsonville strike. Well before that, however, Joint Council 7—and Ybarrolaza in particular—would be playing an increasingly big role, both publicly and behind the scenes.

Chapter 5

The Strikers' Committee

The strike was in its second week when Manuel Díaz arrived in Watsonville from San Jose. In his capacity as paid organizer for the Cannery Workers Organizing Project (CWOP), he regularly made the rounds of the various cannery workers' organizations across the state. If a crisis arose in a particular community or plant, it was his job to provide support and guidance and spread the word to other local organizations, which would do what they could to help out.

The situation in Watsonville qualified as a crisis. Even before the walkout formally began, Frank Bardacke called CWOP's Michael Johnston with a request for help. The workers had few resources at their disposal. Enormous demands were being made on local activists, whom Díaz believed "did not have a whole lot of organizing experience." Certainly, none had ever seen a struggle of such magnitude break out in Watsonville.

The cannery workers' network had a history with Watsonville activists—most specifically with José López, who sat on the CWOP board—going back to the late 1970s. "We were comrades, despite some differences," Díaz said of López and Bardacke. "We had a good relationship with them before the strike." López, in his view, was "a very sharp thinker. He had a lot of courage, a lot of heart. But he didn't want to accept any kind of collective leadership. He was so spontaneous, so undisciplined that he couldn't be trusted. He was an anarchist in more than name—he had an anarchistic personality."[1]

Díaz was the eldest of seven children. His mother, Reina Díaz, had

71

worked for years at the Libby's cannery in San Jose and now served as president of Raza Sí, a San Jose–based Chicano community organization that focused on immigrant rights. She was a seasoned organizer, something of a legend in her local community. Her eldest son had hired on at the warehouse in his mother's plant when he first got out of high school; later he did farm labor, tended bar, worked as a teacher's assistant, and spent a year at Stanford University after graduating from the local community college. At Stanford, he became involved with Seize the Time, a Marxist-Leninist organization that would eventually merge with the League of Revolutionary Struggle. Since 1978 he had been a seasonal worker at the Del Monte plant in San Jose and a leader of the organization that eventually became the TDU-affiliated CWOP.[2]

Díaz regarded TDU as "an organization of white truck drivers" and his own association with it mainly as a convenience: it allowed him to keep doing what he had been doing all along and still support his family, which required more income than a seasonal cannery job provided. TDU national organizer Ken Paff was not particularly happy when Díaz was placed on the TDU payroll. Díaz had been candid about his politics when he applied for the job; Paff felt that in supporting his application Michael Johnston was advancing his own agenda, raising questions about the strength of his commitment to TDU.[3]

In the end Paff had to swallow his misgivings. Díaz had the support of the CWOP board, including José López, and no other candidate emerged who could match his experience or qualifications. "Ken Paff is a very smart man," Díaz recalled. "He understood better than anybody that TDU needed us more than we needed them." Díaz was happy to leave the task of haggling with him to Michael Johnston.

Having arrived in Watsonville, Díaz hit the ground running. He met with López and Bardacke and got the names of several workers who had spoken up at union meetings or volunteered to take on responsibilities once the strike started—serving as picket captains, overseeing the strike fund, organizing the food bank. They included Guillermina Ramírez, Chavelo Moreno, Gloria Betancourt and her older brother Armando Morales, Carlos Hernández, and Henry Celis, who offered up his home for the first of what became a series of house meetings. "Each person we met gave us more names," said Díaz, and over the next three weeks the group expanded rapidly.[4]

Díaz became disturbed by what he perceived as a failure of López and Bardacke to give the rank-and-file activists more direction and support, or to prepare them for actual leadership in the strike. (He had no such expectations of Joe Fahey, an anglo who had never worked in the industry.) He respected López but did not feel he had the people skills the situation required. To a degree, Joe Fahey shared this assessment: "José was very impatient when people disagreed with him, and people picked up on that."[5]

Early in the strike TDU had issued a leaflet, written by Frank Bardacke, calling on Local 912 to convene "a mass meeting of all workers on strike," which would, among other things, set up "a strike committee, elected by the people on strike, to help lead the strike."[6] The union predictably failed to act on the idea, and TDU did not pursue it—something Bardacke would sum up years later as a serious error. Díaz spent much of September and early October making up for lost time. His house meetings began with a briefing on Robert's Rules of Order and then got into the more complex aspects of running a meeting, handling a sound system, providing translations, assigning tasks, following up with volunteers, and dealing constructively with conflicts and disruptive individuals. He used role-playing exercises to develop people's skills.

His efforts did not sit well with José López. As a CWOP field organizer, Díaz was expected to concentrate on getting outside support for the strike and leave the job of working with strikers to the local people. He was unwilling to accept such constraints, especially since from his perspective the necessary local work was not being done. "From that point on," he recalled, "it became a contentious relationship." His encounters with José López at the union hall or on the picket line were "cold and negative. He didn't give a damn that I was in the League. He wasn't anticommunist, he was just anti-me."[7]

Part of the problem was the chaotic situation inside Local 912. An effectively functioning union would have had trained leadership in place to take charge of strike activity. TDU's program had always been geared toward exposing the incompetence of the local's officers with the goal of eventually replacing them, taking control of Local 912, and making it into a fighting, democratic organization. The strike seemed the perfect opportunity to do this: Richard King and Fred Heim were thoroughly discredited, workers were angry and ready to fight, a power vacuum in the local was waiting to be filled. And so each of the Sunday meetings that López and Joe Fahey organized during the summer was geared toward preparing workers for the monthly membership meeting two days later. There was an implicit assumption that union meetings were the place for activist workers to assert themselves and TDU the proper vehicle for them to do so.

Now something else was happening: a move by strikers to organize themselves outside the formal structure of the union. The motion was driven largely by necessity: there were urgent tasks to be done, and the union was not doing them. For all practical purposes it was consistent with what Bardacke wanted to see happen. But neither he nor Joe Fahey was in a position to work closely with the strikers who were trying to bring it about. Bardacke had surrendered his Local 912 membership when he left his job at the Hansen's bottling plant in 1983. Fahey had his day job at UPS, and much of his work in TDU had been with fellow UPS drivers and other delivery drivers, mostly men. As for the struck plants, "I didn't know a lot of people," Fahey recalled. "I was good in group situations, where people were raising their ideas," but one-on-one organizing required more time, more contacts, and perhaps more experience and better Spanish than he had at that point.[8]

José López was in a far better position to help activist strikers get organized. Not only was he one of them, he was also well-known as a fighter, both in the plant and in the union. But for all his intelligence and charisma, he was temperamentally unsuited for the task. His confrontational approach put some strikers off, but it did influence others to carry out daring, surreptitious attacks on scab trucks and company property. This was high-risk activity, which by its very nature had to be done by isolated individuals. It could not substitute for the kind of mass organizing required to sustain the walkout.

Bardacke saw his own role as one of "thinking outside the box," contributing to the strikers' efforts by coming up with ideas that broadened the parameters of the struggle and took it beyond what he called "the ordinary rules of 'labor-management' disputes." Ideally, this would have entailed a general strike, with workers in all eight of Watsonville's frozen food plants walking off the job at once. Short of that, Bardacke had two specific suggestions: demanding that the Teamsters increase the $55-a-week strike benefits to $100, and calling on field workers who supplied the struck plants with produce to stage a short work stoppage in a demonstration of solidarity.[9]

The first of these was of mainly agitational value: it exposed the extent to which the infrastructure of the Teamsters union was not set up to deal with the needs of its lower-paid members. As a rule, union truck drivers who walked out off the job did not need to rely solely on strike benefits to sustain them while they were on strike. But members of Local 912 had little else. Most of them had few assets and no savings to speak of, and many had house or car payments to make. Their local did not even have an ongoing strike fund. It was obvious to everyone that $55 a week was pitifully inadequate.

The problem was that increasing strike benefits would have required action by the IBT convention. For the moment, at least, there was little anybody in Local 912 could do about the situation except ponder their own lack of standing in the international union. From a purely practical standpoint, the main value of raising the issue was to highlight the need for aggressive fundraising from sympathetic supporters.

The second idea was to come up from time to time during the course of the strike. Many of the strikers had worked in the fields or had family or friends who still did. They were aware of the history of jurisdictional warfare between the Teamsters and the UFW, a conflict that had never been fully resolved. Frank Bardacke himself had spent several years working the lettuce and celery harvests in the Salinas Valley and had good relationships with a number of UFW militants there, though by the time of the Watsonville strike they had been largely marginalized in their union.

However, an effective sympathy strike would have required serious preparation and organizing in the fields. The initiative would probably have had to come from within the UFW, and in the past several years internal problems, together with a massive reorganization of California agribusiness, had left the union with far fewer workers under contract in the area. One can only speculate whether Cesar Chavez would have been willing to take the legal and jurisdictional risks of a sympathetic work stoppage, since, as Manuel Díaz pointed out years later, "No one ever asked him to."[10] Throughout the strike, the UFW would be supportive of the strikers, but its support consisted mainly of advice, encouragement and contributions to the food bank. Juan

Cervantes, the UFW field organizer from Salinas, offered to monitor the buses bearing strikebreakers from Salinas and talk to any of them who were known to the UFW.[11]

While Frank Bardacke pondered ways to expand the struggle, Joe Fahey was preoccupied with preparations for the Solidarity Day action on October 6. The flier announcing the rally appealed for outside supporters to stand with workers who had, almost overnight, become virtual outlaws in their own community:

> Strike supporters may not walk down public sidewalks, walk down the street to a restaurant, visit residents of the street, or use the public telephone. . . . There are several city blocks where it is against the law for anyone but a scab or a resident to walk that street. The police are picking up scabs in prearranged locations, escorting them down police-controlled streets, and taking them through court-limited picket lines. Sections of Watsonville are under virtual martial law.[12]

Both TDU and the League were a good position to build turnout. TDU enjoyed considerable prestige among sectors of the Bay Area left, and its work on behalf of Juan Parra had made it enough friends in Watsonville and Santa Cruz to inspire strike support committees in both communities. Santa Cruz was a college town with a progressive city council and a respectable number of left activists. The Communist Party (CP), once a serious force in the area's fields and packinghouses, had barely survived the McCarthy era, but the county chapter was now undergoing something of a revival. Its work focused mainly on Central American solidarity and campaigns against the militarization of police; its interest in Watsonville, first engaged by the Parra case, ramped up considerably with the outbreak of the strike. Its chairman, Jim Brough, was never able to persuade the national leadership of the party of the strike's importance, but that did not stop him from heading up the Santa Cruz Strike Support Committee.[13]

In Watsonville, the most prominent member of the local support committee (apart from Frank Bardacke) was an immigrant rights activist named Cruz Gómez; she was the plaintiff in a 1985 voting rights lawsuit that would transform the town's political landscape four years later by forcing court-ordered district elections.[14] In both Santa Cruz and Watsonville, there had been angry protests over the heavy-handed and frequently racist behavior of local immigration agents. TDU became involved with these protests after la Migra made its clumsy attempt to intervene in the Parra case.[15]

The League had its own network of contacts, apart from those it had built up through its work in the Northern California canneries. It could draw on its connections in several Bay Area unions, most notably San Francisco's largest, Local 2 of the hotel and restaurant workers, where it had organized a sizeable Latino caucus called Raza Unida. It could mobilize the membership of community organizations like Raza Sí in San Jose and the Chinese Progressive Association in San Francisco. On university campuses, it maintained an active presence in several chapters of MEChA, the nationwide Chicano student organization. All told, it was able to fill five buses that rolled into town for the rally on October 6, besides many more who made the trip down in private cars.

The influx of outside support, however encouraging for the strikers, made life more complicated for Joe Fahey. "I was just looking at the mechanics of what needed to be done," he recalled. He believed he had a reasonably good grasp of things in Watsonville, but once people started coming in from out of town he felt out of his depth. His main exposure to the organized left had been as a student at UC Santa Cruz, and he had found it hard to identify with the educated middle-class radicals he met there.

Fahey was fearful that the rally would erupt into violence. It was being held without the approval of local authorities and was likely to be treated as a violation of the court injunction. He worried about outside supporters being needlessly provocative or usurping the rally for their own purposes, leaving the strikers alienated and prone to taking things into their own hands without leadership or direction. As word of the rally spread, he was being bombarded with requests from different organizations for time on the program to make solidarity statements.

All this took a toll on Fahey. As October 6 drew near, he ran into Manuel Díaz at the office of the local teachers union, where TDU made copies of its leaflets. In the course of their conversation, he fretted that he felt "completely responsible for what was happening, like it was all up to me."

"I don't," said Díaz.[16]

The day before the rally, Díaz's mother, Reina, arrived in Watsonville with company of Oscar Ríos, a League activist from San

Francisco who had been working with Raza Unida. Her son Manuel was in Chicago with Gloria Betancourt, making an appeal for support to the TDU convention, but he had advised the two of them to hook up with Guillermina Ramírez when they got to town. They did, and she took them to the union hall, which was full of strikers. After introducing themselves and talking with people, they asked to go to the picket line. The answer, as Ríos recalled, was "Sure, but watch out, because the cops are really, really mean." Sure enough, as soon as they were within two blocks of the strikebound plants the two were accosted by police and ordered to leave the area.[17]

They returned to the hall and began asking questions about the rally scheduled for the next day. Guillermina Ramírez described her conversation with Reina Díaz: "She asked me, 'Where's the leadership here? Where's the agenda? Where are the security committees?' I didn't know."[18] Ríos was told by several people to talk to Joe Fahey, who was supposed to be in charge. But Fahey, harried and distracted, was too busy to talk to an inquisitive outsider.

Ríos spent the night at a striker's home, asking questions and making suggestions. "This is not well organized," he remarked. He advised Guillermina Ramírez to round up ten friends and have each of them recruit ten people they could trust to act as security at the rally.[19]

As for Joe Fahey, he got very little rest that night. "I was worried that the whole thing was going to go down in flames," he recalled. "I spent an hour and a half sleeping and the rest of the time in the toilet with the dry heaves."[20]

Much to his relief, the demonstration went off without a hitch. Starting mid-morning, busload after busload of supporters began arriving for the noon rally at the town plaza on Main Street. A sizeable portion represented Chicano campus and community organizations, which had turned out in force. The UFW had a visible presence. So did Teamsters Local 890 in Salinas, where an insurgent slate, backed by the CWOP, had just swept into office.[21]

By the time the program started, the crowd had swollen to two thousand people. To protect them from a possible police attack, the impromptu security committee linked arms, forming an unbroken line between the cops and the crowd that would be maintained for the entire event. After a short rally, the crowd marched to the plant gate in deliberate defiance of the injunction. The police, about 150-strong, did not interfere. There was no violence and no arrests.

Fahey and Bardacke, sensing that the strikers would be eager to march on the plant and would not have the patience to sit through a lot of speeches, had made a point of keeping tight control of the program. It consisted mainly of a brief performance by the Freedom Song Network from San Francisco and a speeches by TDU cochairs José López and Joe Fahey.

Some feathers were ruffled in the process. There had been little or no consultation with strikers in planning the program. Outside groups had worked hard to build turnout and expected at least some acknowledgement. Manuel Díaz, just back from the TDU convention in Chicago, wanted to take the mic to announce that he had passed the hat there and raised $2,200 for the strikers. He was pushed off the stage. After some arguing back and forth, he was allowed to speak briefly. Later Fahey apologized to Díaz, who laughed off the incident. But too many people had seen it, and those whom Díaz had been working with for the past several weeks were not inclined to forget it.

The next day at the union hall Guillermina Ramírez denounced Joe Fahey as a "racist dictator." Her reaction was particularly intense, and particularly disturbing to Fahey, whose personal history must have made the charge of racism rankle. Ramírez had worked faithfully with Watsonville TDU for three years—one of a relative handful of women in a largely male-dominated group. But talking to Ríos and Reina Díaz had made her question her association with the organization, how seriously she had been taken, how much (or how little) it had prepared her to assume leadership responsibilities.[22]

There was a more general feeling, which Ríos did his best to encourage, that the strikers needed to pick their own leadership body. TDU had attracted some of the most visibly militant people in the plant, but it hardly represented the strikers, and to many of them its assumption of responsibility was presumptuous. "I felt like they had no respect for the workers," said Gloria Betancourt. "They wanted to be the leaders." Looking back, Frank Bardacke did not spare himself on this point: "The crucial mistake TDU made was not understanding that they could not lead the strike. I don't know how someone as politically sophisticated as I was at the time did not get this. It's basic democratic process."[23]

A belief in the importance of procedural democracy was central to Bardacke's political perspective, but the objections of strikers like Guillermina Ramírez and Gloria Betancourt undoubtedly went deeper. They had a gut feeling that if they were to hold their ranks together and weather the ordeal that awaited them, they would ultimately have to rely on themselves and the resources and understanding they brought to the strike. Politically sophisticated outsiders could offer help and advice, but the final responsibility had to rest with those whose view of the struggle was shaped by direct experience, not only as workers in the plant but also as Latina women.

In any case, Bardacke's assessment came years later. For now, Fahey simply found himself wondering if the house meetings Díaz had with the strikers had been a calculated effort by Díaz and Michael Johnston to discredit him. Hoping to mend fences and to clear up any misunderstandings that had come out of Solidarity Day, he decided to pay a call on Gloria Betancourt. She had, after all, sided with TDU on key votes at union meetings prior to the strike.

As he approached her house, he saw her two young sons roughhousing in the front yard. The boys rolled around in the dirt, pummeling each other with their fists and calling each other the worst name they could think of: "Joe Fahey! Joe Fahey!" The real Joe Fahey, standing a few feet away, had a sinking feeling that his diplomatic mission was not going to go well.

He was right. The reception he got from the boys' mother was polite but cold.[24]

Several days later a leaflet circulated, in Spanish and English, bearing the signatures of six strikers from Watsonville Canning and seven from Richard Shaw. Among the signers were Gloria Betancourt, Guillermina Ramírez, Aurora Trujillo, Armando Morales, and Chavelo Moreno. It read, "We call for a strikers only meeting for the purpose of electing a STRIKERS' COMMITTEE. We urge all strikers to come. Our future is in our hands." The meeting was to be held at 6:30 p.m. on Tuesday, October 15 at the Assumption Church in nearby Pajaro.[25]

The leaflet got an electric response. More than five hundred workers from the two struck plants showed up at the church on the appointed evening. No outsiders were admitted. When the meeting adjourned, a nine-member Strikers' Committee had been elected. In addition to four conveners of the meeting—Gloria Betancourt, Chavelo Moreno, and Armando Morales of Watsonville Canning, and Aurora Trujillo of Richard Shaw—it included Henry Celis and Arnold Highbarger from Watsonville Canning and Shaw strikers Linda García, Manuel Ybarra, and Victoria Benavidez. Gloria Betancourt received the most votes and assumed formal leadership of the committee.[26]

"I didn't know what it meant," said Chavelo Moreno. "None of us did. But they had faith in us, so we couldn't let them down."[27]

The formation of the Strikers' Committee was not only necessary but overdue. Still, the way it happened made many of TDU's friends and community supporters uneasy. For those inclined to view the strike mainly as a battle for the soul of Local 912, the committee's readiness to distance itself from TDU implied both a conciliatory attitude toward the union and a rejection of worker militancy.[28] The roles played by Manuel Díaz and Oscar Ríos in getting the committee off the ground, for those who were aware of their association with the League, conjured up suspicions of a hidden political agenda. Thus Cruz Gómez, deeply mistrustful of the Teamsters, could charge that the Strikers' Committee had been "hand-picked" by forces that "followed the union line." Jim Brough of the Santa Cruz Strike Support Committee noted that non-English speaking strikers had been reluctant to put their names in nomination at the October 15 meeting, and as a result "the women put in semi-leadership positions are all fluent English speakers, more anglicized and less militant."[29]

In fact, the range of views on the Strikers' Committee was too broad to represent any particular agenda. Gloria Betancourt, for one, was far more alienated from Local 912's leadership than someone like Arnold Highbarger would have been. And whether fluency in English translates into lack of militancy is debatable.

What is true, however, is that by and large those elected were not typical line workers. Armando Morales was a working foreman. Henry Celis was a skilled mechanic whose job gave him the run of the plant. Both men were well-known to the plant's workers. The same was true of Chavelo Moreno, who had earned his promotion to line foreman on the cleanup crew years ago by going to night school and learning English.

Moreno was a soft-spoken man, not given to fiery rhetoric, and in tense situations it would generally be his role to try to calm things down.

But he was intelligent, steadfast, and utterly selfless. He approached his new responsibilities with an attitude that bordered on self-effacing: "If you are a leader, you don't necessarily have to know how to resolve all problems . . . another brother or sister may think of something that hadn't occurred to you. You present the problems to the people, and someone among the people comes up with a good idea, which is then approved by the majority and is carried out."[30] He had a deep respect for the women strikers, believing them to be the heart and soul of the struggle. His attitude was remarkable in a community where men were apt to be threatened by the notion of women in leadership.

He was given the challenging job of administering the hardship fund, which the Strikers' Committee set up for those in difficult financial straits. There was no way to accommodate everyone who needed help, and Moreno had to determine whose needs were most urgent, how much help the fund could afford to give them, and where else they might get assistance. However difficult his choices, he could usually explain them in a way that made sense to people and preserved group solidarity. He was able to account for every nickel of the $12,000 fund. Esther Gonzalez remarked, "I don't think he ever slept. He was at the union hall 24/7."[31]

Gloria Betancourt had likewise been one of the higher-paid workers in the plant before the strike. During her twenty-three years at Watsonville Canning, she had mastered every kind of production job and worked her way up to floor leader, responsible for training and overseeing the work of 100 to 120 people. As she readily acknowledged, floor leaders were a frequent target of worker resentment. But she made a point of being fair and treating those working under her as her equals, with whom she shared the common bond of doing a demanding job and doing it well. She prided herself that her team invariably yielded good production.

She also functioned as a kind of de facto shop steward. Under Richard King's leadership, the union simply could not be counted on to help women workers with grievances, so they came to her with their issues instead. She intervened on their behalf with middle management and tried to get things resolved.[32]

During the strike she would emerge as the strikers' most visible spokesperson. A tall woman with platinum blond hair and a compelling presence, she did not back off from confrontations and was a superb extemporaneous speaker in her native tongue. "Of all of the ladies," Alex Ybarrolaza remarked, "she was the best rabble-rouser." On the picket line she was fiery and combative; at one point in the strike the *Watsonville Register-Pajaronian* apologized to its readers for running a front-page photo of her greeting strikebreakers with an obscene gesture. When called upon to address a crowd in English, however, she chose her words carefully, and felt comfortable only when she had written them out in advance.[33]

An outsider might find it hard to understand why these four, better paid and presumably more assimilated, would be selected to lead a strike of mostly lower-paid, non–English speaking women. Years later, as he neared the end of his Teamster career, Joe Fahey would take a cannery job for the first time in his life, needing extra hours to qualify for his union pension. He quickly grasped the dynamics of in-plant leadership, something he had not had the opportunity to learn while driving a UPS truck:

> The people who have respect inside a plant tend to be the mechanics, the foremen. They're not company people. They're competent, they've got a big investment in the work, they know everybody and they know what they're doing. . . . There's a quiet, conservative guy [in my plant] who's a mechanic, and I find myself saying, this guy is really smart, he's really sharp, and if I have a question I'm going to go to people like him for an answer. Because these are the people paying the most attention, taking the most responsibility . . .
>
> If this were a non-union plant and I was trying to organize it, the people I would be trying to organize would be some—not all, but some—of the key leaders in the plant, who happen to have a title given them by the company. . . . The angriest people might be the most willing to act, but they're not necessarily the best leaders.[34]

Conceivably, critics of the Strikers' Committee might have been more sympathetic had they not been so suspicious of the League activists who worked with it. As Oscar Ríos put it, "They regarded us as interlopers." It did not help that Ríos and Manuel Díaz did not seem particularly interested in repairing the rift that had developed between the strikers and TDU. The left newspaper *In These Times* quoted Fahey as complaining that "their style of work has been to attack all the local organizations doing strike support and replace them with local people directed by Manuel."[35] His words reflected a belief on the part of some left activists in Watsonville that the League had intervened in a local struggle where it had no business, and the Strikers' Committee was being manipulated by outsiders driven by narrow factional interests.[36]

Watsonville was a small, insular community whose longtime anglo residents were uneasy about the town's burgeoning Latino population and deeply suspicious of "outside agitators." Jim Brough described it as "a difficult place to be a leftist." Though the CP was active in strike support work, Brough made sure it kept a low profile; he figured the last thing the strikers needed was to be exposed to red-baiting attacks. He noted that every time he drove down to Watsonville from Santa Cruz he immediately attracted a police escort, although the one time the cops actually confronted him, it was to advise him that his teenage daughter had just been caught shoplifting and he needed to come to the police station and pick her up.

Unlike some local left activists, Brough had no problem with outside groups getting involved in the strike and trying to influence the strikers. As he put it, "You've got to have outsiders with other points of view and enough moxie to push things to the next level." But he was adamant about such groups not projecting themselves into the limelight.[37]

As for Frank Bardacke, he knew enough of the League's work in the California canneries not to view Manuel Díaz and Oscar Ríos as outsiders. But he did take issue with what he saw as the League's failure to confront the Teamster leadership, and he would later argue that the Strikers' Committee discouraged rank-and-file participation and had become "another bureaucratic formation."[38]

The League had, in fact, decided to make Watsonville a major focus of its energy and resources. It saw the situation as an opportunity to raise its ongoing cannery work to a higher level and link up its Latino community organizing to a workplace struggle with national implications. More specifically, the League hoped that out of the Watsonville strike, strong leaders would emerge who could make the union more responsive to its Latino members and at the same time positively influence the political direction of the Chicano movement. If the "strategic alliance of workers and oppressed nationalities" was to become a reality, it was not enough for the labor movement to embrace the struggles of people of color. As far as possible, the Latino, Asian, and African American movements had to develop working-class leadership.

What the League brought to the strike, apart from its Chicano movement contacts and some experienced and energetic organizers, was not a developed strike strategy so much as a political perspective and style of work out of which such a strategy could emerge. The League's labor organizing had always made a priority of "lower-strata workers" and people of color (or "oppressed nationalities," as the League preferred to call them). Seeing these workers as the key to a rejuvenated working-class movement in the United States, the League poured its energies into their struggles—immigrant women in the garment sweatshops of New York Chinatown, undocumented workers in the metal fabrication shops of greater Los Angeles, "back of the house" workers in the hotels of Honolulu, San Francisco, and Boston.

More than anything else, these workers needed allies. To assert their power, they had to break out of their social and political isolation, and that meant learning to work across class lines when necessary. While the League's advocacy on behalf of those whom the labor movement had marginalized or ignored often brought it into conflict with union officials, it did not share the single-minded focus on union reform that characterized some left groups. It placed equal emphasis on connecting lower-strata workers with the larger Asian, Latino, and African American movements. This required a "united front" approach, which usually involved navigating the often disparate interests and agendas that characterize coalition politics, and finding a way to do so without unduly compromising one's own principles or independence.

Applying this approach in a union context, particularly one as autocratic as the Teamsters, posed a whole new set of problems. So long as Richard King was running Local 912 it was out of the question. As higher levels of the Teamsters organization got involved with the strike, however, "how to relate to the union" would emerge as the strikers' biggest strategic challenge. The League's approach would evolve from a largely oppositional stance toward one of uniting with union officials when possible, challenging them when necessary.

In making the transition, the League drew increasingly upon its experience in the Chicano struggle. Not surprisingly, its most prominent activist in Watsonville had come to the labor movement after a rigorous apprenticeship in Latino community politics.

Oscar Ríos was born in El Salvador and came to the Bay Area with his family at age eleven. After graduating from high school, he tried to join the air force, only to be rejected because of his immigration status. He was recruited into the College Readiness Program, an effort by Black and Latino activists at nearby College of San Mateo to encourage youth to pursue an undergraduate education. Attacks on the program by the college administration provoked a brief but bitter strike by students of color on the campus.

Five months later several students in the program, including Ríos's brother José, were indicted for murder after a violent encounter with two police officers in San Francisco's predominantly Latino Mission District left one of the officers dead. The case of Los Siete de la Raza, as the seven defendants were called, attracted the attention of the Black Panthers. The Panthers offered up the services of their attorney, famed trial lawyer Charles Garry, who won an acquittal with a defense that dramatized the bullying and brutality routinely endured by Mission District youth at the hands of police. Soon afterward several of the dead officer's colleagues, incensed at the verdict, tracked down José Ríos and put him in the hospital with a broken jaw.

Oscar Ríos witnessed his brother's ordeal and worked on the defense effort. From that point on, "everything in my life changed." Los Siete's defense committee blossomed into a community organization that launched a health clinic, a food cooperative, a legal aid service, and a newspaper called *Basta Ya!* Its work showed the unmistakable influence of the Black Panthers. Oscar Ríos became deeply involved; the experience turned him into a revolutionary.

Like Joe Fahey, Ríos was on the payroll of UPS when the Watsonville strike began, but an on-the-job injury had placed him on disability. While he recovered, he was helping out his friend Rafael Espinoza, the head of Raza Unida, who had recently been elected vice president of Local 2. In late September Espinoza arranged for a public meeting with the strikers at the union hall. Guillermina Ramírez and several other strikers came, accompanied by Manuel and Reina Díaz.[39]

Ríos was so impressed with the strikers that he volunteered to move to Watsonville to help out Manuel Díaz. The League's decision to send him proved fortuitous. His big-city ways amused the strikers at first: when he showed up in town wearing shorts, sandals, and a Hawaiian shirt, Gloria Betancourt concluded that he was a hippie.[40] But it did not take him long to win people's confidence. He was resourceful, charming, and politically astute. More important, he knew how to listen. He made a point of telling people that "we're not here to take over, we're here to help." He urged the strikers to take charge of security on October 6 and to elect their own leaders on October 15. His main message seemed to be that it was time for them to stop taking their cues from others and assume responsibility for the conduct of the strike. Whatever larger agenda lay behind it, the message resonated with the strikers, especially given the circumstances.

At the same time, he and Díaz gave the strikers access to needed resources and outside support, making them feel like what they did had consequences far beyond Watsonville. A Northern California Strike Support Committee (NCSSC) was set up to connect the strikers with community and labor struggles in the Bay Area. Ríos took Guillermina Ramírez to a meeting with Chinese restaurant workers at San Francisco's Commercial Club, on strike themselves for fourteen months. "If all we have is one bowl of rice, we will give you half," they told her.[41]

Gloria Betancourt readily acknowledged her debt to Ríos. She was a natural leader, but before the strike she had never seen herself as an activist, much less a spokesperson for Latinas. She credited Ríos with helping the strikers "make connections and links that served us through the strike. . . . [He] taught us how to organize, helped us to relate ourselves to other groups, like students and political organizations." These contacts, she said, were often indispensible to the strikers as they tried to figure out their next moves.[42]

She had several run-ins with the police early in the strike but was eventually persuaded that she was more effective if she stayed out of jail. The League arranged a number of speaking engagements for her, and she used them to raise funds and spread the word about the struggle. On the platform, she would invariably portray the strike as a "fight for all Latinos." She remembered an appearance at Boston University: "It's not easy to stand in front of educated people and make a good speech. My English has never been so great. But I was so mad at the time, it gave me courage." Most likely, her audience was as in awe of her as she was of them.[43]

Usually, she chaired the Monday night meetings at the union hall, with Chavelo Moreno filling in when she was on the road. The meetings were informal at first, publicized largely by word of mouth; most likely this is what prompted Frank Bardacke's claim that they were "invitation-only meetings" that "did not build democratic structure into their activity."[44] High-level strategic discussions generally took a back seat to day-to-day problems of keeping the strike going: organizing picket duty, providing help for destitute strikers facing eviction or medical bills, making sure that those who left town to find work would be kept in the loop. As Gloria Betancourt put it, "We sort of made things up as we went along. We spent a lot of time talking to each other. We asked people on the picket lines for their suggestions."[45]

A typical meeting included a financial report from Chavelo Moreno and a discussion of the work of the food committee, led by Lydia Lerma and Reyna Guzmán. A system of rotating picket captains was set up to cover round-the-clock shifts at the plant gates. Since everybody had to do picket duty to qualify for their weekly strike benefits from the union, people were constantly coming by the hall to get their assignments and touch base.

Attendance at the meetings fluctuated from twenty or so, when nothing unusual was happening, to more than a hundred when there was a crisis. The lines of communication were no less real for operating informally: Watsonville had a remarkably effective grapevine. If someone had left town, people made sure the Strikers' Committee knew who they were and how to contact them. If the committee learned that an employer in a nearby town was hiring, carpools were arranged. Leaflets went out bearing pictures of strikebreakers, who could usually count on unwanted escorts when they left town to return home at the end of the shift.

Shiree Teng, who headed the NCSSC, called it a "total social network. . . . Word of mouth was all they needed, because everybody was related to somebody else. Between Chavelo, Gloria, and Lydia, they knew everybody." Written communications from the Strikers' Committee were often included in the bags of food that strikers picked up weekly at the local food bank.[46]

Two problems beset the Strikers' Committee. One was keeping open lines of communication with the union without being seen as being a part of it. Oscar Ríos thought it important that the Strikers' Committee "utilize the union." He would tell them, "The union is yours. Make Sergio and the rest of them accountable."[47] And Sergio López did occasionally sit in on the Monday night meetings. As a rule, he did not play an active role, but his mere presence made some people uncomfortable, especially in the first phase of the strike when many workers still regarded him as Richard King's proxy.

The other problem was turnover. "It was a hard job," said Shiree Teng. "And it was thankless. People were not vying for places on the Strikers' Committee; they were drafted." Three of the elected members from Watsonville Canning, all men, dropped away within a few months. Invariably, women strikers such as Lydia Lerma and Cuca Lomeli stepped into the breach and began functioning as de facto leaders. No one elected them; as Esther Gonzalez put it, "Nobody wanted the dirty jobs; they were willing to do it." Shiree Teng noted that while the Strikers' Committee provided formal leadership and assumed administrative responsibilities, a core group of forty or fifty of the most active women did most of the work and engaged in much of the practical decision-making, often meeting in small groups in each others' houses.[48]

The neglect of the larger strategic discussions Frank Bardacke wanted was not due just to the pressure of daily events. Left activists involved in the strike might have driven such discussions, but in the first months of the strike they were not talking to each other. TDU's leaders and some of their supporters in the local community were angry and resentful of the League, believing the League had deliberately set out to undermine them. By extension, they were ready to believe the worst about the Strikers' Committee. For their part, League activists in Watsonville stopped trying to work with TDU after Solidarity Day. Having concluded that the group lacked a real base in the plants and was unpopular with many strikers, they simply did not take it seriously—at least not until TDU's allies began publicly attacking them.[49]

Manuel Díaz and Oscar Ríos had poured their energies into developing relationships with the more active strikers and encouraging them to take charge of the strike. Some time would have to pass before they began paying serious attention to relations with local left groups and the support committees that had formed in Watsonville and Santa

Cruz. As for the Strikers' Committee, the League maintained that, as a democratically elected body, it reflected the will of the workers and had thus had a mandate to represent them. When the committee came under fire, the League newspaper *Unity* made a pointed reference to "some leftists . . . [who] would prefer it to include only those they consider to be the most 'politically advanced.' Others talk as if they themselves ought to be running the strike. Such actions not only do a disservice to the strikers; they discredit the left as well."[30]

The big strategic question, of course, was how and when the union would start running the strike, and what kind of leadership it would provide when it did. With Local 912 due to elect new officers in December, this question was about to move to the top of everyone's agenda.

Chapter 6

Exit the King

Before the strike, Guillermina Ramírez attended Local 912 meetings regularly. Most of the time, she left feeling frustrated and bitter. She was in a radically different frame of mind when she left the October 15 gathering at Assumption Church, where the Strikers' Committee had just been elected: "Everyone was smiling. Our spirits were renewed. And for that reason I say that instead of hurting us, the companies have given us something. The blindfolds are coming off, and we are unmasking the union officials. We want to continue having our union, but not with the same representatives. . . . When union elections come, we are going to kick out all of them and put in persons who will stand with the people."[1]

As it happened, union elections were less than six weeks away. Nominations were to be held on November 24, and ballots had to be mailed by December 28. Sentiment among the strikers was virtually unanimous that Local 912 could not continue as before. At the Solidarity Day rally on October 6—boycotted by Local 912 officers because TDU had organized it—José López had drawn cheers when he called on workers to "throw out all those union officials who do not support us."[2] Watsonville's TDU chapter had been advocating for a change in union leadership for its entire four years of existence; now, thanks to the strike, it seemed like a real possibility.

Such sentiments reflected a newfound sense of power on the part of workers who had, for the most part, felt they had no role to play in their union before the walkout began. Suggesting that the strike was "a blessing in disguise," Chavelo Moreno explained, "Being on strike has forced us to see it is possible to do new things. . . . We may not be experienced, but we are certainly learning fast."[3] The fledgling Strikers' Committee organized a rally and march on November 3 that drew four thousand people. Strikers provided food for the large crowd and maintained a 150-strong security force, which linked arms as the half-mile long column of people, walking 16 abreast, filed past the "black-helmeted officers [who] carried 3-foot riot-control sticks and stood, unsmiling, at parade rest."[4]

The rally, endorsed by a range of Bay Area unions and union officials mobilized by the Northern California Strike Support Committee, was designed to highlight growing outside support for the strikers. It featured speakers from MEChA and Raza Sí, as well as statements of solidarity from Congressman Ron Dellums and Mario Obledo, president of the League of United Latin American Citizens. Significantly, Bill Walsh spoke, representing Joint Council 7. So did Sergio López.[5] Leon Ellis, Local 912's other business agent, marched at the head of the line, though *San Jose Mercury News* reporter Jim Dickey noted that he was visibly uncomfortable. President Fred Heim was present but kept a low profile.[6]

Notwithstanding the apparent ambivalence of Local 912 officers, responsible people in the Teamsters were clearly trying to reassert the union's leadership role in Watsonville. Besides supporting the November 3 demonstration, Joint Council 7 announced its own rally for the following Sunday. A letter from Chuck Mack, dated October 29, went out to Bay Area unions and Central Labor Councils, emphasizing the police attacks on strikers and charging the strikebound companies with an "increasingly obvious" attempt at union-busting. "The results of this strike will affect all of organized labor in California," wrote Mack. "Please send a delegation from your Local Union and your Labor Council. We need your presence, your input, and your donations—including food for the Local 912 Food Bank."[7]

Sergio López, meanwhile, was engineering a break with the man who had launched his union career fourteen years earlier. Years later he would recall what must have been an ugly conversation with Richard King: "He felt that I'd pushed him out of office. All I said to him was, 'Richard, I just want you to know—nominations are coming up and I'm here to let you know that it doesn't matter who the people nominate.

Whoever is nominated is going to beat you. You're not going to win.' And he said, 'OK, you ungrateful son of a bitch, son of a whore, but let it be known—you didn't run me out. I quit.'"[8]

Personal loyalty matters in union politics. For King, already smarting from what he regarded as his betrayal at the hands of Mort Console, the defection of his longtime union protégé must have been the unkindest cut of all. He would not even show up at the nominations meeting on November 24, sending word that he was sick in bed and would in any case be retiring at the end of his term, as would Fred Heim. The two business agents, Sergio López and Leon Ellis, wound up running for their offices. Contacted by reporters, King said simply, "I just got tired. . . . The people wanted a change and they got what they asked for."[9]

The abrupt departures of the man who had run Local 912 for eighteen years and his highest-ranking associate indicated the growing power of the rank and file. It also complicated the task of developing a unified strategy in the forthcoming election. Sergio López was tainted in the eyes of many by his connection to the old administration; the assumption was that he had been handpicked to succeed King. But he differed from the rest of the current officers in several important respects. Not only was he bilingual and a native of Mexico, but for better or worse he had—unlike King—been enough of a presence at the union hall to function for years as the effective face of Local 912. In that capacity he had helped many members, handling their grievances and dispensing advice.

No one could match his experience at contract administration or his familiarity with the mechanics of running the local. Even those who believed the union had fundamentally failed them felt uncomfortable entrusting such tasks to inexperienced people, let alone taking them on themselves.

Joe Fahey was one of those who thought it pointless to challenge Sergio López in a head-to-head contest. This put him at odds with his TDU cochair José López, who wanted to finish the job that had begun with TDU's nearly successful campaign in 1982.[10] For her part, Gloria Betancourt believed women had been excluded from leadership of the local for far too long; even the slate TDU had run three years earlier had been all male. She was determined to run for high office herself,

and she urged fellow members of the Strikers' Committee to pull together a full slate of opposition candidates.

Her efforts to persuade them were only partly successful, as indicated by the eventual decision of Henry Celis, also elected to the Strikers' Committee from Watsonville Canning, to run for business agent
on Sergio López's slate. Alfonso Torres, one of the conveners of the
October 15 meeting, also wound up running with Sergio López.[11] Victoria Benevidez, a Strikers' Committee member from Richard Shaw,
ran as an independent candidate for trustee.

A pair of November meetings at the Assumption Church failed
to resolve these differences. A hastily assembled slate of candidates,
called La Planilla del Pueblo (People's Slate), emerged from the meetings. In addition to Gloria Betancourt, it included Chavelo Moreno,
nominated for business agent, and Guillermina Ramírez, running for
trustee. It did not include anybody from Watsonville TDU. Manuel
Díaz's recollection, nearly thirty years later, was that TDU could have
gotten representation on the slate had its leadership been willing to
compromise and accept candidacy for lesser offices, but José López was
as determined as Gloria Betancourt to run for president.[12]

The rift between José López and Fahey prevented TDU from offering a candidate for the top spot of secretary-treasurer. Gloria Betancourt's brother Armando Morales, a member of the Strikers' Committee
and a popular figure in the Watsonville Canning plant, was persuaded
to challenge Sergio López for the job and head up the People's Slate. Joe
Fahey had real misgivings about this decision; he recalled trying to warn
Manuel Díaz that Morales was not a reliable candidate.[13]

Fahey's misgivings, it turned out, were well-founded. Morales worried about his lack of qualifications, despite assurances from Díaz and
other League activists in Watsonville that he would have the help and
support of experienced people from other unions. His wife was reportedly unhappy with his growing level of involvement in the strike and
wanted to move the family back to Mexico.[14] But it was the influence of
Joint Council 7, in the person of Alex Ybarrolaza, that proved decisive.

Since arriving in Watsonville at the beginning of October, Ybarrolaza had become close to Morales. "He was a very intelligent,
straightforward individual," Ybarrolaza recalled. "I liked him a lot."
He felt Morales could have beaten Richard King easily and might be

strong enough to defeat Sergio López as well. But he worried that Morales, despite his lack of any connection to TDU, would be viewed with suspicion and possibly red-baited by the Teamster hierarchy: "If he got in as an opposition candidate, it would have been bad for international support." The initial dilemma posed by the situation was resolved, at least for Ybarrolaza, when Richard King retired.

Ybarrolaza and Morales both believed that, however strong the solidarity of the strikers, they could not win unless the Teamsters made a serious commitment to the strike. Making sure that commitment was forthcoming was Ybarrolaza's paramount concern. For that reason, "I talked him out of running against Sergio. I told him, 'You're both great guys, but it will be easier for the Teamsters to work with him.'"[15]

Morales, a reluctant candidate to begin with, was persuaded. Barely a week after the formal nominations meeting he had withdrawn from the race, ensuring that Sergio López would succeed Richard King as Local 912's top officer. In ending his candidacy, he also dealt the People's Slate a body blow before its campaign had fairly begun. Gloria Betancourt was furious; she believed her brother had "chickened out."[16]

As hopes for a unified opposition slate vanished, TDU tried mounting a slate of its own. It had even less success, fielding only five candidates for the nine open offices. Joe Fahey decided to run an independent campaign, standing for both recording secretary and the paid position of business agent. Though he put out his own literature, he was endorsed by TDU. So were two members of the People's Slate, though neither had consented to be part of the TDU's campaign: Eddie Torres, mechanic and shop steward at Smuckers, who was challenging John Bubich for vice president, and Reyes Jiménez, a cleanup crew foreman at the Crosetti plant, who was running for trustee. Enrique Torres, who together with his wife Esperanza were longtime TDU supporters, also ran for trustee as a TDU candidate.[17]

The League, which regularly put out a bilingual newspaper and several journals, had a well-developed publishing apparatus. This was placed at the disposal of the People's Slate, which had a leaflet ready for the nominations meeting and soon produced a four-page tabloid promoting its candidates and laying out its platform. Its literature called for "a just resolution of the strike" and declared bluntly that "women need to lead our union." It also called for workers' committees in every plant ("Our current shop steward system is too weak"), rank-and-file contract education, and drastically reduced officers' salaries. (David Gourley, the young forklift operator from Smuckers who was the slate's candidate for recording secretary, noted that "Richard King makes in three years what I make in eighteen years.")[18]

TDU literature hammered away at what it saw as Local 912's long tradition of one-man rule, corruption, and coziness with the cannery owners. It portrayed the incumbents as "puppets dancing to King's tune," and added, "King inherited his position and NOW, in the tradition of Mexican politics, the position is AGAIN BEING IN-HERITED." Since striking workers were not being paid, TDU called on officers to forego their own paychecks until the strike was settled: "Union dues are to be used to help the strikers." But the heart of its platform was a call for a by-law change that would effectively transfer power in the local from the secretary-treasurer to the executive board, which would be charged with setting officers' salaries. (The majority of the executive board positions were volunteer.)[19]

Joe Fahey felt that TDU's literature put too much emphasis on Richard King. He issued his own trifold mailer that echoed important aspects of the People's Slate platform: membership education and participation, lower salaries for union officials, and a better system of representation on the shop floor. He also reiterated TDU's proposals to win the strike: stopping the flow of produce into the struck plants, raising strike benefits to $100 a week ("with help from our friends in the labor movement," since at the moment there was no way to get it from the Teamsters), stronger ties to outside supporters, and "a decent contract—the same as the others—$7.06 an hour. Not a penny less!" The mailer gave TDU's return address, and its text cited Fahey's role in founding the Watsonville chapter, but apart from that it did not mention his ongoing connection with the organization, much less his status as its cochair. Frank Bardacke thought the trifold was inappropriately self-promoting and told Fahey so.[20]

After some internal discussion, the League had decided to put its resources at the disposal of the People's Slate while leaving it to the strikers to decide who would be on it. This was in keeping with the League's belief that the strikers should choose their own leaders. Looking back, however, Manuel Díaz concluded that it was "idealistic" to think that he and Ríos should not try to influence the slate's composition. Not only was it a mistake to run Armando Morales, but "we didn't struggle enough with the candidates to get them to accept Joe's candidacy. Gloria wouldn't hear of it." Since there were two open slots for business agent, theoretically both Chavelo Moreno and Joe Fahey could have run on the ticket.[21]

Frank Bardacke believed it was a "bad mark against the left that there wasn't a united slate," suggesting that differences among strike activists could have been overcome were it not for the failure of the League and the leadership of Watsonville TDU to thrash out their own differences.[22] A front-page story in *In These Times*, which generally took a jaundiced view of the Marxist-Leninist left, characterized the differences Bardacke referred to as "nothing but sectarian." Author Joan Walsh noted that, with union elections looming, the conflict was "of more than prurient interest because . . . sectarian battling has so split the opposition that mainstream Teamster candidates are expected to win easily." The article also took a swipe at Gloria Betancourt, remarking pointedly that she denied belonging to TDU even though she had traveled to the organization's national convention to seek financial support for the strikers.[23]

Both TDU and the League had reason to be dismayed by Walsh's story. Since it made a point of saying that both Díaz and Michael Johnston were on the TDU payroll and operated out of its Western Regional office, the implication was that the nationwide rank-and-file group was being rent by internal conflict—yet another effective grassroots organization being compromised by the struggle of competing left groups to control it.

The League, concerned about its standing on the left, was also worried that Walsh's assertions would undermine its efforts to rally more labor and community allies to the strike. It solicited supportive letters to the editor of *In These Times* and suggested to Fahey that such public bickering was harming the strikers. (Walsh had quoted Fahey at length while getting "the other side of the story" from Manuel Díaz.) Fahey, Díaz, and Michael Johnston cosigned a letter suggesting that Walsh's piece had made far too much of their differences. Internally, the League engaged in some soul-searching about its failure to take Watsonville TDU seriously or to develop a clear strategy to guide its dealings with TDU.[24]

TDU's national office resorted to a different form of damage control: coverage of the Local 912 elections in its nationally circulated newspaper, *Convoy Dispatch*, barely acknowledged the existence of the People's Slate. For Michael Johnston, who had been quarreling with Ken Paff for some time, this proved to be the last straw.[25] He ended his six-year association with TDU a few months later and took an organizing job with Teamsters Local 890 in Salinas. Local 890's newly elected Chicano leader, Frank Gallegos, identified with the opposition movement in the union but was never part of TDU.

It is doubtful that many strikers had heard of either *In These Times* or *Convoy Dispatch*, much less read them. Their hopes of transforming their local union faced a far more serious obstacle than the "sectarian battling" Joan Walsh described in such detail. Even with Richard King out of the picture and women taking on most of the responsibility for keeping the strike going, Local 912 continued to function as a largely male domain.

A favorite refrain of Sergio López and his supporters during the election campaign was that, if Gloria Betancourt won, "We'll have to install a beauty parlor in the union hall." This sort of sexist talk appealed to deeply ingrained attitudes among many workers, including some women as well as men. Chavelo Moreno, who was unusually sensitive to the plight of women strikers, remarked, "In Mexico, the unions are run by men. In politics too. . . . A lot of the men felt that. They made it hard on their wives."[26]

Manuel Díaz felt that what he termed "sexual politics" represented the most serious barrier to organizing in Watsonville. Oscar Ríos recalled being taken around and introduced to people by one of the women strikers when he first arrived in town. When they returned to the woman's home, her husband took him aside and said, "Brother, I don't want you to take this the wrong way, but I can't have my wife going around town with you. People will talk."[27]

Fidelia Carrisoza, who joined some of the "scab hunts" shadowing the strikebreakers as they were bussed out of town after a shift, went to considerable lengths to conceal such activity from her husband. One night they had a furious argument because he heard their three-year-old daughter repeating slogans she had heard when her mother took her to the picket line.[28]

Gloria Betancourt's marriage was only one of many that broke up under this kind of strain. After nine months on strike, her husband gave her an ultimatum: either she had to give up her activism or he was leaving her. "Go ahead, get a divorce," she told him angrily, and he did. "You know how men from Mexico are," she lamented later to a woman reporter from the *San Jose Mercury News*. "They want their women to stay in the home."[29]

Such attitudes prevailed even when the women were, in fact, working. Two incomes were necessary for families with children, Guillermina Ramírez pointed out, because "you can't get a place for less than $500 a month if you have kids. We work, and we come home tired. . . . The men, they come home to eat after work and just sit there."[30]

Nor did the pressure come only from husbands. Women active in the strike often contended with judgmental mothers and mothers-in-law: "They said awful things, like 'What kind of a mother are you? You should be taking care of children, not striking!'"[31]

Such comments hurt, because the children did suffer. They went without new clothes for school. Socorro Murillo's eleven-year-old son complained about the powdered milk from the food bank. Emma Jiménez remembered breastfeeding her baby in the cold and rain on the picket line. Strikers with older children saw them drop out of school and take jobs to help pay the bills; for many families, this was all too reminiscent of the days when they were migrant farm workers and moved constantly, making regular school attendance impossible. Testifying before the city council on September 23, Aurora Trujillo burst into tears as she described her daughter's decision to leave school and go to work.[32]

Enrique and Esperanza Torres and their five young children were evicted from their home when they fell five months behind with their rent. To avoid the same fate, Margarita Martínez and her husband had to sell off most of their furniture, exhaust their savings, and secure last-minute loans from her parents and three sisters.

Margarita Paramo's situation was especially painful. Abandoned by her husband when she still lived in Mexico, she had left her children in care of relatives and moved to Watsonville, where she worked for seven years before she could save enough money to send for them. Now she had to send them back for the duration of the strike; only the youngest stayed behind, sleeping in a car with her mother after they became homeless.[33]

Evictions and utility shutoffs became a problem almost as soon as the strike began. On September 25, the *Santa Cruz Sentinel* profiled a striker who was living in her sister's garage and a striking couple with two children who had to take out a loan to get their water turned back on. Watsonville Canning striker Carmen Guardado and her six children wound up jammed into an eight-by-ten-foot trailer with a single twin bed and a mattress on the floor. Socorro Murillo, an eight-year veteran of Watsonville Canning, eventually lost her house and spent several months sleeping in a van. She kept clean by showering every day at houses of friends and fellow workers. "It was terrible, so humiliating," she recalled. "I felt dirty. But I kept my mind on the strike."[34]

Pacific Gas and Electric soon agreed to allow strikers to defer their bill payments, and in mid-November county welfare officials publicly encouraged them to apply for food stamps and Aid to Families with Dependent Children.[35] Unemployment benefits were another story. Teamster attorneys maintained that, because returning to work on the companies' terms would reduce their income by more than 20 percent, the strikers were legally entitled to collect them.[36] But the local unemployment office did not agree, and the state Employment Development Department delayed hearing an appeal, prompting several angry demonstrations by strikers and supporters.

Of all the survival issues the strikers faced, the housing situation was perhaps the most critical. By the end of November at least thirty families had been evicted. Ten more had their evictions forestalled when Catholic Social Services paid their rent, but ten similar requests for help had to be turned down because the agency had run out of money. Two months later the agency calculated that more than 70 families, including 246 children, had been evicted or received notices to vacate since the strike began.[37]

In a town of 25,000 with 1,700 people on strike, the prospect of large numbers of striking families becoming homeless represented a civic crisis of grave proportions. Still, when strikers appealed for a moratorium on evictions at the November city council meeting, the council unanimously turned them down.

A month later, the *Register-Pajaronian* wryly noted that "council members may have caught a dose of the holiday spirit." At its December meeting the council voted to ask the county housing authority to let strikers use the Buena Vista labor camp. The camp housed migrant farmworkers during the harvest season but was empty between October and April; it could accommodate as many as thirty families. Mayor Ann Soldo continued to maintain that such actions were tantamount to the city taking sides in the labor dispute. But at least one city councilman, Roy Ingersoll, told the strikers in attendance that "I will work with you, with or without the council's blessing."[38]

Ingersoll was disturbed enough by the situation to conduct his own personal investigation that winter. What he found appalled him. He saw "a tremendous amount of doubling up. . . . People are living in cars, in campers taken off trucks and placed in a corner of a backyard. . . . I don't think in our society we should have working people wandering the streets with no place to stay except doubling up in garages, especially when you have standing houses available." A former deputy police chief, Ingersoll warned of growing public health and public safety costs to the city if the ranks of the homeless continued to swell.[39]

While city officials debated what to do about the homeless population, the Watsonville Strike Support Committee did what it could to stave off more evictions. Sympathetic clergy made themselves available to mediate between landlords and tenants who had fallen behind with their rent. Two local attorneys who worked with the committee set up a legal aid hotline to counsel those who had received eviction notices. Cruz Gómez could be seen bustling around town with a huge stack of leaflets under her arm, knocking on doors of people having landlord problems and offering advice.[40]

The leaflet she was distributing was almost a tenants' rights primer. It was both informative and concise. It offered "free legal and moral support to anyone who is having trouble with their landlord." It advised tenants of what to expect from a landlord bent on evicting them and detailed how they should respond. It emphasized that tenants could contest an eviction in court and, in so doing, drag out the process long enough that it would no longer be worth the landlord's while to pursue it. "Remember," it concluded. "No one need be evicted because of the strike. Do not ignore any legal documents or notices from your landlord. You will have the support of the Watsonville community." It provided a pair of phone numbers to call "as soon as you receive any notice."[41]

The Watsonville Strike Support Committee included social studies teacher Delia Mendez, Frank Bardacke, local Unitarian minister Dave MacMillan, documentary filmmaker Jon Silver, attorney Sherry Lessen, and several members of the local Communist Party. Cruz Gómez was arguably the committee's most prominent member. A college-educated Chicana from Santa Barbara, fluent in English and Spanish, she often translated for strikers at city council meetings. She had a gut-level identification with women's issues: like many of the strikers, she had married young, seen her marriage break up, and raised her children alone.

She was already a single mother when she began taking Chicano studies classes at the University of California at Santa Barbara. She rediscovered her Chicana identity, joined MEChA, and became an itinerant community organizer, eventually landing in Watsonville in 1979. Delia Mendez, a farmworkers' daughter like herself, had first gotten to know her in a local women's consciousness-raising group.[42]

Cruz was, in the words of Manuel Díaz, "a one-woman social service agency." Jon Silver, who regarded her as a mentor, said she taught him that attending directly to people's needs was a crucial part of organizing. Prior to the strike, she had directed her considerable energies toward advocating for the undocumented. She worked with a local free clinic that served migrant farmworkers; later she was hired by Food and Nutrition Services, whose office would provide the space for the Watsonville Strike Support Committee's regular Thursday meetings. She was instrumental in setting up People's Immigration Services, which held biweekly clinics to assist people with legalization while collecting personal testimony about INS abuse. Its crowning achievement was a day-long public hearing at Watsonville High School, cosponsored by Congressman Leon Panetta. Attended by five hundred people, it featured a parade of witnesses, who painted a compelling picture of la Migra as a rogue agency waging a reign of terror in Watsonville. The upshot of the hearing, according to Jon Silver, was that "we ran the INS out of town."[43] Immigration raids in the fields, churches, schools, and soup kitchens tapered off drastically.

When People's Immigration Services became involved with the Juan Parra case, Cruz Gómez got her first real exposure to union politics. She was appalled at Richard King's refusal to help Parra and came away from the experience with an almost reflexive hostility to the Teamsters. During the strike, this translated into a suspicion of anybody who tried to work with the union. The striker she felt closest to politically was José López, with whom she had worked on Leon Panetta's immigration task force. She admired López for his fearlessness: he never allowed his undocumented status to temper his militancy. During the strike he would be arrested repeatedly on weapons and drunk driving charges; Cruz was convinced that "the union fingered him."[44]

She had the kind of intense personal investment in her own work that often led her to question the motives and commitment of others. Though she collaborated with left activists on the Santa Cruz Strike Support Committee, she complained to a reporter that "sometimes I feel like Central America is more important to [them] than Watsonville." Santa Cruz homeless advocates, she added, were more concerned with local street people than with dispossessed strikers. After the strike ended, Shiree Teng of the Northern California Strike Support Committee told an interviewer that when she first arrived in town in December 1985, she and Reina Díaz had gone to a meeting of the Watsonville Strike Support Committee and gotten a chilly response: "Cruz told us that we were stealing their ideas, and that we were not welcome. . . . That backed us off a lot." Cruz Gómez told the same interviewer that the Northern California Strike Support Committee was "impossible to work with. They were embracing the union line."[45]

Coalition politics may not have been her strong suit, but Manuel Díaz readily acknowledged that Cruz Gómez "helped a lot of people." Her tireless efforts to provide aid and comfort to the strikers made it easier for them to weather the sometimes terrifying hardships they faced. What mattered most, however, was the help that the strikers— the women particularly—were able to give each other. They coped by treating their fellow strikers like an extended family. "We rely on each other to take care of our children," said Lydia Lerma. "We help each other out. It's a deep feeling of *confianza* [trust]. I know if there's any kind of a problem, I can count on them and they can count on me." Socorro Murillo added, "We had lost everything . . . but we supported each other. The whole community became una familia."[46]

"The ones who impressed me the most," Manuel Díaz reflected years later, "were the older women—their steadfastness, their clarity, their good judgment in making decisions. They were hard-working, non-complaining, sharing, and nurturing. They held the strike together. They noticed everything. No matter what was going on, they were there."[47]   .

Initially, many of the women were reluctant to go to the union hall. "I just stay right here on this line," said one picket. "That's what counts."[48] Men used the hall as a place to meet, socialize, play cards. If the women needed to meet, they preferred the picket line or someone's house. "We could talk there among ourselves and feel comfortable," one of them said.[49] Visiting the picket line, Manuel Díaz noticed that "there was always somebody getting married, getting pregnant, breaking up with somebody. I didn't pay enough attention to this. We felt the pressure of strategizing and coordinating outside activities and neglected to get to know people."[50]

On principle, the Strikers' Committee had insisted on having its weekly meetings at the union hall. At the outset, the decision may have adversely affected attendance. Two of the most active women, Fidelia Carrisoza and Esperanza Torres, both recalled feeling unwelcome at the hall. Committee members often had to seek people out on the picket line to get needed input on decision-making. Esperanza Torres relied on Joe Fahey and Chavelo Moreno to keep her posted on what the union was up to; she would then relay the information to fellow strikers.[51]

Over time this began to change: women would bring their children with them to the hall, changing diapers or feeding them on the tables, trying to quiet them when they cried. Gloria Betancourt noted that many of the men didn't like it. She asked rhetorically, "What did they expect? You have to take care of your children."[52] Eventually the men learned to live with it; some rose to the occasion by taking on a bigger share of the childcare responsibilities themselves.

But these changes did not happen overnight. In building its campaign around the principle of women in union leadership, the People's Slate faced an uphill fight. Many women strikers appreciated Gloria Betancourt's willingness to run for president, believing that she was standing up on their behalf. "I know Gloria," one of them remarked. "She has the same problems that I do. She's got to take care of her kids. But she's there every day, and I know she's making sacrifices for us."[53]

But if her sacrifices encouraged many of the women to take on new responsibilities themselves, few of them were prepared to extend that to candidacy for union office. Only one other woman, Guillermina Ramírez, was willing to run on the People's Slate, and she had a history of union activism. For the others, being on strike was apt to be a matter of holding their ranks together, confronting the scabs, and helping each other cope with the hardships of the struggle. The women strikers performed impressive feats of self-organization—running the food bank, coordinating the "scab hunts," cooking food for hundreds of outside supporters who came to town for the big rallies. But little in their past experience suggested that their efforts in these areas would be significantly helped by day-to-day involvement in the union. At best, it was a low priority; at worst, it meant putting themselves in a position where it would be hard for them to be taken seriously or function effectively. Accordingly, only a relative handful were predisposed to see the Local 912 election as a critical arena of struggle.

The incumbents capitalized on the situation, stressing that holding union office required people with experience. Leon Ellis argued that candidates on both the TDU and People's slates were not proficient enough in English to handle the business of the local. Generally, the "Progress Slate"—as the candidates running on the ticket with Ellis and Sergio López called themselves—walked a fine line. On one hand, they promised continuity of leadership, arguing that the union could not afford officers who had to learn on the job in the middle of a strike. At the same time, they tactfully tried to distance themselves from Richard King.[54] In his comments to the press, Sergio López portrayed King as a man who had served the members well in the past but had outlived his usefulness to a union whose membership had changed since he first took charge.[55]

It was a delicate balancing act, but it appeared to work. Joe Fahey was the only opposition candidate to be elected, easily winning both the business agent and recording secretary positions. Eddie Torres, running for vice president on both the TDU and People's slates, took 42 percent of the vote. Chavelo Moreno also made a respectable showing, drawing nearly 40 percent of the votes cast for business agent. But José López got less than 20 percent of the votes for president, and Gloria Betancourt's total was under 10 percent. The People's Slate candidates for trustee, Guillermina Ramírez and Reyes Jiménez, each garnered more than twice as many votes as Gloria Betancourt had received, but were still well back in the pack.[56]

Outside supporters of the strike struggled to make sense of the election results. For many, the situation had posed a ready narrative: a corrupt union, an embattled and angry rank and file ready to rise up and assert its power. When reality failed to conform to people's expectations, it was perhaps too easy to assume that factionalizing, opportunism, and general bad behavior on the part of left activists was to blame. Either they had failed to resolve their differences in a principled way, as Frank Bardacke believed, or they had sought tactical leverage by making an unprincipled accommodation with the union, as some of TDU's more partisan sympathizers seemed to think.

The reality was far more complicated. And while Richard King was a good enough villain for anybody's narrative, the Teamsters union itself was a bundle of contradictions that resisted facile generalizations. The deeply ambiguous character of the Teamsters' role in the conduct of the strike would become increasingly apparent in the weeks to come.

Chapter 7

The Shaw Settlement

lex Ybarrolaza was a quick study. Once he'd arrived in Watsonville on October 2, he took barely forty-eight hours to size things
up. He saw a local that had all but ceased to function; its leadership was incompetent and had lost the confidence of the rank and
file. Its striking members were ready to hold out as long as necessary
but had been forced to rely almost completely on their own resources
and whatever outside support they could muster. The strikers had the
sympathy of much of the community, but a sweeping restraining order,
issued by a local judge and zealously enforced by local police, made the
situation volatile and potentially explosive.

The Teamsters union had never paid much attention to its frozen
food workers, trusting Richard King to take care of things. Ybarrolaza was convinced that it could afford to ignore them no longer.
It was critical that the higher levels of the organization—from Joint
Council 7 in San Francisco to the Western Conference of Teamsters
to the International itself—inject itself into the strike and provide
some leadership.

Ybarrolaza did not simply report on what was going on and urge
Teamster involvement. He also began sketching out a strike strategy. It
was apparent to him that a victory over Watsonville Canning was not
only possible but critical. But the conflict at Shaw, in his view, should
never have happened. It was a direct result of Richard King's decision
three years earlier to hand Mort Console a forty-cent-an-hour wage
advantage over his competitors. Much of what Ybarrolaza would do

in Watsonville in the ensuing months amounted to damage control, doing his best to clean up the mess King had left behind.

Maintenance of a uniform wage standard among competing employers—what labor economists call "pattern bargaining"—emerged in the post–World War II boom years as a major weapon in labor's arsenal, one which did much to raise working class living standards in those years. Typically, a union would identify a firm that was particularly vulnerable to pressure and come to a wage agreement with it. The union would then "whipsaw" the firm's competitors into accepting the same terms rather than risking a strike that would divert their business to the company with which the union had already settled. Once a wage standard was established in an industry, the union would do all it could to make sure no employer deviated from it.

The principle of uniform wages strengthened union solidarity by preventing employers from playing workers in competing firms against each other. It also gave top union officials greater control over their organizations, centralizing responsibility for bargaining and deflecting the complaints of members who might otherwise have felt the union neglected their particular needs. No one employed the pattern-bargaining strategy more skillfully than Jimmy Hoffa, and for years the Teamsters' Master Freight Agreement served as a model of how a union could use an industry-wide contract to keep its members satisfied and keep employers in line.[1]

But an inherent contradiction in pattern bargaining became apparent in the late 1970s. Deregulation of interstate trucking during the Carter administration, and the accelerating decline of US manufacturing generally, persuaded many union negotiators that contract concessions were necessary to reduce layoffs and protect union jobs. Under such conditions "wage parity" invariably meant lower wages for everybody.

Conflict within union ranks was inevitable. Critics like *Labor Notes* editor Kim Moody argued that pattern bargaining no longer functioned as a weapon in the fight for higher wages but had become "a top-down conduit for further concessions" and "negotiated retreat."[2] At the Hormel plant in Austin, Minnesota, members of UFCW Local P-9 felt they were strong enough to resist company concessions demands. Just a few weeks before the strike in Watsonville began, the Hormel workers walked out, effectively challenging the UFCW's strategy of enforcing a reduced wage standard throughout the industry. After a bitter and highly publicized conflict with its national union, Local P-9 was placed in trusteeship and its strike effectively broken.[3] Pattern bargaining was supposed to be a means to an end; the fate of the Hormel workers showed that, once it became an end in itself, it could extract a stiff price—not only in the size of workers' paychecks but in the internal life of their unions.

When pattern bargaining was first established in Watsonville in the 1950s, the balance of power between labor and management in the frozen food industry favored the Teamsters. The industry was rapidly expanding, highly competitive, vulnerable to market pressure, and desperate for workers. To protect themselves against Teamster whipsaw tactics, local employers banded together in the Watsonville Frozen Food Employers Association, and for the next twenty-five years frozen food workers were covered by multi-employer collective bargaining agreements.

By 1985, however, the fabric of labor relations in the industry had begun to unravel. Richard King's concessions to Watsonville Canning three years earlier had created a powerful incentive for other frozen food companies to break ranks and see if, like Mort Console, they couldn't get a better deal by going it alone. The threat loomed of a "race to the bottom," with employers vying to see who could get away with paying their workers the least.

It didn't help that King had broken the industry-wide wage standard on behalf of the one employer in town who was effectively committed to driving the union out of his plant and driving at least some of his unionized competitors out of business. Clearly, the multi-employer agreement could no longer be counted on to protect frozen food companies from mutually ruinous cutthroat competition. They could hardly be blamed if they began to wonder what they gained playing by the union's ground rules. Richard Shaw, for one, felt that Local 912 had thrown him under the bus and was not bashful about saying so.

How to repair the damage? The task for the union, in Ybarrolaza's view, was to mend its fences with the other unionized employers while isolating Watsonville Canning.[4] Local 912 would have to reestablish its commitment to wage parity, even if it meant accepting a cut in pay. King's 1982 deal with Watsonville Canning had effectively knocked the ground out from under the old $7.06-an-hour wage for production line workers. Restoring it would be difficult at best, particularly when at least one other employer claimed that Local 912's preferential treatment of Mort Console three years before was threatening to bankrupt him.

As soon as Richard King was out of office, Ybarrolaza approached Richard Shaw and indicated that the union would be open to a wage cut if Shaw could demonstrate financial need. He asked Shaw to open his books. Shaw agreed. Ybarrolaza had made a similar request of Watsonville Canning, but Mort Console's lawyers demanded that the union put up $500,000 in security, "fair compensation for the foreseeable losses which might result" in the event of any breach in confidentiality. With that, any semblance of serious negotiations between the two parties was over. Union lawyer Duane Beeson forwarded the terms of Watsonville Canning's proposal to the NLRB as evidence of unfair labor practices.[5]

Ybarrolaza quickly assembled a fact-finding team to inspect Shaw's financial statements, payroll records, tax returns, and other documents that indicated the state of the company's health. He had Bill Walsh contact Bishop Shubsda of the local Catholic Diocese, which had been sympathetic to the strikers. Walsh also approached Robert Crall of the Federal Mediation and Conciliation Service and Lawrence Taber, president of the California League of Food Processors. Crall and Bishop Shubsda both agreed to send a representative; Taber would participate directly. The three met at the Shaw plant on January 22, having secured permission of the picket captains to enter the premises.[6]

They spent the next two days poring over the books. They concluded that Shaw had, indeed, been hemorrhaging cash since 1982, even though the company appeared to be well-run, its administrative overhead was modest, and its management salaries were "on the low side." Fixed costs such as utilities, payroll taxes, and insurance were likely to increase, as was competition from low-wage plants in Texas and Mexico. The committee concluded, "There is a serious need to be concerned about the company's financial ability to continue to operate. The need to reduce operating costs is clear and self-evident."[7]

No doubt Richard Shaw was in trouble, but at least one aspect of the committee's report may have been open to question. Both Shaw and Smiley Verduzco of Watsonville Canning were fond of invoking the menace of Mexico and Texas to justify their wage cuts.[8] But a rival frozen food executive, who gave a long interview to the *Santa Cruz Sentinel* in mid-November on condition of anonymity, considered the issue a red herring. He pointed out that in Texas "their productivity levels are probably half of what ours are . . . we have maybe one crop failure every 20 years in California, while in Texas, sometimes three crops in five years fail." Favorable growing conditions in the Pajaro Valley allowed local plants to run broccoli year-round; for plants along the Rio Grande, the work remained seasonal.

"All businesses have competition," said the executive, but Watsonville frozen food firms were "our own worst enemy. We have over 100 million pounds of overcapacity, which is a hell of a surplus." Put simply, local plants were producing far more than the market could absorb, and the executive placed most of the blame squarely at the feet of Mort Console.[9]

Typically, frozen food companies based their production targets on anticipated sales. Not so Watsonville Canning. For the past two years, the executive pointed out, the largest of Watsonville's eight frozen food companies had been running its plant at peak capacity. No sooner was the ink was dry on the 1982 wage deal than Mort Console had doubled his production of frozen broccoli, dumping it on the market at bargain-basement prices when there were no ready buyers. Richard Shaw, who produced for the same market, had panicked and slashed his prices as well, to the point where the more broccoli he sold, the more money he lost.

The strategy of the Watsonville Frozen Food Employers Association going into 1985 contract talks had been to hold the line on employee compensation while gradually working to reestablish wage parity. If the union resisted, the employers were prepared to take an industry-wide strike. But the unilateral wage cuts by Console and Shaw, besides provoking walkouts at their respective plants, had sabotaged the association's united front and created a situation that threatened to become unmanageable.

The executive's parting shot suggested that it was not just the Teamsters who regarded Mort Console as a rogue employer. "I have a lot of respect for Dick Shaw," he said. "He hasn't accomplished what he has by trying to destroy the industry. I can't say the same for Watsonville Canning."[10]

The Teamsters' bargaining strategy was too heavily invested in the fact-finding process at Richard Shaw to allow for much questioning of the committee's conclusions, and Ybarrolaza shared Shaw's concerns about Mexican imports.[11] Nevertheless, union officials apparently felt comfortable with the *Sentinel*'s analysis. Chuck Mack sent copies to both the Western Conference of Teamsters and Jackie Presser, general president of the International. "Of all the media coverage," his accompanying letter said, "these stories are probably the most accurate."[12]

Down in the trenches, the strikers were not privy to this high-level strategizing, but their own frustrations were mounting. The fall peak season had come and gone without any hint of a settlement. The privations endured by the strikers continued; only the Thanksgiving and Christmas turkeys, collected for every striking family by the Watsonville Strike Support Committee, kept the holiday season from being completely bleak.

The ranks of the Watsonville Canning strikers held firm, but some Shaw strikers had begun returning to work, among them mechanics whose skills were key to the plant's operation. The court injunction was restrictive enough to prevent strikers from blocking access to the struck plants, and the police enforced it aggressively. Occasionally Watsonville Canning managers Ron Trine and Larry Vawter would point out certain pickets and demand that police arrest them.[13] The police usually complied. Few things infuriated the strikers more.

The injunction inhibited strike activity at the plant gates, but it did nothing to make things peaceable. The *Register-Pajaronian* routinely carried reports of scab cars whose tires were slashed and windshields broken. Strikebreakers responded in kind: a striker who lived across the street from Watsonville Canning and let pickets use her bathroom found her house bombarded with ball bearings, apparently fired from a slingshot inside the plant. One twenty-three-year-old male plant supervisor confronted Socorro Murillo while she was doing picket duty. In the scuffle that followed, the *Register-Pajaronian* reported, she spit in his face, kneed him in the groin, and was arrested for battery. Another striker, Lourdes Sanchez, was arrested on the same charge when she hurled an apple at the driver of a scab truck and hit him in the shoulder.[14]

In Gilroy, fifteen miles to the east, eighteen strikers were arrested after a confrontation in a supermarket parking lot where company vehicles were waiting to transport scabs to work at Watsonville Canning. During the melee a company driver pulled a gun on the strikers.[15] On November 8, a bus from Salinas carrying forty strikebreakers to the Shaw plant was ambushed at a stop sign on the edge of town by a dozen strikers who, in the driver's words, "jumped out of the weeds and started throwing rocks."[16]

Esperanza Contreras had no compunctions about fighting the police. She recalled with pride how she and her fifteen-year-old daughter had wrestled a cop to the ground when he put another striker in a chokehold. She described another incident where she was part of a group confronting a busload of scabs in Salinas. Watsonville Canning plant manager Bill Lackey was on the scene and pointed her out to the police. She promptly took off her sweatshirt and baseball cap and lost herself in the crowd. "I was too smart to get arrested," she said with a smile, adding that she "never felt fear during the strike." But she also said soberly that she was "grateful that for all we went through, no one was killed."[17]

The most dangerous incidents did not involve violations of the court order, which accounted for most of the arrests, or even the sort of carefully orchestrated actions described above which, in Manuel Díaz's words, "put the fear of God into the scabs."[18] Rather, they were isolated, random acts of violence that took place under cover of night.

Fernando Ramírez, night shift supervisor at Watsonville Canning, had belonged to Local 912 until the company reclassified him as a salaried employee and rendered him ineligible for union membership. Accordingly, he remained on the job after the strike began—only to be fired in September 1986 for refusing to order his crew to process contaminated produce. Well before that happened, however, his house was targeted twice within a period of several days by person or persons unknown. A firebomb was hurled at the house one night in late December. Then, in the wee hours of the morning on January 4, shots were fired from a high-powered rifle which pierced the bed where Ramírez and his wife were sleeping. Bob Johnson of the *San Jose Mercury News* reported three other shootings and a barroom fight involving knives and tire irons during the same period.[19]

Strikers were not spared this kind of violence. Gloria Betancourt's house on Elm Street was shot up one night, a bullet shattering the window of a room where her infant grandson lay asleep. She believed one of the Watsonville Canning managers was responsible.[20]

The *Register-Pajaronian* carried items almost daily about strikers, usually male, being arrested for setting fires or shooting off weapons; frequently, alcohol was said to be involved. On one occasion police arrested José López for driving under the influence and found a loaded twelve-gauge shotgun, a .380-caliber semiautomatic, and spent shells in the back of his car. As one of the most militant and visible strike leaders, López was a natural target for police harassment, but he did little to protect himself. He wound up going to jail for several months at the height of the strike after he slugged a reporter for the *Register-Pajaronian*. (The incident arose out of yet another instance of manager Ron Trine's fingering of a striker who Trine claimed had vandalized his car; the reporter was attempting to photograph the striker's arrest.) Manuel Díaz, who respected López, found it sad that his leadership skills were lost to the struggle because he could not control his temper.[21]

The most serious charge brought against a striker involved Amadór Betancourt, Gloria's husband. He was held on $250,000 bond after allegedly hurling a firebomb (which failed to ignite) at a busload of scabs. Though police were unable to confirm that he had thrown the bomb, he ended up pleading no contest to possession of an explosive device in return for serving time in the county jail rather than state prison.[22] The evening after his arrest, someone set fire to a Watsonville Canning cold storage warehouse. Strikers were assumed to be responsible, but when the company tried to put in an insurance claim months later, evidence surfaced that supported suspicions of an inside job.[23]

For the most part, the local criminal justice system concerned itself with lesser offenses, finding more than enough of these to keep busy. By January 20, the district attorney's office had handled more than three hundred strike-related cases, and the police department had spent over $100 million on overtime pay—enough to make city funding for routine police activity problematic.[24]

Law enforcement was becoming almost as much of a sore spot for the larger community as for the strikers. Enforcing the sweeping court injunction had placed a considerable burden on local police. Early in the strike they had the benefit of reinforcements from the departments of Santa Cruz and neighboring Capitola, but effective lobbying of the city councils of both communities by the Santa Cruz Strike Support Committee succeeded in putting an end to it.[25]

In mid-October, after an unusually rough several days, the *Register-Pajaronian* ran the sort of "a plague-on-both-your-houses" editorial that newspapers often run in such situations in an effort to appear even-handed. It cited confrontations at the plant gate and several cases of arson, and advised strikers that "violence and vandalism are wrong and will not be tolerated in the community." But then it addressed Mort Console and Richard Shaw in remarkably sharp language:

> For years the Pajaro Valley has been subsidizing your businesses. . . . You've continually gone before the government, begging for (and usually getting) special privileges, on the grounds that you were providing well-paying jobs. Now, you're not providing jobs, and it's costing the taxpayers a small fortune to support police protection for your strikebreaking efforts. Maybe this would be a good time to reflect upon your responsibilities to this community, get back to the bargaining table, and make a deal you and your workers can live with.[26]

The *Register-Pajaronian* was not about to criticize the police, whom it typically described as "caught in the middle." And though it decried the cost to taxpayers of enforcing the court injunction, it never really questioned either the appropriateness or the fairness of the injunction itself. But others did. Outside supporters might not always understand the technical aspects of contract negotiations or feel a visceral identification with the strike issues, but they readily perceived the injustice of a biased court system and repressive police. In October Cruz Gómez and José López made an appeal for support from students at the UC Santa Cruz campus. When the students asked what they could do to help, López told them, "You can challenge the injunction." Forty-five students dutifully travelled down to Watsonville, assembled at the plant gate, and submitted to arrest. As they were being loaded into paddy wagons, an approving López told reporters that their act of civil disobedience was "just what the strikers need." Moments later he himself was arrested, presumably for instigating the demonstration.[27]

To a very real degree, Watsonville Canning's strategy revolved around using the legal system to drain the union's resources and raise the cost of the strike to the point it could no longer be sustained. Littler, Mendelson, Fastiff, and Tichy specialized in this sort of thing: on a regular basis, they tried to get the court order made even more restrictive and filed million-dollar damage suits against the union, charging that it had "encouraged and incited violence among the mobs of pickets" and "planned, approved, encouraged, participated in and/or ratified the violent conduct, property damage and unlawful acts."[28]

Local 912, of course, did not have the resources to fight these court battles; in truth, when Sergio López took office at the beginning of 1986 he found that his predecessor had left the local treasury virtually empty. It fell to Duane Beeson, attorney for Joint Council 7, to handle the local's legal issues, and by and large he took a defensive approach. Beeson's office was able to thwart company efforts to tighten up the injunction. When strikers were arrested or cited for violating it, Beeson tried to take advantage of the city attorney's crushing workload, which had increased exponentially since the strike started. Initially, he sought indefinite continuances in strike-related cases, figuring that eventually there would be a decision not to prosecute most of them. Failing that, arrested strikers were encouraged to take plea deals that got them off with token punishment and a promise that the offense would not be repeated. Generally, Beeson tried to protect Local 912 from legal liability when violations of the injunction occurred.[29]

This approach did not sit well with some members of the Watsonville Strike Support Committee, who wanted to confront the legal system and expose its bias. Jon Silver, who regarded the Teamsters as a "company union," cited Beeson's plea bargaining approach as a brake on worker militancy and another example of the union's failure to represent its members.[30]

For the strikers themselves, it was not so much a matter of curbing their militancy as of not getting caught. Benjamin Torres was six years old when his parents, Esperanza and Enrique, were on strike. He remembered the men who would show up at his family's house, across the street from the plant, with slingshots under their coats and their pockets full of rocks. Sometimes the men would scale the chain-link fence in front of the plant under cover of night and sabotage company trucks. If the police came to the house, they escaped by a side door. Esperanza Torres recalled earnest conversations in which the men would remind each other to be careful, that any arrests would simply add to the union's expenses and make it harder to sustain the strike.[31]

Among other things, such activity reflected a growing frustration on the part of many strikers. The frustration was heightened after a union meeting at the county fairgrounds at the beginning of January failed to reveal any clear plan on the part of Local 912's new leaders to win the strike.[32]

Joe Fahey, newly installed as Local 912's recording secretary as well as business agent, was a minority of one on the local executive board. He looked for an approach that relied on active strikers rather than Teamster officials, one that could attract a broader base of support than TDU was capable of mustering. He appears to have been the author of a leaflet distributed toward the end of January, calling for "an organization of members to take the actions necessary to win the strike and save our union . . . open to all Teamsters who want to be an active force in winning the strike."

The call, issued after several informal early meetings, was reminiscent in tone of the flier that had called for the formation of the Strikers' Committee three months earlier. It was signed by four Strikers' Committee members—Gloria Betancourt, Chavelo Moreno, Aurora Trujillo, and Manuel Ybarra—as well as TDU stalwarts Enrique Torres and Fidelia Carrisoza. "We thought that things were going too slow," said Gloria Betancourt, "so we decided to get all of our forces together." Local 912 members were urged to attend a February 8 meeting at the Veterans Hall.[33]

The meeting drew 150 to 200 people, including local supporters as well as strikers. The plans that emerged were nothing if not ambitious. The group, which decided to call itself Teamsters United 912, called for a full week of coordinated action. It would begin on February 17 with a rally at Callaghan Park followed by a march to the plant gates in defiance of the injunction. It would conclude with a rally on February 22, which was already in the works: sponsored by the Teamsters and endorsed by much of the Bay Area labor movement, this was the latest in a series of regular events that Bill Walsh used to drum up union contributions to the food bank.[34]

Frank Bardacke worked on the leaflet that came out of the February 8 meeting, and his influence over its style as well as its content was unmistakable:

A new processing season is about to begin. There is no other way to

win this strike than to stop the scabs, gain the direct support of other frozen food workers in Watsonville and prevent the raw product
from ever leaving the fields in Salinas. . . . We will do whatever is
necessary to achieve these goals.

February 17 we will have a rally and march. . . . For the next
four days we intend to do everything possible to shut down Watsonville Canning and Richard Shaw's. We will picket the fields and the
trucks to stop the product; we will seek support from workers at other
plants; and we will prevent scabs from going to work. We will do all
of this in a spirit of militant, disciplined non-violence. We hope you
can join us.[35]

Joe Fahey showed a draft of the leaflet to Sergio López, who was
worried about legal repercussions for the union and urged Fahey to
dissociate himself from the group. Fahey responded that the event was
going to happen with or without his participation. By taking part in
the planning process, he said, he might be able to exert enough influence to keep things from getting out of hand.

Gloria Betancourt would maintain that Fahey's actual role was
minimal. "We were mad," she said, "because, you know, we were supposed to stay together" and Fahey had "backed out." She dismissed
assertions by Sergio López and Leon Ellis that Fahey had either insti-
gated or controlled the week's events. "Nobody was a leader," she said.
"We all participated."[36]

Fahey did do one thing that left him open to disciplinary action
by the union. Since the new administration had taken over, Local 912
had been meeting weekly at the hall. At the February 11 meeting Fahey got a vote through that gave the local's formal blessing to the week
of protest. Owing to a city council meeting that night, which was to
take up strike-related issues, the meeting of the local was sparsely
attended and may not even have had a quorum. Joe Fahey was the
only officer present, forcing him to chair the meeting and write up
minutes, in his capacity as recording secretary, after the fact. The upshot was that the final version of the Teamsters United 912 leaflet,
not yet available when Fahey and Sergio López spoke, contained the
Teamster logo and the words, "Officially endorsed by the membership
of Teamsters Local 912."[37]

While Teamsters United 912 was making plans to dramatically
escalate the strike, Alex Ybarrolaza was simultaneously engineering

what amounted to a tactical retreat. Since late January he had been negotiating with Richard Shaw in hopes of bringing the conflict there to a speedy conclusion. He viewed Shaw as someone the union could work with, and the fact-finding report had confirmed his suspicions that the company was in serious trouble. He also suspected that necessary support for Local 912 from the higher levels of the union was far from assured and would be much easier to secure if the Teamsters had to bankroll a strike at only one plant instead of two. He may have realized something else that was lost on many others at the time: the Shaw strikers were starting to break ranks. Time was not on the union's side; the longer the Shaw strike lasted, the harder it would be for the union to salvage anything from the negotiations.[38]

The deal that Ybarrolaza negotiated with Shaw was remarkable in that it allowed wages for production workers to fall even lower than the $6.66 an hour that Shaw had initially demanded, and the union had rejected, the previous summer. The proposed new wage of $5.85 an hour was to be projected by the union as the new standard for the industry. For everyone except the Watsonville Canning workers, who had already taken a pay cut in 1982, this amounted to a 17 percent drop in their hourly earnings. As a "fail-safe against windfall profits from reduced wages," as Ybarrolaza put it, net earnings above the first $2.25 million would be equally divided between the company and the workers should Shaw return to profitability. Strikers were to be granted amnesty and returned to work with full seniority.

Sergio López would say years later that he thought Ybarrolaza had given up too much. If he felt that way at the time, however, he kept his reservations to himself. Even Ybarrolaza conceded that the proposed deal was "nothing to be proud of." Its most disturbing provision gave Shaw the right to reopen the contract should Watsonville Canning settle for less than $5.85. This language was supposed to protect Shaw from a replay of 1982; it was hard for union negotiators to oppose it, since Local 912's failure to maintain wage parity three years before was at least partly to blame for the company's current financial woes.[39] But it put the Watsonville Canning strikers in a difficult position: henceforth everything would depend on them—and on their ability to hold out indefinitely against a company that had thus far showed no interest in settling the strike.

The tensions that resulted were fully in evidence at the ratification meeting February 14. Chavelo Moreno was among those distributing a flier to the 650 workers filing in to hear the terms of the proposed agreement, which until then had not been made public (though the previous day Sergio López indicated that workers would be asked to "bite the bullet for a couple of years"). In the absence of specific information about what was being voted on, the flier simply said, "No to a bad contract," and emphasized two points. First, it stressed that it made no sense to give ground when the new production season was about to begin and the company needed workers. Second, it warned Shaw workers not to make the same mistake that Watsonville Canning workers had made three years before, when they allowed themselves to be misled by Smiley Verduzco's poor-mouthing. The last sentence of the flier would prove prophetic: "The wages that you accept will be forced on all of us."[40]

The meeting began with a presentation on the fact-finding committee's report. Then the proposed contract terms were explained by Leon Ellis, who made no attempt to sugarcoat the situation. "It's not very pleasant to sit before you and read this," Ellis said. "Every item on this contract was fought for. We wish we could say there is more, but there isn't." Angry shouts greeted him as he announced the proposed wage settlement. They grew louder when Paula Hernandez, a member of the rank-and-file negotiating committee who worked at the food bank, argued, "The company can't afford to give us what they don't have." Whatever difficulties Shaw faced, the strikers had endured far worse, and the conclusions of the fact-finding committee were not enough to persuade everyone present that their own sacrifices would have to continue. At least one Shaw striker cited the committee's report as evidence that the company's agreement to profit-sharing was a meaningless concession.[41]

Watsonville Canning strikers were particularly incensed, and they became so vociferous that finally Ybarrolaza ordered the room cleared and only Shaw workers readmitted. After that, however, the outcome of the meeting was probably inevitable. With only ninety minutes to consider the actual contract terms, the argument by the Watsonville Canning strikers that the Shaw workers had a responsibility to maintain solidarity and not break ranks had been perhaps the most compelling reason not to ratify.

Local 912 recording secretary Joe Fahey, who was taking minutes of the meeting, was unable to get the floor to speak against the agreement: "Alex wouldn't call on me." Afterward Fahey was sharply criticized by Frank Bardacke and others on the Watsonville Strike Support Committee for not being more aggressive. But it is doubtful that he could have turned the tide. The vote, when it came, was decisive—the Shaw workers voted by a 2 to 1 margin to accept the terms and go back to work.[42]

"Shaw workers railroaded," said the front-page headline in *Unity* a few days later. The mainstream media was not so harsh, but with the exception of the *Register-Pajaronian*, which welcomed the settlement, news accounts generally portrayed the Shaw agreement as a major setback for the union.[43] Bart Curto, head of Teamsters Local 865 in Santa Maria (and one of the founders of Local 912 more than thirty years before) sent a letter to IBT president Jackie Presser complaining that the Shaw settlement was "harmful to all Local Unions with contracts in the same industry." He asked the international union to exercise its power to intervene in such situations and "stop [the] problem in California from escalating. . . . I respectfully request the nullification of that contract and the establishment of a Frozen Food Council in California to oversee the Frozen Food Industry in the state." There is no evidence that Presser gave this request any consideration, but Chuck Mack got a copy of the letter, and it remains in Joint Council 7's files.[44]

Gloria Betancourt spoke for many Watsonville Canning strikers when she said the Shaw workers had "sold themselves," and the agreement amounted to a betrayal by the union. The Shaw workers remained deeply divided. Sandra Perez, who had voted against the settlement, described the atmosphere in the plant after she returned to work as "very tense" and complained that coworkers who had crossed the picket line were "always snitching on us." Having ended their own walkout, Shaw workers were supposed to contribute five dollars a week to Local 912's strike fund to help sustain the ongoing struggle at Watsonville Canning. Sergio López complained that far too few of them did.[45] After five months without a paycheck, some of them may have simply felt they couldn't afford it; on the other hand, the terms of their contract were such that if the Watsonville Canning strike was lost, their own wages would fall even further. Two elected members of the

Strikers' Committee from Shaw, Linda García and Aurora Trujillo, understood this well enough to remain active on the committee after going back to work; Aurora Trujillo in particular remained close to the Watsonville Canning strikers and was a visible and outspoken presence in their struggle to the very end.

Why did the Shaw strikers break ranks while the Watsonville Canning strikers stayed together? One explanation is obvious: the latter never really had the option of settling. Mort Console, unlike Richard Shaw, was not interested in negotiating with the union. What he demanded of his workers was nothing short of capitulation. And while working conditions in the Shaw plant were far from pleasant, those at Watsonville Canning had become virtually unbearable in the weeks before the strike, as workers had endured a brutal speedup, harassment, arbitrary firings, and a climate of constant fear.[46]

There may have been another reason as well. Watsonville Canning's workers were overwhelmingly local people. But Richard Shaw's plant, the newest of Watsonville's eight frozen food operations, was less than ten years old. When it was established, the industry was still scrambling for workers, and the availability of local labor was limited. Shaw thus had to hire a large percentage of his workers from out of town.[47]

Skilled mechanics were indispensible to a plant's operations, and the willingness of some mechanics at Shaw to cross the picket line made the strike there much harder to sustain. Knowing this, Watsonville Canning would offer its own mechanics a bonus and a wage hike in June 1986 if they abandoned the strike and returned to work. None of them did, and Frank Bardacke had a revealing conversation with one of them:

> I asked him why he didn't accept.
>
> "Do you think I should go back?" he asked unbelievingly.
>
> "No, I just want to know why you don't."
>
> He gave the question some thought. "There is no way for a striker to cross that picket line and live in Watsonville."
>
> "Do you mean that you are afraid that people would attack you? Shoot up your home or throw rocks at your kids or something?"
>
> "No, I don't think anyone would hurt me. But I couldn't go anywhere in town with my head up, on the chance that I might have to look some striker in the eye . . . I couldn't shop at the grocery store, I couldn't go to the bingo game. For the rest of my life I would be the mechanic

who betrayed my people. No money is worth that. I will go back to work at Watsonville Canning with everybody else, or not at all."[48]

For someone who commuted to work, crossing the picket line meant enduring a few unpleasant minutes each day entering and leaving the plant. But local people would have to face their neighbors constantly, as long as they lived in Watsonville. They risked the kind of ostracism that can make life in a small town unbearable.

The Shaw strikers were to return to work on Tuesday, February 18. The week of protest activities was scheduled to begin the previous day. Police were aware of the planned activities and were already implementing what might be considered preemptive action. On January 28, Sergio López got a letter from police operations captain Terry Medina complaining of "continued violations of the court order on the part of your members":

> As soon as we are not physically present, the rules are ignored. Drinking continues to be a problem on your property outside the Union Hall. Rock throwers still run to the Union Hall as a sanctuary to escape identification or apprehension. Please be informed that effective this evening, our officers will be ... expecting strict "letter of the order" compliance of all court orders. . . . It will be up to the discretion of the officer or supervisor on duty as to whether we issue a citation or make physical arrests.
>
> Outside the area of the court order limits at Watsonville Canning, we will disperse crowds gathering on the corner of West Lake and Walker Streets. . . . Any person drinking alcohol in a public place or in an automobile will be arrested. We expect you and your employees to exercise maximum control over your members . . . [and] over your building and property.
>
> Please advise your members and supporters that the place to defend people that [sic] are being arrested is in court, not in the street. [Anyone] gathering around officers who are writing a citation or making an arrest . . . is subject to arrest under section 148 of the California Penal Code.

Medina's letter got coverage in the local press, which referred to it dryly as a "no more Mr. Nice Guy policy."[49]

Joe Fahey was the first to feel its effects. On February 3, an administrative appeals judge commenced hearings on the denial of unemployment benefits to strikers, taking testimony from Watsonville Canning strikers at the Veteran's Hall. A crowd of about four hundred showed up to testify; they found themselves cheering when Watsonville Canning managers Larry Vawter and Ron Trine testified that the company was shorthanded and unable to do routine maintenance. Trine and Vawter, of course, were trying to persuade the judge that strikers were not entitled to unemployment because there was plenty of work for them at the plant. But they were flatly contradicting their earlier claims, made repeatedly to the media, that Watsonville Canning was getting along fine without them.

Local 912's newly elected business agent had to miss the hearing, because he unexpectedly found himself in police custody. He had been in the middle of a group of seventy people who walked together from the union hall to the Veteran's Hall for the hearing that morning. Before the group got very far, however, police picked Fahey out of the crowd, handcuffed him, and took him to the county jail, where he was booked for unlawful assembly and interfering with an officer.

"It was our interpretation that he was leading a parade for which he did not have a permit," said a police spokesman. "He appeared to be the one controlling the group." Chavelo Moreno, who was walking with Fahey, had assumed at first that the police were there to direct traffic for the crowd. He was astounded by Fahey's arrest. "It was an insult," he told a reporter.[50]

It was also a portent. With the February 17 rally and march looming, the Watsonville police drew up a detailed battle plan to keep anything from happening. Once again, they assumed Joe Fahey was the ringleader. Anticipating the police, a tactical committee met the morning of the rally. According to Gloria Betancourt, "We were just discussing how we were going to get to the plant, which street we were going to walk, because we didn't have no permit for marching. . . . If we were going to walk in large groups they were going to stop us right away."[51] The committee decided to break the crowd up into small groups as soon as the rally ended, with each group taking a different route to the plant gate.

But the rally never really got started. As a crowd gathered in Callaghan Park, it was welcomed by Chavelo Moreno and serenaded by a pair of musicians; the *Register-Pajaronian* called it a "party atmosphere."

Then the police moved in. They ordered the public address system shut down and the crowd dispersed: "They didn't even let us step on the grass," said Gloria Betancourt. The tactical committee did not want "any confrontations with the police before getting to the plant," so they complied with police orders. But there was an undercurrent of anger in the crowd. In the past police had allowed rallies in the park; this time, Chief Belgard cited the leaflet from the February 8 meeting, with its vague language about "doing whatever is necessary," as a justification for not permitting it. "It sounds chicken shit, but the reason we did it was to absolve liability," he said.[52]

The crowd was not finished. The musicians continued to perform from the back of a flatbed truck, providing a distraction for police as demonstrators broke into small groups and dispersed. A half-hour later, people began converging on the Watsonville Canning plant from different directions, forcing police to redeploy there. Knots of people briefly blocked traffic, retreating as the police pushed them back. One reporter noted that the crowd's chanting effectively drowned out the orders to disperse that issued from a police loudspeaker.

Ron Trine stood inside the plant gate videotaping everything, with leashed guard dogs at his side. On the other side of the chain-link fence, Jon Silver and his cameraman Joe Dees were also filming the action; they got footage of Cruz Gómez being arrested as she urged the crowd to move back from police lines. Minutes later Silver and Dees were themselves placed in custody; somehow they managed to get footage of their own arrests, which would feature prominently in Silver's documentary *Watsonville on Strike*. Police seemed to be targeting certain people whom advance intelligence had identified as instigators.

At two o'clock Watsonville was hit by a violent winter storm. As rain pelted the streets, Ron Trine retreated inside the plant, but rain-drenched strikers and police continued to face off. As the crowd was slowly driven back, rocks and bottles began to fly. It was time for shift change at the plant, but the chaos made it temporarily impossible for anyone to enter or leave. A truck from Gilroy bringing a load of broccoli to the plant gunned its motors and ran a red light to get through the crowd; its driver was cut by broken glass as he ran the gauntlet. "I didn't stop because those people would have killed me," he said. A company security car riding shotgun for the truck was attacked as well; all of its windows were shattered.

Aggressive police tactics made it impossible for rally organizers to exercise any discipline over the crowd. The plan had been for people to reconvene at the union hall to plan the rest of the week's activities. But when they got there the police routed them with tear gas, and the hall had to be evacuated. After that things spiraled out of control. Small groups of people ran up and down Main Street, smashing windows at random with their feet and fists. Among the shops targeted were a restaurant, a camera shop, a jeweler, and an office-supply store. "Bewildered motorists and shoppers seemed to freeze as they watched the unrestrained destruction," reported the *Register-Pajaronian*.[53]

The violence on Main Street was pointless, especially since at least some of the targeted merchants considered themselves strike sympathizers. There is no way to know who was responsible, since the police made no arrests. In fact, they made no attempt whatsoever to stop the vandalism; as Jim Brough of the Santa Cruz Strike Support Committee acidly remarked, "They were too busy lobbing tear gas grenades at the union hall." Summing up the day's events, the *Register-Pajaronian* noted that it was "obvious that the police strategy of making a show of force to curb any movement toward violence did not work."[54]

Union officials were appalled by the incident and tried to blame it on outsiders. "We've been infiltrated by every leftist-socialist-communist group that ever took a breath," said Sergio López. Frank Bardacke, at home nursing a cold when the rioting broke out, recalled getting a frantic phone call from Joe Fahey. Fahey told him that "things were out of control" and even an ambulance taking an injured person away was being pelted with rocks. "What do you want me to do about it, Joe?" Bardacke asked.[55]

Gloria Betancourt told the *Register-Pajaronian*, "They should have directed their anger at the plant, not the town." But she could not resist adding, "Maybe this will make people realize the pressure is on the city." Echoing what many others were saying, she indicated that the crowd's anger had been fueled by the Shaw settlement no less than the provocative tactics of the police.[56] Much of her energies in the days that followed were spent encouraging fellow Watsonville Canning workers to focus their anger on Mort Console—and move on.

In the meantime, though, the union had to engage in damage control. Sergio López sent a letter to the *Register-Pajaronian* asserting that the union had nothing to do with the violence and had "no connection, formal or informal," with Teamsters United 912. Joe Fahey said he understood López's responsibility to protect the local and was prepared to serve as a fall guy. "Let's just see what happens, Joe," López remembered telling him. "Maybe it will all go away."[57]

But it didn't. Chuck Mack was worried about possible blowback from the higher levels of the union, and Bill Walsh was afraid the violence would discourage labor support for the food drive and the support rally scheduled for the following Saturday. Mack sent López a letter that stressed "the importance of taking all necessary steps to dissociate [Local 912] from any group calling itself by the Teamsters' name, but engaging in activities of an illegal or unauthorized nature." The local executive board brought formal charges against Fahey, which were sustained by the executive board of Joint Council 7 when it finally heard them on June 4.[58]

By that time the local courts had dismissed charges against Fahey and others singled out for arrest during the February events. Mack's tone at the conclusion of the June 4 hearing was almost paternal, as he patiently explained to Fahey that as an officer in the local he had new responsibilities and no longer had the same kind of freedom to act that he enjoyed as an ordinary rank and filer. Fahey got off with a formal reprimand.

As far as strikers were concerned, responsibility for the February 17 violence rested squarely with the police. But their attempt to make their case before the city council on February 25 proved less than satisfactory. Some two hundred strikers showed up for the meeting, but Mayor Ann Soldo refused to allow Spanish translations. She said it would be a waste of the council's time.[59]

Chapter 8

Enter the Teamsters

On March 9, a group of women strikers and the NCSSC took over the Watsonville High School auditorium to commemorate International Women's Day, a holiday not normally observed in Watsonville. The *Register-Pajaronian*, still fretting over the civil unrest a few weeks before, noted the "positive tone" of the event and stressed that it was peaceful: "The speeches were spirited but not venomous. The closest thing to a march came at the end . . . when everyone headed to the cafeteria for some food." The three hundred strikers and strike supporters in attendance were treated to music, dance performances, a juggling act, and speeches that were clearly meant to be a show of unity and morale in the wake of the Shaw settlement.

Guillermina Ramírez shared emcee duties with Linda García, who had just returned to work at Richard Shaw. Putting aside their differences, Cruz Gómez and Shiree Teng gave solidarity statements on behalf of their respective support committees. The presence on the platform of Bea Molina, state president of the Mexican-American Political Association, served notice that the strike was becoming a cause célèbre in the California Chicano movement.

But the most enthusiastic response was reserved for three visitors from Austin, Minnesota. Skinny Weis, white-haired and smiling, was an officer of UFCW Local P-9, which had walked out at the Hormel meatpacking plant in Austin a few weeks before the start of the Watsonville strike. He was joined onstage by a younger couple, Bud and Barb Miller. Bud was a P-9 rank and filer; Barb belonged to the United

Support Group, made up mainly of strikers' wives who had taken on many of the day-to-day tasks of the strike. Shouts of *"Huelga! Huelga!* (Strike! Strike!)"* greeted the three when they declared, "Hormel and Watsonville are hand in hand in the fight against concessions."

Their own struggle had just entered a difficult period. They were touring the West Coast as part of a concerted effort to build national support. They got a particularly warm reception in Watsonville, where they also addressed a February 22 rally at the county fairgrounds—the latest of Bill Walsh's mobilizations in support of the food bank.[1]

Watsonville was something of a revelation for the three Midwesterners. Culturally as well as historically, it was a world apart. Austin had been settled in the early years of the century by Scandinavian immigrants whose grandchildren would become leaders of Local P-9 and whose politics had often included a powerful dose of old-country radical syndicalism. The town became a union stronghold in the early 1930s, when an old Wobbly named Frank Ellis made the hog kill department at the Hormel plant the nucleus of a citywide general union that would soon organize packinghouses across northern Iowa and southern Minnesota.[2] If, as some believed, the Watsonville strikers were the future of the labor movement, the Hormel strikers represented some of the best things about its past. They were descended from a generation of European immigrants and their children who were the heart and soul of the Depression era movement to organize basic industry, and were in fact its main beneficiaries.

Though meatpacking has always been dangerous work, it paid well as long as strong union contracts prevailed in the industry. For years Austin's workers had enjoyed a decent standard of living. Hardy Green, historian of the Hormel strike, noted that "the town's several thousand trim houses and manicured lawns . . . seem immune to the passage of time."[3]

Actually, though, the passage of time had brought wrenching changes. The industry was in the midst of a radical restructuring that threatened to drive the union out of its plants. In the 1960s, the advent of the interstate highway system allowed packinghouses to begin a long process of decentralizing production. Agricultural conglomerates ConAgra and Cargill bought up old-line meatpackers and began closing unionized plants, typically reopening them in remote rural areas with low-paid nonunion workers.[4] By the late 1970s, packinghouse unionism was a shadow of its former self.

In 1979, membership losses induced the United Packinghouse Workers of America to merge with three other struggling unions to form the UFCW. Retail clerks were the biggest component of the new union, and their old officers dominated its leadership; within its ranks, meatpackers were a small and relatively powerless minority. Hoping to stem the hemorrhaging of packinghouse jobs, and apparently bowing to pressure from UFCW President William Wynn, the head of the UFCW meatpacking division had embraced a strategy of "controlled retreat," allowing wages in the industry to fall to a level that the union felt it would be able to enforce at all of its packinghouses.

The strategy wasn't working. In a scenario remarkably similar to what occurred a few years later at Watsonville Canning, workers at the Austin Hormel plant had made wage concessions to keep their plant from relocating, only to have the company come back for more three years later. Instead of caving this time, Local P-9 elected new leadership and hired labor consultant Ray Rogers, who had engineered the successful "corporate campaign" against anti-union textile manufacturer J. P. Stevens in the late 1970s.

When their contract expired in August 1985, P-9 members walked off the job, despite the insistence of the international union that Hormel was "the wrong target at the wrong time." Pointing out that Hormel's profits had risen more than 80 percent the previous year, local president Jim Guyette retorted, "If concessions are going to stop, they'll have to stop with the most profitable plant of the most profitable company."

Five months into the strike, Hormel "permanently replaced" the striking workers. The National Guard was called out to stop mass picketing at the plant. Ray Rogers was arrested on "criminal syndicalism" charges, under an archaic statute passed during World War I to stop the IWW from interfering with the war effort. Defying the International, Local P-9 sent roving pickets to other Hormel plants that were doing work farmed out from Austin. In the face of a UFCW propaganda barrage denouncing the strike as a "suicide mission," P-9 members fanned out across the country giving their side of the story.[5]

It was not hard for the Watsonville Canning strikers to identify with the Hormel workers. They, too, had made wage concessions that they had come to regret. They had gotten the same kind of treatment from Mort Console that the Austin workers had gotten from Hormel. Police had broken up their picket lines, just as the National Guard had done in Austin. A leadership change in their local had been necessary to resist company attacks. And while they had thus far been spared the kind of ugly breach with the Teamsters that the Hormel strikers had experienced with the UFCW, many were unhappy with the concessions granted to Richard Shaw, especially since workers in other frozen food plants would likely be pressured into making the same concessions in the interest of "wage parity." They could not help but notice the parallel with the bargaining strategy employed by the UFCW meatpacking division.

They were also coming to understand, as the Hormel strikers had, that to win their strike they would have to do more than simply withdraw their labor. As Ray Rogers conceived it, the corporate campaign strategy had two key components. One involved the full mobilization of union members in generating public sympathy and support, on the assumption that, if the boss had the money and the media access, the union had the troops. The other was a matter of heightening the economic pressure on the company by identifying and exploiting its vulnerable "pressure points," often through a skillful use of negative publicity.

J. P. Stevens was brought to the bargaining table through pressure on its major creditor, Metropolitan Life. Pro-union policyholders threatened to take advantage of a rarely exercised legal right to demand a new election for Met Life's board of directors. The election would have been costly, and Met Life found it more expedient to pressure J. P. Stevens into coming to terms with the union.[6]

Not all corporate campaigns were as successful; a 1990 study suggested that they often failed to locate a big enough chink in the corporate armor to give unions the leverage they needed.[7] But when conditions were right, corporate campaigns could be invaluable, and nowhere more so than in farmworker organizing drives. Both the UFW in California and the Farm Labor Organizing Committee in the Midwest used consumer boycotts to generate the kind of sustained pressure that their members, most of them seasonally employed, could not bring to bear at the point of production. The UFW became so proficient at the tactic, and so dependent on it, that critics charged it was neglecting its primary responsibility to represent workers in the fields.[8]

Back in November Cesar Chavez had appeared unexpectedly at a support rally in Watsonville. He did not, as some local left activists hoped, pledge to pull workers out of the fields to stop the flow of produce into the struck plants. The UFW probably did not have enough Watsonville Canning suppliers under contract to make much of a difference if he had.[9] But he did suggest that the strikers step up the pressure by targeting their adversaries' sources of financial support. The UFW, he noted, had plenty of experience in this area and would gladly help develop an economic boycott plan should the Teamsters choose that route. Given the history of antagonism between the two unions, his comments were, if nothing else, a welcome show of readiness to bury the hatchet.

By late February they had taken on new relevance, even urgency. Morale had been low among the strikers following the end of the Shaw strike and the disappointment of the Local 912 election two months earlier. Some way had to be found for them to regain the initiative.

An idea that Frank Bardacke had been floating since the earliest days of the strike was to spread the walkout to other frozen food plants. To win, he believed, the workers needed a show of solidarity that embraced the entire industry. Curiously, the Watsonville Frozen Food Employers Association had also wanted an industry-wide resolution of the strike issues, but any prospect of that happening had disappeared when Richard Shaw decided to take on the union alone.

In settling with Shaw, Local 912 had effectively committed itself to an industry wage floor of $5.85 an hour for production workers. The previous fall Green Giant had quietly signed a new three-year agreement, identical to the old one, and was still paying $7.06. But Green Giant was not typical. It was a multinational company, a sizeable portion of whose productive capacity was already in Mexico. Locally owned firms were apt to be struggling and had more to lose by keeping the old wage.

Crosetti, Smuckers, and Naturipe had agreed to maintain the terms of their previous agreement in a one-year contract, due to expire on June 30. Del Mar and New West, both of which packaged frozen fruit, had simply extended the old agreement until things were resolved at Watsonville Canning and Richard Shaw. The union was handling them the same way it handled Shaw. First, it asked to see their books; having seen them, it was prepared to offer $5.85 an hour, with the option to reopen the wage package should any of the other frozen food plants settle for less.

Expanding the strike to other plants over union opposition posed obvious difficulties. "When Frank talked about a general strike," said Joe Fahey, "Workers didn't know what it meant. I didn't know what it meant." There was not even an active presence in Local 912 to push for it; Watsonville's TDU chapter had been inactive for five months, never having recovered from the setbacks of the previous fall.

Jim Brough of the Santa Cruz County Communist Party also hoped the strike would spread, but he recognized that any movement in that direction would have to come from the workers themselves. The party lacked a base inside the plants and had only a half-dozen members in Watsonville, none of them frozen food workers. The bulk of its members were from Santa Cruz and its most effective work was in a strictly supportive capacity, mainly through the Santa Cruz Strike Support Committee.

The League, though it had established good relationships with key Watsonville Canning strikers, also lacked a presence in the other plants. It made no attempt to influence events there. After Shaw settled, League activists in Watsonville initially concentrated on holding the ranks together at Watsonville Canning, maintaining morale and providing material support.

The national leadership of the League, which was following the situation closely, concluded that more was needed. The Teamsters organization, it believed, had far more firepower at its disposal than had been thus far brought to bear; the trick was to get the union to use it. A boycott campaign, if the Teamsters could be prevailed upon to support one, could dramatically broaden the strikers' base of support. In particular, it could be used to build alliances with the Chicano movement, where the League could exert some influence.

The challenge was to push the union as far as possible without overplaying one's hand and giving it an excuse to abandon the strike—a possibility the League did not dismiss. The strike was winnable "IF we could force the Teamsters to more actively pursue a boycott and . . . IF we could more fully mobilize the Chicano and larger community for more support and also to put more pressure on the Teamsters." Since the union's continued engagement was critical, care would have to be taken to avoid "tactics which would have forced the union out of the strike, turned the strike into a wildcat, and dissipated the energy of the strike in long and futile court proceedings." Among other things, that meant avoiding needless police confrontations—especially incidents like the February 17 riot on Main Street, which alienated community sympathy and caused a noticeable falling off in contributions to the food bank.[10]

Some members of the Watsonville Strike Support Committee were only too happy take on the legal system. They were among the nineteen defendants, arrested as a result of the police department's February "no more Mr. Nice Guy" policy, who refused to plea bargain and insisted on a public trial. Dan Siegel, the attorney in the Juan Parra case, came down from Berkeley again to head up the defense effort in his usual aggressive style: Jon Silver, one of the defendants, admiringly recalled how Siegel stood down the city attorney in a heated argument outside the courthouse. In the end, all nineteen had their charges dismissed or were acquitted by a jury.[11]

A *Register-Pajaronian* editorial found the acquittals disturbing: "How can [the police department] head off potentially violent strike situations without the likelihood that the violators they arrest can be successfully prosecuted?" The editorial worried about the implication "that police are arresting strike sympathizers without sufficient cause. . . . Strike support leaders go so far as to say that the police are in cahoots with the management of Watsonville Canning and Frozen Food Co., a charge we find patently ridiculous."[12]

Meanwhile the boycott idea was getting some traction. Following up on the offer Cesar Chavez had made in November, campus activists with ties to the League traveled to the UFW field headquarters in Salinas. Acting on behalf of the NCSSC, they asked questions and took copious notes. Shiree Teng wrote up their findings in a detailed proposal and submitted it to Alex Ybarrolaza. He appears to have taken it seriously: a copy wound up in Duane Beeson's files, suggesting that the Joint Council 7 attorney was asked to give it a legal review.[13]

The proposal laid out several possible strategies. One was to have Local 912 members picket the distribution points for the struck product in the hope that at least some drivers would refuse to carry it. A second was to leaflet stores that carried the product, asking customers not to patronize them. A third would be to set up an ad hoc boycott committee, not formally affiliated with the union; presumably it would be able to operate more freely than the Teamsters, without running afoul of federal law that enjoined unions from secondary boycotts. A fourth suggestion was a "pre-boycott scare campaign to the distributors and the retail stores," warning them that as a boycott was in the offing they could save themselves some trouble by acting now to end their business dealings with Watsonville Canning. A detailed budget was included in the proposal, along with drafts of a leaflet for consumers and a letter for store managers.[14]

Fortunately, Ybarrolaza did not need to be persuaded that a boycott was needed. "I did not think the local would win without it," he recalled. "The picket line was symbolic at that point—union trucks weren't going in, but scab trucks were."[15] Both he and Sergio López were well aware that, particularly after the Shaw settlement, the union needed to regain the workers' confidence: "They are questioning the lack of activity by all levels of our union other then the physical picketing of the plant and its very limited effectiveness."[16] The level of mistrust was bound to increase as Local 912 set about imposing the new $5.85 wage standard at other plants, something that could only foster more resentment.

The problem was persuading the Teamster hierarchy to go along with the idea. They had to be convinced that it would pay off for the union, and they had to be reasonably confident that the union would not be exposing itself to legal difficulties.

The Taft-Hartley amendments to the NLRA, enacted in 1947 by a Republican Congress over President Truman's veto, represented the wild card in the deck. Drafted by the National Association of Manufacturers, the Taft-Hartley law included a wide range of provisions that sharply curtailed unions' ability to represent worker interests. It empowered states to effectively outlaw the union shop by passing "right to work" statutes; it withdrew NLRB protection from unions that failed to demonstrate that none of their officers were Communists; and its strictures against secondary boycotts made it risky for unions to engage in solidarity actions, or indeed resort to any tactic that could be interpreted as involving a "neutral third party" in a labor dispute.[17]

The law's language on secondary boycotts was confusing enough for one legal scholar to characterize it as a "dreadful mess . . . applied freely to all sorts of situations never before thought of as secondary boycotts. The authors of this measure . . . were so cagey in drafting it that they produced something virtually unworkable." He noted that it was all but impossible to predict how either the NLRB or the courts would interpret the law in any given situation.[18]

Farmworkers did not need to worry because farmworkers had never been covered under the NLRA and were therefore not bound by its restrictions. But the ban on secondary boycotts had been a huge headache for the Teamsters from the start. Among other things, it effectively outlawed what had been one of the union's most effective weapons: declining to handle "hot cargo," that is, cargo originating with a strikebound or nonunion firm. If Teamster drivers refused to deliver Watsonville Canning products to the supermarkets that had hired them, they might be accused of engaging in a "hot cargo" strike and expose the union to legal action.

By offering to set up an independent, ad hoc boycott group, the NCSSC hoped to give the Teamsters a measure of protection against secondary boycott charges. But if the Teamsters could not be held legally responsible for such a group's activity, neither would they be able to control it. NCSSC activists wanted the Watsonville strike to galvanize constituencies outside of Watsonville, in much the same way that the UFW grape boycott had inspired a nationwide Chicano movement in the late 1960s. Needless to say, this went well beyond the Teamsters' agenda.

Ybarrolaza had worked up his own plan by early April. While it incorporated some of the support committee's ideas, generally it put less emphasis on the mass mobilization aspects of the corporate campaign model, and more on the exploitation of economic pressure points. More than anything else, he wanted to convey to all parties with ties to Watsonville Canning that the Teamsters were in for the duration. Thus, he suggested a visible union presence in Salinas and Monterey, where many of the scabs were being recruited, to counteract claims of company recruiters that the jobs being offered at Watsonville Canning were permanent. He wanted to put both Wells Fargo Bank and the growers who had extended credit to Mort Console on notice that the company was a poor credit risk. Noting that "most of the company's raw product is coming from the greater Salinas valley," he indicated that "some picketing activity in the fields would be appropriate"—not to stop production but to warn growers that they might not be paid for it. (He also noted, "The UFW has pledged support, and while this is desirable it is not really necessary.") Meanwhile, major food distributors that put their brand on Watsonville Canning products were to be advised that they were likely targets of a consumer boycott.[19]

This last aspect of the plan was the most problematic, and not just because of the secondary boycott law. Duane Beeson had advised the Western Conference of Teamsters that the union could engage in two activities and remain in compliance with the law: it could throw up an informational picket line at stores, asking customers not to buy Watsonville Canning products, or it could distribute leaflets asking them not to shop there until Watsonville Canning products were taken off the shelves. The union could not, he stressed, do both, and if it opted for the latter, "it would be imperative to maintain strict control over the handbillers to insure that they do not contaminate the lawful activity by handbilling at the wrong locations, interfering with deliveries to the stores, or making improper comments . . . regarding the purpose of the handbilling." Care would have to be taken that the activity was directed strictly at consumers and would not interfere in any way with the stores conducting their normal business.

The first course, an informational picket line, was less fraught with legal pitfalls, but it was far more difficult to carry out. Watsonville Canning products were marketed under a profusion of brand names, many of which were also attached to the product of other frozen food companies. Through careful research, the union had learned to identify the company's product by the bar code on the packaging, but it did not seem realistic to ask consumers to do likewise, especially when the bar code was not always visible on the outside of the package. Beeson recommended against it.

Beeson did put his stamp of approval on Ybarrolaza's other ideas— attempting to dissuade the growers and the bank from doing business with Watsonville Canning—as long as they didn't involve direct economic pressure. The union could, however, ask people to withdraw their accounts from Wells Fargo.[20]

Ybarrolaza continued to believe that at the end of the day a consumer boycott would be the most potent weapon in the union's arsenal. But he also acknowledged that "while this is the most visible part of our program, with great public relations exposure for the Teamsters, it is also slow moving and the most costly." An effective boycott would require the active, enthusiastic support of the international union, something far from assured. And time was an issue as well: Ybarrolaza was well aware that if Watsonville Canning could make it through the spring and summer peak production season, it could move to decertify the union in September.[21]

Since the better part of Ybarrolaza's game plan involved exerting pressure behind the scenes, it was all the more important that "the morale of the strikers . . . be kept high with support programs, food drives, rallies and marches." The strikers were already taking on much of this responsibility themselves, but many were starting to question why the union wasn't doing more. Ybarrolaza wanted the Teamsters organization to assume a much higher profile, to the point where Joint Council 7 would "assume control of both the conduct of the strike and the negotiations." For different reasons this, too, would prove an elusive goal.[22]

Sergio López laid out the proposal in general terms at a meeting with the strikers on April 11. At a rally the next day, Chuck Mack made it sound like it was already operational. "We are digging in for the long haul," he told the crowd. "We are boiling it down to a program of economic sanctions that will isolate Watsonville Canning from the community. . . . We want to persuade people that it is not good business to do business with that company." But when the full executive board of Joint Council 7 met the following Tuesday, it insisted on attaching a pair of conditions: Local 912 would have to get the board's approval before any boycott activity was carried out, and the board would not associate itself with any effort to get the international union or the Western Conference of Teamsters on board. The initial reaction of the Western Conference was less than enthusiastic: when Ybarrolaza first broached the subject with them, he was told, "That's farmworker stuff."[23]

Even before Ybarrolaza's proposal had taken shape, the Teamsters' effort to impose an industry-wide wage standard was generating real tensions in Local 912. Negotiations with Del Mar had begun almost before the ink was dry on the Shaw agreement. They were conducted hastily and in secret; workers knew nothing about the terms of the settlement until they were called together to ratify it.[24]

"NOT SO FAST . . . LET'S THINK IT OVER" said a leaflet (signed "Members of Teamsters Local 912") that was distributed as the Del Mar workers filed into a meeting on March 7. Pointing out that the union had departed from its usual practice of having rank-and-file members on the negotiating committee, the leaflet urged them to move "to delay the voting at least a week. This . . . will give you time to study and discuss the offer and ask your questions." The leaflet pointed out that "a NO vote only means you want negotiations to continue. It does not mean strike."[25]

But the company insisted that $5.85 was its "final offer," meaning under Teamster bylaws it would have required a two-thirds majority to reject it. The Del Mar workers, who were being asked to take a 17 percent pay cut, did indeed vote to reject it on March 7, but not by a big enough margin. Fewer than a hundred workers were present at the meeting to cast ballots; at peak production the company employed four times that many.[26]

Sergio López noted that the company was losing money and was seriously considering selling its plant to a nonunion firm based in Fresno. The agreement specified that anyone who bought the plant would be required to honor the union contract. He told the *Register-Pajaronian* that any company expecting concessions from the union would need to demonstrate financial hardship first.[27]

New West was not losing money. It employed two hundred workers and contracted with roughly one hundred local growers to process their strawberries. But its management made clear that it was not about to give Del Mar a competitive advantage by agreeing to a higher pay scale. New West had two nonunion plants in Orange County, several hundred miles to the south, and was prepared to shut its Watsonville plant and ship its strawberries to Southern California if the union did not give it what it wanted. Five days after the settlement at Del Mar, workers at New West voted narrowly to accept $5.90 an hour, along with elimination of shift differential and straight time for Saturday work ten weeks out of a year.[28]

It was precisely the kind of concessions bargaining that had bedeviled the Hormel workers. And it belied claims that the union's stance in negotiations was determined strictly by company balance sheets. The truth was that both Ybarrolaza and Sergio López were trying to isolate Mort Console by coming to a quick settlement with his competitors. Indeed, there was already speculation in the media that Crosetti was getting much of the business that would normally have gone to Watsonville Canning.[29]

Whatever the logic of the union strategy, it still required workers to take a substantial pay cut, and it still required the union to persuade them to do so. The worst thing about it was the language in the new contracts, which left open the possibility that wages could fall even further if the Watsonville Canning strike was defeated. Ybarrolaza's economic sanctions campaign was intended to keep that from happening, but Local 912's members had to take it largely on faith. The campaign was still in its early stages, much of it would take place behind the scenes, and there was, as yet, no assurance that the higher levels of the Teamsters union would go along with it.

Apart from a firm commitment from the union, a boycott campaign would require publicity and a significant broadening of outside support. The League concentrated its efforts on trying to build it. League activists had worked on Jesse Jackson's 1984 presidential campaign and had good contacts in Jackson's Rainbow Coalition; by early March a move was underway to bring Jackson to Watsonville.[30] Arrangements were also made for Chavelo Moreno to address the MEChA state convention in Bakersfield on April 26; he traveled with the student activists to the UFW headquarters in La Paz, where he was granted a personal audience with Cesar Chavez.

The growing involvement of the Bay Area labor movement in the strike owed much to the efforts of Lou Gray, who had made it a personal cause. Gray was the director of Community Services for the Santa Clara County Labor Council, none of whose meetings were complete without one of his impassioned speeches on behalf of the Watsonville strikers. "These people are barely out of the miseries of migrant farm life," he would say, his voice rising with emotion. "They've been able to rent a little house around here, live here year round; the kids can go to the same school year round . . . and the greed of this one miserable little owner is gonna destroy whatever progress they've made. We can't permit this to happen!"[31]

Every Monday, Lydia Lerma and her husband drove their truck from Watsonville over the Santa Cruz Mountains to Gray's house in San Jose, where they picked up any contributions to the food bank that Gray had collected the previous week. Knowing the Lermas to be short of money, he hired them to do yard work for him so they could take some extra cash back to Watsonville along with the canned goods.[32]

Gray was also a driving force behind one of the more ambitious solidarity actions. Since their arrival in the area in March, the Hormel strikers had continued to make the rounds in the Bay Area, pleading their case wherever they found an audience. By now the UFCW had placed Local P-9 in trusteeship, frozen its assets, and was moving to end its strike, but the Bay Area labor movement remained generous in its support of the beleaguered local. Meanwhile flight attendants at TWA were in a desperate battle with owner Carl Icahn, a corporate raider who was spearheading a movement to drive unions out of the airline industry. Over Memorial Day weekend, TWA strikers joined the delegation from Austin for a three-day, fifty-five-mile pilgrimage, much of it on foot, from the Teamsters Hall in San Jose to the county fairgrounds in Watsonville. There they were greeted by hundreds of strikers and supporters who had gathered for a rally and barbeque. The event was endorsed by the state labor federation, the UFW Chicano and religious groups, and virtually every central labor council in Northern California.

From the IBT, however, the strikers needed more than solidarity statements and donations to the food bank. They needed assurances that the union would continue to back the strike and put its considerable muscle behind the economic boycott campaign. Neither was a foregone conclusion when delegates assembled at Caesar's Palace in Las Vegas on May 19 for the union's national convention.

On the eve of the convention, Michael Johnston, writing under the pseudonym Mark Johnson, published a front-page article in *Unity* that portrayed the IBT as a union in deep trouble. Johnston cited a 20 percent decline in membership since 1979. The National Master Freight Agreement, he wrote, was "disintegrating," and a 1982 decision to allow UPS to institute a two-tier wage structure meant that more than half of the company's workers were now making five dollars an hour less than coworkers doing identical jobs. Turning the union around, he asserted, would "require uniting traditionally well-paid, overwhelmingly white workers in freight and other 'basic jurisdictions' . . . with thousands of lower stratum workers, many of them minorities, who by now make up the bulk of the Teamsters membership."

Johnston saw reasons for hope in the West Coast canneries and bottling plants, grocery warehouses, and "giant, heavily minority locals in cities like Los Angeles and New York" where Latino Teamsters were starting to flex their muscle. His personal frustrations with TDU notwithstanding, he praised its increased influence in the traditional Teamster jurisdictions where workers were seeing "a lifetime investment in seniority, skills, and pension benefits slip from their grasp." He noted the election of TDU leader Linda Gregg to head the largest local in the Rocky Mountain region.[33]

Johnston's optimism was not shared by the mainstream media, which generally echoed the position of federal authorities that the IBT was too thoroughly penetrated by organized crime to be reformed from within. Typical coverage called the convention "carefully orchestrated" and made an issue of the fact that Jackie Presser was re-elected to a five-year term as general president of the union despite having been indicted on federal racketeering and embezzlement charges a few days before. Presser's own conduct at the convention seemed almost calculated to reinforce the media stereotype. The three-hundred-pound general president was carried onto the convention floor in a sedan chair borne by four burly Teamsters dressed as Roman centurions, while trumpets blared and the PA system repeatedly declaimed, "Hail, Caesar!"[34]

Chuck Mack tried in vain to pass a resolution empowering seasonal workers to serve as convention delegates and run for union office. Alex Ybarrolaza had better luck with his own resolution, committing the IBT to carry out the economic boycott campaign against Watsonville Canning. It passed unanimously, thanks to some adroit behind-the-scenes maneuvering on Ybarrolaza's part:

> You can't get these things past the people in charge, so I approached John Blake, who headed up the Resolutions Committee. I hand-delivered it to him the day before the committee met. These things are all about access. The new head of the Western Conference, Arnie Weinmeister, liked me. He'd always wanted to hire me. . . . He asked me if we could win the strike, and I said yes—the workers are there,

and that's the key. But we need a boycott. . . . I explained my strategy: target the customer base, the product source, and the financiers. Arnie liked it.[35]

With Weinmeister's support and a favorable recommendation from the Resolutions Committee, the boycott resolution sailed through the convention without opposition. On June 5 a five-man task force from the Western Conference was convened and assigned to Watsonville. It was headed by John Blake, who was to take charge of the Economic Boycott Campaign; Blake eventually set up a dozen boycott offices in key Teamster locals around the country. Helping him out was Vince Aloise of Joint Council 7, who was familiar with Teamster trucking, grocery, and warehouse contracts in the Bay Area; he was to provide expertise in developing a local consumer boycott. Eddie Rodríguez and J. C. Lendvai were supposed to work with the strikers. Lendvai was close to Jackie Presser and had something of a reputation in the union as an enforcer; the strikers do not appear to have paid much attention to him. Rodríguez made more of an impression, on Chavelo Moreno at least: Moreno described him as "the kind of guy who'd come up behind you while you were eating your lunch and help himself to a taco off your plate."[36]

Alex Ybarrolaza, who had worked hard to get the four to Watsonville, remarked that "there's not much arguing with these guys," adding wryly, "I was the lowest paid one of the bunch." The International did agree to reimburse Local 70, Ybarrolaza's local, for paying his salary and that of Bill Walsh.

For his part, Sergio López viewed the arrival of the task force with decidedly mixed feelings. On the one hand, he welcomed the International's commitment to the strike. On the other hand, he felt the task force was looking for an excuse to relieve him of authority over the local. Once the four set up shop in the union hall, "I was under constant surveillance. . . . They were here supposedly to give advice, but they were really here to just let that little Mexican's foot slip one time and he's gone, he's in trusteeship. . . . It was a nightmare."[37]

John Blake believed that, for the boycott strategy to work, the union had to come to terms as quickly as possible with Watsonville Canning's competitors, as anyone honoring the boycott would need someplace else to take their business. In particular, the Crosetti contract was "of major importance." Crosetti employed almost as many union workers as Richard Shaw, and a significant number of them were prepared to resist the kind of concessions that the Shaw workers had been forced to accept after five months on strike.[38]

Blake was worried that Local 912 had lost control of the situation. On May 15 Naturipe workers had overwhelmingly rejected their contract. "Even though the union leadership pushed it a lot," said one of them, "we figured why not negotiate instead of just accept it. At other companies workers got scared, moved too fast, and didn't take time to think." The workers wound up settling for $6.00 an hour. It was still a substantial pay cut, but at least they had settled on something resembling their own terms. In the much larger Crosetti plant, meanwhile, a core of fifteen to twenty workers was actively organizing against concessions.[39]

Crosetti made its "final offer" to its workers on June 26. It was virtually identical to the Shaw contract. The union was pushing for an immediate vote. The workers expressed their unhappiness at a well-attended meeting at the Assumption Church, across the street from the plant in Pajaro. They decided to ask for a two-week extension so they would have more time to consider the proposal. Esperanza and Anita Contreras were among the Watsonville Canning strikers who attended and advised the Crosetti workers to stand their ground. So did Joe Fahey. He had been sharply criticized by Watsonville Strike Support Committee members for not opposing the Shaw settlement more vigorously. Now he was now making up for it.[40]

The company agreed to extend the old contract for two days, and a ratification vote was scheduled for the plant on July 2. Three hundred workers promptly signed a petition asking the union to move the vote to a "neutral location." Local 912 officials said it wasn't necessary.

Members of the Watsonville Strike Support Committee agitated openly against the contract. In the past, the committee had been praised in the Local 912 *Weekly Bulletin* for its work, which had kept many strikers from losing their homes and purchased $34,000 worth of milk and eggs, as well as fresh vegetables, for the food committee.[41] But the committee did not confine itself to providing strikers with material aid. It tried to influence contract negotiations and was publicly critical when it felt the union was mishandling them.

"We are not sheep," said one of its leaflets. "When we have seen your union and its officials take the wrong path . . . we have spoken up. We cannot and will not remain silent about this kind of neglect, indifference, and incompetence." At one point in the Crosetti negotiations Cruz Gómez accused Sergio López in the press of "selling out his people."[42] Years later, she would attribute the committee's adversarial stance toward the union to Frank Bardacke's influence. "You can't have a meeting with Frank in the room and not discuss strike strategy," she said smiling.[43]

Local Communist Party activists likewise opposed the settlement, though they were far more discreet about it. Mainly, they stationed themselves outside the plant and engaged the workers in one-on-one conversations about the new contract terms. Unlike many people, Jim Brough was not worried about the Teamsters abandoning Local 912 if the members got out of line. True, the UFCW had turned on the Hormel strikers, but Brough had a gut feeling that the organizational culture of the Teamsters would not allow the union to accept a humiliating defeat at Watsonville Canning that could jeopardize its presence in the frozen food industry.[44]

The roiling tensions around the Crosetti contract remained beneath the surface when Jesse Jackson arrived in Watsonville on June 29. The visit of the 1984 presidential candidate was supposed to attract media attention, and it did. Up to that point the Watsonville Canning strike had been largely ignored by all but the local press. The struggle at Hormel, taking place in the "American heartland" and featuring a dramatic confrontation between a hidebound international union and a rebellious local, was considered much better copy than a strike by Spanish-speaking immigrant women whose most remarkable quality appeared to be their endurance.

In April Jackson himself had visited Austin. But he also understood the importance of the Watsonville strike, precisely because it involved people of color whose struggles had been too long ignored. Jackson's 1984 campaign had begun as an attempt to energize the African American electorate. By 1988, with his second run at the Democratic nomination, he would be making a full-blown effort to reconstitute a liberal–labor coalition that had been a major force in the party before the political realignments of the late 1960s. With his visits to Watsonville and Austin, he was just beginning to establish his credentials as a labor candidate.

His speech in Watsonville reflected it: its most compelling passages sought to elevate the struggle with language borrowed from the civil rights movement. "Watsonville is today to economic justice what Selma, Alabama, was to political justice 20 years ago," he said, providing the media with a proper sound bite. He paid tribute to the women strikers, saying, "They represent the highest and best in all of us." He addressed the actual strike issues in the words of a peacemaker, calling for "new cooperation between workers and managers. . . . If workers take concessions, it ought to be as an investor with stock in the company."

But the heart of his speech was a call for Latino political power. He denounced the system of at-large elections that had left Watsonville's Latino voters effectively voiceless in city government. "Hands that once picked cucumbers and broccoli can pick governors and presidents," he declared. "It's time for a new course and new coalitions. If we turn to each other, we are the new majority. We can redirect the course of our nation."

Several thousand people attended the rally, which gave Jackson an opportunity to pose not only with strikers but also with Chuck Mack and other prominent labor officials. Before the rally the strikers prepared flan, fruit salad, and homemade donuts for six hundred people at a breakfast reception that raised over $5,000. In addition to the splash of publicity, the day's events provided the strikers with a valuable morale boost, although Gloria Betancourt would privately express irritation that Jackson expected to be paid for his visit.[45]

Three days later, some two hundred Crosetti workers rallied at the Assumption Church and then marched across the street to the plant to cast ballots against their proposed contract. The final tally was 313 to 117 to reject, well above the two-thirds margin required. Workers interviewed in the media afterwards cited the contract's "most-favored nation" clause, which left open the possibility of further wage cuts should Watsonville Canning settle for less than $5.85 an hour. A leaflet urging rejection had called it a "contract without a floor."

Crosetti demurred, pointing out that the company retained the right to renegotiate the wage package only if the union were decertified at Watsonville Canning. Under the circumstances, it is not surprising that the workers treated this as a distinction without a difference. September was just two months away.[46]

The company responded to the vote by stopping production and locking out the workers. A memo from John Blake to Arnie Weinmeister indicates that this was not a unilateral decision:

> Ratification was continuously threatened by outsiders, non-Teamster groups, communist groups, Latino groups, and others. . . . The first ratification meeting of Crosetti was completely out of control. . . . The vote was lost and with the cooperation of the company and meetings with John Blake, WCT [Western Conference of Teamsters] boycott coordinator, and Alex Ybarrolaza, JC7 [Joint Council 7] boycott director, the company agreed to shut down until we felt everything was under the local union's control and an effective vote could be held.[47]

Sergio López was supposed to be handling the negotiations with Crosetti. If the Blake memo is accurate, the meetings referred to were conducted without his knowledge.[48] Weinmeister certainly would have wanted assurances that Local 912 was subject to Blake's oversight if the Western Conference was to maintain support for the boycott.

López was in a difficult situation. The union had been granted access to the company's books, and López had concluded that its financial condition was indeed precarious. The company insisted that it did not want to operate with nonunion labor; López feared it would close for good without a stable work force governed by a collective bargaining agreement.

Moreover, his credibility as the union's designated representative was undercut by Fahey's outspoken opposition to the contract. A Crosetti spokesperson told the *Santa Cruz Sentinel*, "It's very frustrating to sit at the bargaining table and know our workers are getting different messages from the men we're negotiating with." The same reporter overheard Sergio López venting on the phone to a company official about "that damn Fahey, talking the same old crap."

López had even less patience with Bardacke and Cruz Gómez. He pointed out that, not being members of the union, they had "nothing to lose" if negotiations failed. López had a grudging respect for Bardacke, an educated man who had chosen to become a working Teamster and whose views, however much López disagreed with them, were at least grounded in actual experience in the union. He had no such respect for Cruz Gómez. Publicly, he said she was "divisive"; privately, he called her "a pain in the ass." He sent letters to both of them after the vote, formally barring them from the union hall. Meanwhile the Crosetti workers were left to apply for unemployment benefits.[49]

The lockout lasted sixteen days. As early as July 8 the *Register-Pajaronian* reported that talks were under way between the company, union representatives, and the rank-and-file bargaining committee. The Crosetti workers had voted to reject the contract, not to go on strike, and they were not prepared to deal with the lockout. They had already lost two weeks' pay and their August medical benefits.[50] On July 14 they met among themselves to discuss the situation. Union officials were not admitted to the meeting. Bardacke and Cruz Gómez were also asked to stay away. "We wanted to meet alone with no one telling us what to do," one worker said.

Three days later the Crosetti workers narrowly voted to accept same contract they had rejected on July 2. Sergio López praised the company for allowing the workers to reconsider their initial decision: "They didn't seek to punish the workers" for their earlier vote, he said. In his memo to Arnie Weinmeister, John Blake attributed the company's magnanimity to "the relationship of trust and credibility" that he and Ybarrolaza had established with Crosetti's owner.

Paul Meza, a member of the rank-and-file negotiating committee, urged fellow Crosetti workers to rally behind the Watsonville Canning strikers, who now held the key to stopping the further erosion of wage standards in the industry. Cruz Gómez told the *Register-Pajaronian* that the while the vote was not unexpected, neither was the fight over: "I know there will be another battle in four or five months, once Watsonville Canning decertifies."[51]

Her choice of words suggested that, as far as she was concerned, the Watsonville Canning strike was all but lost. Joe Fahey felt some of the same pessimism. He wondered if it might make sense for the strikers to return to work unconditionally in advance of a decertification vote, and continue the struggle from the inside. He had read an article by Tom Balanoff of the Boilermakers Union that described an "in-plant strategy" the boilermakers had used successfully against an employer who had hoped to force a walkout and use it to break the union. But when Esperanza and Enrique Torres raised the idea to the more active strikers, the response was chilly and in some cases downright hostile.[52]

Fortunately, the Teamsters discovered they still had one more card to play. Prior to the Crosetti settlement, Duane Beeson had filed a petition with the NLRB, formally requesting that Local 912 be certified as the bargaining agent for Watsonville Canning workers. Under the law, the NLRB's response was supposed to be determined by a legally binding vote of the company's workers. The law also said that after one year on strike union members lost their eligibility to cast ballots.

Strictly speaking, the union was legally recognized at Watsonville Canning, but after the strike's first anniversary on September 9 the company could petition for a decertification election in which only strikebreakers would be allowed to vote. Beeson had been racking his brains for a way to keep it from happening, when an inspiration came to him out of what he called "pure fear." Watsonville Canning, he realized, had entered into its collective bargaining relationship with the Teamsters voluntarily, back in 1949. There had never been a certification vote at the plant. Accordingly, there was nothing to prevent union members from asking for one now, before the September 9 deadline. If they could muster more votes than the scabs, they would keep their right to Teamsters representation.

The strategy had never been used before, Beeson said, because "strikes never lasted that long." In effect, he was setting a legal precedent. But the NLRB went along with the idea. The initial hearing on his petition was delayed because company lawyers failed to show up, but on July 28 the NLRB approved it and scheduled a union certification vote at Watsonville Canning for August 14.[53]

It would prove to be the turning point of the strike.

Chapter 9

Mort Console at Bay

L awyers do not win strikes; workers do. In successfully petitioning the labor board for a certification vote, Duane Beeson had done no more than provide the strikers with a foot in the door. Taking advantage of it would require the most intense and difficult organizing effort of the entire strike.

No sooner had a date been set for the vote than the personnel office at Watsonville Canning lurched into high gear. Hoping to inflate the anti-union vote, the company aggressively recruited new hires. Strike-breakers already on the payroll had their hours cut back. Ron Trine distributed fliers and held a series of in-plant, on-the-clock meetings instructing his workers how to vote and warning of the dire conse-quences of a union victory.[1] Offsetting the votes of all these workers would require close to 100 percent turnout on the part of the strikers.

It was a formidable task. After eleven months, many strikers were no longer in Watsonville. Many had scattered across California's Cen-tral Valley, trying to pick up enough money to live on through farm labor. Others were as far away as Texas. Some had actually returned to Mexico to await the end of the strike. Of those who remained in town, many had lost their homes and were reduced to makeshift living arrangements—staying with relatives, neighbors, or friends, camping out in their cars or trailers.

Strictly speaking, John Blake and the rest of the work team from the Western Conference of Teamsters were in charge of the mobiliza-tion. In actual practice, it was up to the Strikers' Committee to carry it out. Long before the Teamster officials got involved in Watsonville, the committee had made a point of having current contact information for each of the one thousand Watsonville Canning strikers. "Every time we had a meeting," said Chavelo Moreno, "we'd ask people to update their phone numbers and addresses. If we didn't communicate with them, someone else would."[2]

Now it was necessary to reach every one of them and make sure they showed up at the plant to vote on the appointed day. When people had moved without leaving word or otherwise dropped off the radar, help had to be enlisted from relatives and friends who knew how to find them. Once located, many had to be convinced that their votes were critical enough to warrant travelling hundreds of miles to cast them.

Attempts were also made to win over strikebreakers, a good number of whom were newly hired and had no idea what was going on. Labor board rules allowed the union access to the plant under strict controls; Chavelo Moreno was knowledgeable enough about plant operations to know how to take full advantage of it. The union bought spots on local radio stations. Strikers visited local labor camps where new arrivals were being temporarily housed. The Northern California Strike Support Committee and the Santa Clara County Central Labor Council recruited observers to come to Watsonville on the day of the vote to make sure it was conducted properly.[3]

The Western Conference officials were clearly anxious. When he had first arrived in Watsonville, John Blake was perturbed that the union hall was open round the clock and provided a venue for strikers and supporters alike. At the time, the controversy over the Crosetti contract was still raging, and Blake was convinced that outsiders were responsible for it.[4] He prevailed upon Sergio López to bar both Frank Bardacke and Cruz Gómez from the premises, but, apart from that, his concerns were largely brushed aside. In the two weeks leading up to the August 14 vote, said Gloria Betancourt, "We took over the hall." Esperanza Torres recalled that strikers were constantly on the premises, phone banking; Lydia Lerma spent three hours a night making calls, occasionally to Texas and Mexico. By August 13, virtually every striker had been contacted no fewer than three times.[5]

If, as Blake believed, "outside agitators" had nearly sabotaged union efforts during the Crosetti talks, they posed an even greater threat now. As if to confirm his fears, a left group called the International Committee Against Racism (INCAR) distributed a leaflet calling on workers to vote against the union. "No union is bad," the leaflet read, "but the Teamsters are just as bad. They have spent a year isolating the militant Watsonville strikers from their powerful allies. . . ."[6]

INCAR had been a noisy, if marginal, presence in town for some time. "They'd show up with red flags at all the marches," said Joe Fahey. "They were always encouraging people to throw rocks at the cops. They were stupid and irrelevant and nobody took them seriously." But they had also opposed the Crosetti settlement. So had Joe Fahey, and that was apparently enough to convince taskforce member J. C. Lendvai that Fahey was in their camp. A few days before the vote, Lendvai invited the Local 912 business agent to "go for a ride." Fahey obliged, and as the two were driving back toward the union hall Lendvai abruptly turned up the car radio, leaned over from the driver's seat, and said in Fahey's ear, "If you and INCAR fuck up this election, I'm gonna kill you. Got it?"

Fahey was more amused than frightened. As the two men entered the hall, which as always was full of people, he announced in a loud voice, "Guess what J. C. just told me!" "I said it in English," he recalled, "so the workers who didn't speak English wouldn't understand. It was really for J. C.'s benefit."[7]

Lendvai and Blake underestimated the strikers. Labor board protocol required that the balloting take place at the Watsonville Canning plant. On the day of the vote, two hundred strikers lined up at the plant gate before the polls even opened. To avoid potential conflict, strikebreakers were to vote in the plant cafeteria while strikers cast their ballots in a trailer set up in a parking lot outside. Rather than give the police an excuse to interfere, the strikers were to assemble at the Veterans Hall, where they would be briefed on what to expect and how to conduct themselves. Vince Aloise of the Western Conference work team would ferry them over to cast their ballots, then drive them back to the Veterans Hall.

He wound up operating at a frantic pace on August 14. Teamster officials who had gotten their first exposure to the volatile ways of Local 912 during the Crosetti talks had not known what to expect. The massive turnout on the part of strikers elated them: after a day of driving people back and forth from the plant, Aloise told Alex Ybarrolaza he'd "never had so much fun in his life."[8]

When the polls closed that evening, 919 ballots had been cast in the trailer outside the plant. These were all assumed to be pro-union, and the company challenged every one of them. There were 844 strikebreakers who voted at the polling place in the plant cafeteria, considerably more than the 500-odd workers who had been on the job before the election was called. The company had waited until the last minute to release payroll records that would determine whether they had been hired too recently to be eligible to vote. Accordingly, the Teamsters challenged 790 of these ballots; of the remaining 54, 7 were actually cast in favor of the union.[9]

More than 1,700 ballots thus remained in the possession of the labor board, sealed and uncounted, until the challenges could be resolved. Sergio López was confident enough that Local 912 had won to make an initial offer to drop the union challenges if the company would do likewise. However, it was soon apparent that, while a quick resolution was likely to favor the Teamsters, the union lost nothing if the dispute dragged on. For once, the law worked in the union's favor. As long as the final tally remained undetermined, Local 912 retained its bargaining rights. The company's best hope was to successfully contest at least some of the votes cast in the trailer, but that was likely to take months or even years. If the challenge failed, a full year would have to pass before another move could be made to decertify the union. Watsonville Canning was over a barrel.

Flushed with victory, the Strikers' Committee called a mass meeting on Sunday, August 17. More than a hundred strikers met to discuss the terms under which they would be willing to return to work. There was unanimity that, as far as wages were concerned, Mort Console had to pay at least as much as other frozen food processors were paying. Strikers had to be called back to work based on seniority, with full amnesty and their old health and pension benefits intact. As one striker put it, "We want to go back in together, just as we walked out together." The next day Sergio López agreed to incorporate these demands into the union bargaining position, and to put members of the Strikers' Committee on the negotiating team.[10]

As Alex Ybarrolaza saw it, "The certification vote was crucial in terms of giving a truth serum to Wells Fargo." Prior to August 14, Watsonville Canning had spread the word among local growers that the company's outstanding debts to them would be honored once the election was over and the union was out of the way. The outcome of the balloting, inconclusive at best, made it all too obvious that the company's creditors would not be paid off any time soon. In fact, Watsonville Canning's attempt to win the election by padding its payroll in advance of the vote had only served to sink it deeper into debt. So had its mounting legal bills to Littler, Mendelson, Fastiff, and Tichy, which responded to the election with yet another lawsuit against Local 912.[11]

The extent of Wells Fargo's support of the company was now a public issue. The $18 million line of credit extended to Watsonville Canning on the eve of the strike was all but depleted.[12] On September 26, having run out of cash, the company closed the plant for eleven days while Mort Console negotiated a new loan from the bank. The shutdown, at the height of the fall packing season, sparked widespread speculation that Watsonville Canning might not survive and focused unwanted media attention on a company that had been doing all it could to avoid scrutiny.

Resumption of operations on October 6 was accompanied by a flurry of new publicity about the convoluted financial deal that had made it possible. To get a fresh infusion of credit from Wells Fargo, the *Santa Cruz Sentinel* reported, Mort Console and his mother Kathryn had pledged as collateral "virtually every piece of property they own in Santa Cruz County." This included the plant and warehouse facilities, residential real estate, undeveloped industrial land, and a retail store. It also included the family home on Gonzalez Street, which Mort had inherited from his father fourteen years before.[13]

An unnamed banking industry expert said the agreement was highly unusual and indicated "a troubled loan." In a seasonal industry, he noted, bank credits typically represent an advance on anticipated sales. If a bank feels compelled to require collateral, it clearly lacks confidence that anticipated sales will be adequate to pay off the loan. He speculated that "Console and Wells Fargo are each cooperating with the other in an effort to protect their positions." The bank, he noted, "moves to the head of the line of creditors because it now holds secured debts."[14]

Most tellingly, the loan agreement was between Wells Fargo and the Console family. Watsonville Canning was not a party to the transaction; it was described in the legal paperwork as a "lessee." For all practical purposes the company now belonged to the bank.[15]

"Wells Fargo Bank has a lock on everything owned by Watsonville Canning," the *Sentinel* reported. "There appears to be nothing left besides warehoused produce for growers to claim, should Watsonville Canning fail." For growers and harvesters who were still awaiting payment on an estimated $10 million worth of produce, this news was potentially devastating. To make matters worse, prior to the 1985 harvest season some of them had acceded to company demands that they waive their right to file producers' liens should the strike prevent timely payment for their crops. The liens entitled them to preferential treatment among company creditors, and there was some question about whether they could even be legally waived. Growers who agreed to the terms doubtless never expected the strike to last so long.[16]

The Teamsters had given them fair warning. As early as May, the union had obtained a list of growers doing business with the company and had sent out a letter, signed by Sergio López, which warned that by extending credit to Watsonville Canning they were taking a serious risk. A letter dated July 25 was more explicit:

> We have been very patient trying to obtain a contract at Watsonville Canning Company, but our "Economic Boycott Campaign" is now fully staged and underway. In evaluating the potential effect of this campaign, careful consideration must be given to the fact that the retail and institutional food industries are fully unionized and many of them . . . are major employers of Teamsters. Also, virtually all labor unions have already pledged support for our efforts.

This letter, which went out to sixty Salinas Valley growers, was followed by another on September 18 which softened the vaguely threatening tone of the earlier one with a "we're-all-in-this-together" message: "Financially crippling the company . . . is not our goal. If Watsonville Canning goes bankrupt, none of us wins. Many growers could not financially withstand the loss of monies owed them and neither could many of the support companies. The strikers . . . would lose their jobs."[17]

Unfortunately, most growers were not in a position to end their relationship with the company on short notice. Local brussels sprout farmers continued to supply the plant, simply because they had nowhere else to go: the head of the Santa Cruz Artichoke and Sprout Growers Association pointed out that their crops had been planted in January on the assumption that both Richard Shaw and Watsonville

Canning would settle their labor disputes. Shaw was already operating at peak capacity and could not handle any more.[18]

On September 26, the same day the plant shut down, the state Department of Food and Agriculture launched an investigation of Watsonville Canning. The department was charged with protecting the interests of growers and making sure the contracts they signed with processing companies were honored. If the probe revealed that Watsonville Canning was defaulting on its obligation to pay its suppliers, the company could be stripped of its operating license. But George Reese, the state official heading up the investigation, also pointed out, "There is a limit to our power. . . . Watsonville Canning can always file bankruptcy under Chapter 11." If it did, authority of the Department of Food and Agriculture in the matter would be trumped by the courts.[19]

Rather than wait for that to happen, two Salinas Valley harvesters filed lawsuits demanding close to $800,000 in payments from the company. Bonita Packing in Santa Maria, 150 miles to the south, held off trying to recover its $2 million in outstanding debts while it consulted with the seventeen growers whose crops it handled. As much as anything, the new loan agreement between Console and Wells Fargo was an attempt to head off any more such litigation, which could seriously complicate matters should the company's affairs wind up before a bankruptcy court judge.[20]

The growers were not the only ones having trouble collecting their debts. In June the *Register-Pajaronian* reported that a Santa Cruz furniture dealer was suing Mort Console over failure to pay for nearly $200,000 worth of merchandise for his house in Aptos. Console filed a countersuit, claiming the store had overcharged him. The disputed merchandise included a $26,000 Chinese dining set, a $21,000 master bedroom set, $1,400 worth of cutlery, and $1,350 worth of wine, cordial, and highball glasses. Meanwhile, the attorney for Console's ex-wife, who had been battling him over $11 million in personal assets since their 1985 divorce, charged that property that was rightfully his client's was being "used to buoy her husband's floundering food-packing company."[21]

From the beginning, Alex Ybarrolaza saw Teamster deposits in Wells Fargo accounts as an important source of union leverage. Initially, threatening to withdraw these funds was simply a way to exert indirect pressure on Mort Console. But as it grew more deeply involved in Watsonville Canning's affairs, the bank became more than a strate-gic "pressure point"—it was emerging as a primary target of the strike.

Arguing that Wells Fargo had "reached the point in its relationship with Watsonville Canning and Frozen Food where it is dictating busi-ness decisions, including those related to the strike," Alex Ybarrolaza asked Arnie Weinmeister for permission to begin polling Teamster lo-cals about their ties to the bank. Permission came on November 5. "We sent letters to all the Teamster branches asking their relationship to the bank without specifying the reasons for it," said Ybarrolaza. "We never got a complete analysis of how much of our money was involved; locals had bank accounts, health and welfare accounts, pension trusts. . . ." However, he guessed that Teamster funds in Wells Fargo accounts were in excess of $1.1 billion, excluding member accounts.[22]

The problem was that appeals for solidarity were not enough to per-suade many locals to pull their funds. "We have enjoyed an exceptional relationship with Wells Fargo for many years," said a letter to Chuck Mack from Local 36 in San Diego.[23] It would take orders from above to get their support, and here, Ybarrolaza got an unexpected break.

On August 19, five days after the certification vote, union and company negotiators met for the first time in nearly nine months. Ybarrolaza, lead negotiator for the Teamsters, walked into a confer-ence room at the Monterey Hyatt with John Blake, Eddie Rodriguez, Sergio López, and Leon Ellis. The five men found themselves sitting across the table from Mort Console, Ron Trine, and Andy Anderson, former head of the Western Conference of Teamsters. Anderson had lost his union position when Jackie Presser decided to replace him with Arnie Weinmeister. He now revealed himself to be a "labor relations consultant" for Watsonville Canning.

The astonished union team called a brief caucus, then returned to the table. Ybarrolaza described what followed: "I asked Andy if he was representing Console. He said yes. He said, 'I've never heard such BS as a union calling for a certification vote. This is happening because of internal union politics.' He was under the impression that Jackie Presser was out to get him, and 'Mort Console is being targeted be-cause he's a personal friend of mine.'"[24]

"I still don't know why he showed up," federal mediator Robert Crall said of Anderson when a local reporter asked him about it later.

Harry Bernstein, the veteran labor reporter for the *Los Angeles Times*, got wind of the incident and devoted an entire column to it.[25] He cited it as yet another example of Teamster corruption, and speculated that Anderson had been giving Console intelligence about Local 912 since the beginning of the strike.

Anderson's presence played right into Ybarrolaza's hands. From the beginning, one of his main strategic objectives had been to make sure the international union stayed engaged with the strike. The public revelation that one of Jackie Presser's factional enemies was working for Watsonville Canning made it much harder for the general president to consider withdrawing support.

On a regular basis, Chuck Mack had been sending Presser packets of news clippings about the situation in Watsonville. The October issue of *Convoy Dispatch*, the TDU national newspaper, included a tear sheet that featured Anderson's photo above an eye-grabbing headline: "ANDY ANDERSON, UNION BUSTER." The accompanying blurb gave a brief summary of the strike and Anderson's role in it, pointed out that Anderson was drawing four separate Teamster pensions in addition to his consulting fee from Watsonville Canning, and invited union members who found all this objectionable to join TDU. Playing the TDU card for the second time in the strike, Chuck Mack made sure to include a copy of the tear sheet in his next delivery to Jackie Presser.[26]

Presser got the hint. At its October meeting, the Teamsters international executive board approved in principle the strategy of divesting from Wells Fargo. With the support of Presser and Arnie Weinmeister, a proposal was to be submitted to the board at its January 1987 meeting formally directing all Teamster locals to take their funds out of Wells Fargo and requesting that the union's members do likewise with their personal accounts. Ybarrolaza was confident that "even without our solicitation much of Labor in California would follow suit." "The advantage of a top-down union," said Ybarrolaza wryly, "is that you can make things happen."[27]

Ybarrolaza and John Blake had enough confidence in the divestment strategy to make them effectively abandon plans for a consumer boycott. This was frustrating to all three support committees and many strikers, who wanted a visible campaign to rally broad public support. There was widespread concern that the effort to ramp up the pressure on Console was being weakened by the Teamsters' insistence on controlling all aspects of it. "Although the International has allocated $20,000 a month for an economic sanctions campaign against Console, the workers are in the dark about what is being done with that money," *Unity* complained. Calling for public agitation to "raise the stakes" for the union and "political leaders, including Chicano leaders," the article suggested a number of ways by which "the union's vast resources" could be used to strengthen the strike, including a national campaign to solicit donations for the strikers, direct involvement of "Teamster drivers who haul Watsonville Canning products to market," and "provid[ing] workers with research on Console's financial holdings to pinpoint ways to bring economic pressure to bear."[28]

To his credit, Ybarrolaza understood that such criticisms were to be expected given the approach the Teamsters had taken. People outside the union hierarchy knew little or nothing of plans to divest from Wells Fargo, and internal union politics ruled out public discussion of the subject. Ybarrolaza was also well aware that no union approach to economic sanctions would succeed if the morale and confidence of the strikers themselves were not maintained. He therefore did his best to reassure critics that just because the boycott was not a high-profile undertaking did not mean that nothing was happening, or that Watsonville Canning, its distributors, and financial backers were not feeling the heat.

"The Economic Boycott Campaign must, of necessity, maintain a low profile, as it is currently functioning at a corporate level," he wrote to one critical support committee activist. "In order to avoid secondary boycott citations from an unfriendly NLRB and courts that could possibly stall our efforts, no high visibility consumer programs are presently planned." But the corporate campaign was having an effect: the Teamsters, he stressed, had already persuaded a Mexican company, Empacadora de Najarantes Azteco, to cancel its marketing agreement with Watsonville Canning. This was confirmed in the October 21 edition of the *Strikers' Committee Bulletin*, which reported that a "recent trip to Mexico by local and national Teamster officials" had been "very successful in disrupting deals that the company was hoping to make." By December 16, Ybarrolaza could report that the company's customer base had been "decimated, with most of their customers transferring their business elsewhere." Safeway was the exception; the supermarket chain continued to rely on Watsonville Canning to pack its premier Bel Air frozen food line.[29]

Sergio López appears to have relayed rank-and-file concerns about the boycott to Ybarrolaza as well. In his response, Ybarrolaza maintained that the two main targets of the campaign, Safeway and Wells Fargo, were "national in scope and as such not vulnerable to local or regional consumer activities. The only effective way to handle these situations is at the corporate level or on a national scale. That is what we are doing and we have been doing it very successfully."[30]

The strikers had another concern: they needed to know that the Teamsters were doing all they could to ease their mounting financial difficulties. The Strikers' Committee continued to hold weekly mass meetings at the union hall; at a meeting held during the eleven-day shutdown of the plant, when it was unclear if Watsonville Canning would even reopen, sixty strikers voted to demand immediate unemployment benefits, retraining funds, and an end to the blacklists that were reportedly preventing the more active strikers from being hired at other frozen food plants. (Fidelia Carrisoza had actually hired on at Richard Shaw but had lost her job when "somebody recognized me.") The union had been trying without success to get unemployment benefits for the strikers for months. It was also suing Watsonville Canning for the vacation pay the strikers had earned prior to the walkout but never received, and had filed a sex discrimination complaint against the company as well. Before the November 13 union meeting Ybarrolaza asked Beeson for an update on all three cases and a timetable for their expected resolution. "We will draw some criticism from the strikers for dragging our heels on these issues, perhaps deservedly," he pointed out.[31]

The Strikers' Committee put out its own public appeal for help on November 11. "In the next period it will be crucial to continue to broaden support for our struggle," the leaflet read. "For the labor movement under attack, this resistance cannot be left unsupported. It is the duty of all workers and progressive people to make sure it is victorious." It asked for donations to be sent to Local 912 or to the Strikers' Committee at Chavelo Moreno's Castroville post office box.[32]

Two days later the *Santa Cruz Sentinel* launched an explosive three-part series on Watsonville Canning that suggested that the company was implicated in kickback schemes, insurance fraud, and selling contaminated produce. Fernando Ramírez, the night shift supervisor at the plant whose home had been the target of gunshots and a firebombing the previous winter, informed reporters that he had been laid off at the end of September "because he refused to ask production workers to process contaminated or inferior vegetables." Ramírez was a former member of Local 912 who had lost his right to union representation when the company reclassified his job as a management position prior to the strike. The attacks on his home, condemned as "reprehensible" in the Local 912 *Weekly Bulletin*, suggested that there were strikers who saw him as an enemy, and at least one of them was willing to act accordingly. But Sergio López maintained a friendly relationship with Ramírez and encouraged him to go public with his story after he was laid off.[33]

His allegations were enormously damaging to the company. Watsonville Canning was already battling its insurance company over a $6.9 million claim resulting from the fire that had destroyed a company warehouse the night of October 14, 1985. The fire, determined by authorities to be arson, had occurred during a period of daily clashes between strikers and police and was widely assumed to have been set by strikers. Now, the *Sentinel* reported that cauliflower processing equipment had been moved out of the warehouse one month before the fire, fueling suspicions of an inside job.

The company's claim was based on what it characterized as lost sales on 22 million pounds of beans. Explaining his refusal to approve the claim, the insurer investigator said, "It would be very difficult for the market to absorb 20 million tons of beans at any price." Moreover, documentation of the lost sales, bearing the letterheads of various brokers and distributors with whom Watsonville Canning did business, was revealed to have been prepared in the offices of Conco, Watsonville Canning's parent company. The insurer filed fraud charges in Superior Court ten weeks later.[34]

Ramírez gave the story an added twist: the beans in question, purchased four days before the fire from a seed company owned by Smiley Verduzco's father-in-law, were actually seed beans, unfit for human consumption. Ramírez said the company had taken steps to conceal the beans from state Food and Agriculture Department inspectors. He also exposed a complicated kickback scheme, which enabled the company to buy and market inferior produce at Grade A prices. Faced with a glutted market, growers would delay harvesting their crop, causing it to deteriorate. Watsonville Canning buyers would demand payoffs under the table to take the produce off their hands and conceal its inferior quality.[35]

This charge was corroborated by two strikers who had worked in the grading department at the plant. They told the *Sentinel* that two company officials who were successfully prosecuted for falsifying tax returns in connection with the kickbacks had ordered them to falsely grade cauliflower and spinach. More tellingly, Ramírez maintained that the practice continued even after the two officials went to jail. He spoke of coming to work at the beginning of his shift and seeing workers shoveling up broccoli that had fallen on the floor and tossing it back onto the production line. He also spoke of anglo managers subjecting workers to a barrage of racial slurs.[36]

The company denied the charges. "There's been an awful lot of pressure placed on Fernando by union people," said Smiley Verduzco.[37]

The *Sentinel* expose was apparently worrisome enough that Safeway quality assurance officer Tom O'Ban took the unusual step of ordering a quality control check on frozen spinach and broccoli coming out of the plant.[38] The results apparently satisfied him, because John Blake reported that Safeway "seems to have increased its orders to WC&FF despite continuing quality problems." However, Blake continued, "We have been able to ascertain that WC&FF broccoli and cauliflower packs are not up to normal Bel Air quality standards and may seek an independent laboratory to perform an evaluation. We are also setting up a system to monitor inventories of WC&FF packed products at all Safeway frozen food warehouses in California."[39]

By now Watsonville Canning had largely exhausted whatever reservoirs of good will it might once have enjoyed in the community. Ron Trine complained that media coverage had done more harm to the company than the strike itself. The *Register-Pajaronian* answered his charge with a lengthy editorial insisting that the paper had no desire to see Watsonville Canning go belly up and the company had only itself to blame for its image problems. It cited the company's repeated refusal to respond to reporters' queries, and noted that when it did respond, it frequently answered questions with outright lies.[40]

Increasingly, the question no longer seemed to be whether Watsonville Canning would fail, but when. The conditions under which the plant reopened did not inspire confidence. For the time being, the state Department of Food and Agriculture had withdrawn its threat to lift the company's operating license, as growers considered the company's offer of a 49 percent limited partnership in lieu of paying down its debts. At least one grower called the offer "intriguing." But Leon Ellis warned, "If the growers become partners in Watsonville Canning, their fields, sheds, and trucking companies will become part of the strike," and the union would presumably be free to "take economic action against them" without fear of secondary boycott charges.[41]

Meanwhile the strikers' euphoria after the August 14 vote had given way to a nagging anxiety about the future. In the November edition of his periodic status reports on the strike, Alex Ybarrolaza wrote, "The strikers . . . would rather see Watsonville Canning bankrupted than give in and return to work without the dignity of an honest Teamster labor agreement." As far as it went, this statement was correct. But while union standards in the industry would be preserved in the event Watsonville Canning was forced out of business, it was difficult to see how the workers themselves would be better off. A reporter asked Arnold Highbarger, editor of the Local 912 *Weekly Bulletin*, what would happen to the strikers if the company went broke. "What do you think is happening to them now?" he said bitterly.[42]

"The Teamsters Union . . . stands by its own," Ybarrolaza's report continued, "and the strikers are still strong and have not been abandoned." He noted that the union had already invested $5 million in the strike. On September 30, Bill Walsh set up a job placement bureau, which Ybarrolaza claimed found alternative employment for almost four hundred strikers, the majority of them in local frozen food plants which expanded their payrolls as they took on more of Watsonville Canning's business. The Employment Development Department still balked at granting unemployment benefits to strikers, but the union did secure its active cooperation in providing individualized assessment, counseling, and other services at the union hall, aided by translators provided by the union.[43]

But what the strikers really wanted was a just settlement, and there was growing sentiment that the bank held the key. On Saturday,

November 22, the Strikers' Committee travelled to San Francisco to meet with Ybarrolaza. They asked that he attend the Local 912 meeting the following Tuesday and report on "the latest with Wells Fargo."

Ybarrolaza complied. At the meeting he gave a detailed account of Watsonville Canning's financial troubles. He then reported on the ongoing investigation of Teamster funds invested in Wells Fargo accounts, stated that Jackie Presser had the authority to withdraw those funds, and assured his listeners that Presser was prepared to do so. Divestment would be a complex and difficult process, he acknowledged, but "Wells Fargo knows we're serious" and the union would not allow it to avoid the consequences of its actions.[44]

But the bank's agenda remained a mystery, and strike supporters were doubtful that the Teamsters' strategy could be relied upon. Writing in the *Santa Cruz Sun*, Jim Brough of the Santa Cruz Strike Support Committee called on the city of Watsonville to use its powers of eminent domain to "keep the plant open until buyers can be found who would be committed to operating [it] with a no give-back union contract." *Unity* speculated that "Wells Fargo's most recent actions appear to be part of a larger plan to gain control of valuable property in the Salinas/Pajaro Valley, where real estate speculation . . . [has] been stimulated by the expansion of nearby Silicon Valley." Early in the year, the article pointed out, the bank had foreclosed on farm loans and idled four thousand campesinos, prompting the UFW to picket bank offices in protest. The implication was that it might be necessary for striking Teamsters to do the same.[45]

For much of December, negotiations went on behind closed doors between the bank, the company, and the growers. The people whose labor had made the company prosperous before the strike did not have a seat at the table. For that matter, neither did their union. As the new year approached, it was clear that the bank was going to start feeling more heat.

Chapter 10

The Final Days

D avid Gill was a victim of his own success. Of all the growers who sold their produce to Watsonville Canning, his operation was the largest. His ranch was located near King City in southern Monterey County, where labor costs tended to be cheaper than the area around Salinas. UFW efforts to organize the Salinas Valley had never penetrated far enough south to significantly affect him.

Gill was an astute businessman. When the devaluation of the peso sent Mexican wage levels plunging, he did not waste time fretting about unfair foreign competition. He simply began cutting back on labor-intensive crops like broccoli and concentrating more on spinach, which was easier to harvest.

Other growers relied on harvesting companies and middlemen to market their crops. In a bid to reduce his overhead, Gill had worked out an arrangement to sell his produce directly to Watsonville Canning. Until the fall of 1985, the move seemed like a smart one. The company was not always prompt with its payments, but Gill's cash flow was healthy enough that the occasional delays were rarely more than a minor bookkeeping headache, and he was saving plenty of money.

But now Gill had come to regret his decision. "I was one of their largest suppliers at the time," he recalled. "We were shipping them so much that when the strike started we were hung out to dry." Though he continued to supply Watsonville Canning during the strike, he had not been paid since October 1985. Avoiding the middlemen had cost him dearly: the company's debts to Gill came to some $5 million, a sum roughly equivalent to what was owed to all the other growers combined. Should the company's fate wind up in the hands of a bankruptcy court judge, he stood a good chance of losing most if not all of it.

Gill respected Watsonville Canning managers like Ron Trine, whom he considered a hard worker. But he had come to view Mort Console with contempt—an unscrupulous and irresponsible owner who "used his company like a personal cash cow."[1]

Sergio López got wind of Gill's situation and decided to talk to him directly. The two met secretly in a restaurant in King City. López laid out his case: Watsonville Canning was not going to survive the strike. The company had shown itself unable to operate effectively with scab labor. Gill's chances of recovering his money in bankruptcy court were slim at best. His best hope was to buy out the company and come to a quick settlement with the union. López promised Local 912's cooperation in providing a stable and experienced work force. The terms of a collective bargaining agreement had for all practical purposes been established at other frozen food companies, so Gill would be spared the uncertainty of difficult or drawn-out contract talks. Working together, he and Local 912 could make the plant profitable again.[2]

Gill had no desire to go into the frozen food business, but López had a point. There was $5 million on the line, and there seemed no other way to get it back. In October Mort Console had tried to pacify his creditors by offering shares in the company in lieu of payment, but the company was in such dire straits that no one was interested. Subsequently Wells Fargo Bank floated the idea of an actual transfer of ownership to a growers' cooperative. Several weeks of complicated negotiations produced a plan in early February of 1987 to reconstitute Watsonville Canning as a consortium of growers, tentatively called NorCal Freezers, which would take over the plant from Mort Console. Growers who elected not to be part of the consortium would be paid off through sale of the company's frozen food inventory.

All told, some two dozen growers were either directly involved in the negotiations or had a financial stake in the outcome.[3] But for most of them, there were legal as well as financial issues that outweighed any possible advantages of participating in a takeover. One by one, all but David Gill would drop out of the process.[4]

Needless to say, the negotiations were cloaked in secrecy. Media coverage was vague and often speculative. And while the lawyers haggled behind closed doors, the strikers continued to suffer. Another holiday season had come and gone with no indication that their hardships would end anytime soon. By mid-January production at the plant had virtually ceased, but no one seemed to know what this meant in terms of resolving the labor dispute.

"People were desperate economically," Shiree Teng recalled. Since many strikers had taken other jobs, "there were less and less people on the picket line. It didn't seem like the union was doing anything, and they didn't have anything tangible that they were telling the workers, so the rumor mill started working."[5]

One rumor had it that talk of a change in ownership was a charade by the company to escape its collective bargaining relationship with the Teamsters, effectively negating the victory the strikers had won the previous August. All the dickering over the company's future "looks like some kind of a trick," said Chavelo Moreno. "Even if they change the name, it's still the same company—the same bank and the same management."[6] In an opinion piece in the *Santa Cruz Sun*, he and fellow striker Carlos Hernández wrote, "Console, Wells Fargo, and the growers hope to legally deny us our jobs and a contract with the union."[7]

As the strikers' frustrations grew, the union itself became a target. Even before there was talk about the plant changing owners, many of them had begun to question both the effectiveness and the seriousness of the economic boycott campaign. In December, having finished out his jail term from the previous spring, José López went to the union hall and voiced his concerns to local officers. These were promptly forwarded to Alex Ybarrolaza, who tried to address them in a December 19 letter to Sergio López.[8]

Ybarrolaza encouraged Local 912 members with specific proposals to submit them in writing so they could be reviewed by Teamster attorneys; he offered assurances that they would get serious consideration and that "all written suggestions will be responded to." He acknowledged that "it is very difficult for the strikers to understand a program that is not readily visible in Watsonville, and we are also very sympathetic and appreciative of the tremendous hardships endured by the strikers." The Wells Fargo campaign, he insisted, was "moving at a very rapid pace."

The union had "substantial leverage" with the bank, far more than Mort Console, and expected its efforts to bear fruit by mid-February provided it did not "run afoul of secondary boycott laws . . . which could stop all our efforts if we make a mistake or if we get blamed for unauthorized acts." In effect, he was asking the strikers to be patient and have faith that the union had the situation under control.

It was not what people wanted to hear. Ybarrolaza's claims about Teamster leverage with the bank were correct: the international union was, in fact, preparing to pull its funds out of Wells Fargo. But from the vantage point of the workers, the strike was in limbo. There was no indication that the company's imminent failure would leave them any better off. And some felt that the more involved in the strike the Teamsters hierarchy had become, the more their own role had been marginalized.

At a Christmas party organized by the Strikers' Committee and the NCSSC, it became clear that "the frustration of the long strike was beginning to boil over. . . . Many workers began to renew their attacks on the union leadership."[9] There was a resumption of vandalism directed at union officials that had not been seen since the early weeks of the strike: both Sergio López and Leon Ellis had their cars trashed, and one night someone hurled a firebomb at López's house.

Chuck Mack viewed these developments with alarm. A memo to Sergio López cited "recent violence, destruction of union property, and threats to officials" and called for "immediate attempts . . . by Local 912 to improve security." Among other things, Mack wanted the union office, usually open around the clock, to be closed except during normal business hours and when meetings were going on. Night picketing was to be discontinued, as the plant was no longer operational. Nonmembers were not to be allowed in the union hall without López's prior approval, and leafleting on union property by outsiders was to stop. Distribution of strike benefit checks from the union was to be done only by López or his designee.[10] All these measures were presumably motivated by a concern for López's safety, but in practice they would simply make his life more difficult and stir new resentment among the workers.

Two weeks earlier, Mack had written López saying he was "shocked" to learn of the hardship fund operated by the Strikers' Committee. The letter characterized the fund as "highly irregular and probably illegal" and urged the Local 912 executive board to "take whatever steps necessary to correct this matter." The fund's existence should have come as no surprise. Nearly a year earlier, Sergio López had directed Joe Fahey to write Duane Beeson inquiring about its propriety. Beeson had responded that the fund did indeed pose potential legal problems. But until now there had been no move by either Local 912 or Joint Council 7 to do anything about it.[11]

The fund was Chavelo Moreno's responsibility. Both he and Gloria Betancourt had worked hard to impress upon their fellow strikers the importance of maintaining an effective working relationship with the Teamsters. Gloria Betancourt in particular did not come by this position easily: she had been deeply estranged from the union when the strike began. But she gradually came to believe that "we had to unite with the union and try to work with them so that there would be better representation." Without the union's support, she argued, the strike would have been doomed to defeat, because "there were too many enemies against the strikers." The union, she said, "has become stronger because of us."

For his part, Moreno believed that one of the most important accomplishments of the strike had been to force the union to take the workers seriously. "It took a lot of work, right from the beginning," he said. Through "the work we did and in the programs we organized," the Strikers' Committee had opened up lines of communication that had not existed before: "We let [union officials] know what the people need and how the membership is looking at things, and then when they see this they have to work along those lines, because the people are the union."[12]

But the strike had reached a point where, at least for the time being, communication between the workers and the union officials was at low ebb. No one was sure what was going to happen or how Teamster officials would respond. Gloria Betancourt took pride in having managed to work with the union while maintaining "the trust of our compañeras."[13] But she believed she had a responsibility to reflect the sentiments of those who had elected her to the Strikers' Committee, and right now they had less than full confidence in the union. By the same token, Joint Council 7 seemed less inclined to trust either the strikers or the local to manage things without closer supervision.

On January 16, Mort Console startled everyone by showing up unannounced at the union hall. He and Sergio López disappeared into López's office, where the two men talked for some time behind closed doors. When Console finally left, he invited López to continue their conversation the following week at the company offices on Green Valley Road.

It was the first time the two men had spoken in over a year, and it touched off a new flurry of media speculation. One theory had it that Console and Smiley Verduzco were fighting for control of Watsonville Canning. Verduzco was supposedly trying to oust Console and take over the company in alliance with the growers. Presumably, Console hoped to enlist Local 912's help in heading him off. Sergio López was willing to go along with the story, to the extent of telling reporters on January 22 that Console needed to get rid of Verduzco and run things himself. By now any chance of Watsonville Canning's decertifying the union was gone: the NLRB had just upheld union charges that Console had padded his employment rolls prior to the August certification vote. On the other hand, should the company change hands, there was no guarantee that the Teamsters would retain bargaining rights.[14]

A union meeting was scheduled for January 19 at the county fairgrounds. López hoped to explain the significance of his meeting with Console to the three-hundred-odd strikers in attendance. Before they would hear his report, however, the workers insisted on passing a resolution "allowing the strikers to mount a public protest, independent of the union, against the bank." They also requested that the Local 912 executive board designate two representatives to attend the Western Conference of Teamsters meeting in Hawaii the following week. López declined to comment to the media about the vote. Given Teamster concerns about secondary boycott charges, it could not have been welcome.[15]

Since the union would not be associated with it, any public protest would require the help of the support committees. Fortunately, by now all three of them had reached the same conclusion: whether the Teamsters liked it or not, it was time to publicly demonstrate against the bank and call it on the carpet for its role in prolonging the strike. The League had done its own assessment of the secondary boycott statutes and concluded that Ybarrolaza's caution in this area was not only harmful to strikers' morale, but also unnecessary. Frank Bardacke was of the opinion that the strike never should have been bound by the Taft-Hartley law in the first place.[16]

Joint meetings of the support committees were not entirely free of tension, but Frank Bardacke would write that by now they "worked together in something like a principled fashion."[17] The support committees worked in tandem on three January 30 demonstrations. The Watsonville Strike Support Committee took charge of picketing at the bank's Watsonville branch on Freedom Boulevard, which according to press reports drew about seventy-five people. María Corralejo, a local social worker who had worked closely with strikers from the beginning and got on well with all the support groups, acted as media spokesperson. The NCSSC organized a protest at the bank's corporate headquarters in San Francisco; turnout was augmented by the League's contacts from the Bay Area student movement. The Santa Cruz Strike Support Committee staged a smaller protest at their local branch.

At all three demonstrations, leaflets identified the protesters as "Concerned Citizens" and stated that they had no affiliation with the Teamsters, but strikers were prominent in the ranks of pickets in San Francisco and Watsonville. At the Watsonville protest, Gloria Betancourt made a point of telling a reporter she was "not here as a union member but as a community member."[18]

Even before the demonstrations took place, the Teamsters took pains to distance themselves. "I am informed that a group of individuals will appear and demonstrate in front of your bank on Friday," stated Sergio López in a letter hand-delivered to Wells Fargo's Watsonville branch. "Any activity of this kind has not been approved or authorized by Teamster Local 912. The individuals involved . . . are not representatives of our local union and their activities do not reflect the policy of Local 912." Chuck Mack sent his own statement to the bank branch the same day, advising that the pickets "have not been authorized or sanctioned by us." While the union was concerned about the bank's role in the strike, he said, "demonstrations, leafleting, or picketing are not presently on our agenda to deal with this matter." For good measure, he sent copies of the letter to two high-ranking bank officials and phoned in a press release to the *Register-Pajaronian*, the *Santa Cruz Sentinel*, and the *San Jose Mercury News*, all of which could be expected to cover the Watsonville action.[19]

"I ended up in Watsonville on Friday," Alex Ybarrolaza wrote Duane Beeson the following week. "The demonstration was satisfactorily diffused [sic] and it wound up a very low key effort . . . with just a few individuals." The Teamsters appear to have ignored the San Francisco picket line, perhaps because they assumed the big city media would ignore it as well.[20]

There were already indications that union divestment threats had the bank seriously worried. For months, bank officials had steadfastly rejected union requests for a meeting, even after a sharply worded letter from Chuck Mack on October 30 advised them that the Teamsters now saw Wells Fargo as "in full control" of Watsonville Canning and union members found the situation "intolerable."[21] But on January 6, Mack and Mike Riley, who ran the Teamsters pension fund, were finally granted a secret audience with an executive vice president of the bank in Los Angeles.

At the meeting Mack characterized the union's relationship with Wells Fargo as "embarrassing." "How do we explain it to our members?" he demanded. He also asserted that, from a purely financial point of view, the bank's continued support for Console made no sense, because "we're going to put this guy out of business." The conversation ended with nothing resolved, but three weeks later, when the Western Conference executive board was meeting in Hawaii, Mack learned that the bank's CEO, Carl Reichert, was staying in the same hotel:

> We had been talking about the Watsonville strike. I said, "I'm going to call this guy up." Sure enough, he was there. I told him, "I'm just getting back to you. We hadn't heard anything from you." He said, "I'm taking your concerns to the highest levels of the bank. You'll hear from us. . . . Do me a favor, Mr. Mack, and please don't call me again about this matter." The bank took over Watsonville Canning a week later.[22]

Mack's recollection is not entirely accurate: too many other parties were involved for a takeover to proceed that quickly. Farm loans made up a big part of Wells Fargo's business locally, and enough of Console's creditors had sizeable debts to the bank to make an outright shutdown of the plant problematic. A better solution would be to find a buyer or buyers who could make productive use of Watsonville Canning's assets. That way, growers who had sold their crops to Watsonville Canning in the past would not lose their market and would be better able to pay off their loans.

· But finding a willing buyer was a challenge. Navigating the technical details of an ownership transfer was an even bigger one. Watsonville Canning's affairs were in sufficient disarray that any negotiations over the plant's future would be byzantine in complexity. The situation made everybody nervous.

Particularly the strikers. On February 17 a number of them had come to the union hall to pick up their strike benefit checks. That day's *Register-Pajaronian* had just hit the stands and reported that phone calls to the plant's employment office were being answered, "NorCal Freezers." It seemed a confirmation of strikers' worst fear—that the company would change hands and they would be left out in the cold. Furious, a crowd of about fifty surged out of the hall and toward the plant, two blocks away, chanting, "You buy the plant, you buy the strike!"

The police got there a few minutes later and promptly declared the situation a "riot." They called for reinforcements from the county sheriff's office. Larry Vawter pointed out Chavelo Moreno and demanded that the police arrest him for violating the injunction. According to Shiree Teng, who was on the scene, this merely served to inflame the crowd further: "Chavelo was so beloved, so mild-mannered and even-tempered, that for him to be arrested was insulting and infuriating."

Carlos Hernández thought the police might let their prisoner go if he distracted them. He began hurling rocks in their direction, then fled into the crowd. Margarita Paramo described what followed:

> We blocked the way so the police couldn't catch him, because we knew they would throw him down to the ground and beat him. . . . I saw another cop in a police car with someone he had arrested. And I grabbed my one-year-old daughter and stood in the center of the road to block the police car and I told him, "Go ahead and run me over, but I won't let you pass." The cop hit the siren to get me to move, but I stood my ground. When the other strikers saw that I wasn't going to move, they joined me in front of the cop car. So the police had to turn around and take another route.

Later, she was amazed at what she had done. "I don't know where I got the courage to stand in front of a car," she said. "I just had to do it. . . . The strike did that to people."

As the police took the prisoners away, the strikers followed hard on their heels. They massed in front of the police station chanting, "Free Chavelo!" "Free the strikers!" and "¡Queremos justicia! (We want justice!)"

A front-page color photo in the next day's *Santa Cruz Sentinel* captured the scene. The photo shows a crowd of angry women crowded into the station lobby, clapping their hands, shaking clenched fists, standing with arms folded. Gloria Betancourt, wearing a red dress, stiletto heels, and a string of pearls, is shouting something at an officer who is walking away from the crowd. He is young and looks uncomfortable. Oscar Ríos stands off to one side laughing.

"We stayed there screaming all night!" Margarita Paramo recalled. She was exaggerating, but not by much. Late in the afternoon police captain Terry Medina called the union hall and appealed to Leon Ellis to come down and disperse the crowd. He did not get the response he wanted. "We told them not to go," Ellis snapped at him. "They did it anyway. If I go down there, they'll yell at me just like they yell at you." Eventually Moreno and Hernández were released on their own recognizance, and the crowd drifted away.[23]

Three days later, Sergio López received a copy of a memo Chuck Mack had just sent to Jackie Presser. The memo began with an upbeat assessment of the strike's prospects: Watsonville Canning was "for all intents and purposes . . . insolvent. It is now just a matter of time before they either file for bankruptcy or are bought out." But while the strike and boycott campaign had been "very successful," things still needed to be "brought to a proper conclusion, and recent events in Watsonville have caused us considerable concern. Dissident groups within the ranks of the strikers aided by non-Teamster agitators have increased their efforts to disrupt the normal routine of business at Local 912 and instill violence into our peaceful strike efforts."

Mack cited three developments that he found particularly troubling. The first was the violence and property destruction directed at Sergio López and Leon Ellis. The second was the incident on February 17, when "a group of strikers and outside agitators . . . engaged in violent conduct in violation of court injunctions." While Local 912 had not authorized the action, Mack noted, neither had its officers made any real effort to stop it.

Finally, Mack reported that "in contravention of instructions from me, private meetings have also been taking place between Sergio López and Mort Console . . . which could potentially prejudice [our] position . . . in pending litigation."

Mack had "given some serious thought" to placing Local 912 in trusteeship, but had decided against it. Instead, he requested that Presser designate John Blake as his "direct representative" in functioning as a "monitor-advisor" who would "take full control of all facets of our strike effort."[24]

Asked about the memo years later, Mack said, "We did not want a trusteeship and weren't serious about doing it. It was just a matter of exerting leverage with the Local and the members." However, Sergio López took the threat seriously and was not happy about it. He responded to the memo immediately, requesting that Mack "explain in detail" the extent of Blake's responsibilities. "Are you recommending that the Local 912 executive board votes whether or not to voluntarily give up its autonomy to John Blake," he asked, "with the understanding that if we fail to do so, you will request that our local is put in trusteeship?"[25]

Any prospect of a power struggle between the local and Joint Council 7 was quickly overshadowed by developing events. Wells Fargo was prepared to foreclose on Mort Console as soon as the terms of a takeover could be agreed upon. David Gill's attorney, Dick Maltzman, was negotiating with both the union and the bank. Gill needed to close the deal quickly, because the "spring pack" was already underway, and if he was to buy the plant he would have to resume production immediately or risk losing his market. As it was, he would be starting off with some $20 million in debts, above and beyond his legal expenses and the $5 million that Mort Console had never paid him. Theoretically, Mort Console could torpedo the whole process by filing for bankruptcy protection before the bank could foreclose, saddling the bank with the plant's inventory and accounts receivable. It was not the outcome the bank wanted.[26]

On February 27, Wells Fargo pulled the plug on Console. Watsonville Canning was taken over by David Gill, who renamed it NorCal Frozen Foods. Maltzman had secured additional financing for Gill from San Francisco investors, and the foreclosure complaint against

Console was withdrawn in return for his selling the plant's land and equipment to the new owner. Most of the real estate that Mort and Kathryn Console had put up as collateral the previous fall was deeded over to Gill. At least some of the outstanding debts were to be paid off through the sale of inventory.[27]

With Watsonville Canning out of business, the strike was technically over, but Sergio López instructed his members to maintain the picket line until a collective bargaining agreement could be negotiated with Gill. After a mass meeting to discuss the situation, the Strikers' Committee issued a leaflet addressed to all members of Local 912:

> It is imminent that the grower, David Gill, will become the main owner of "NorCal," the new name that's been given to Watsonville Canning. It is possible that he will offer a contract to the strikers. Before this happens we, the strikers, must make our demands clear.
>
> Our officials, jointly with our negotiating committee, must fight for these demands which represent our interests:
>
>> Wages no lower than the other plants; a union contract with seniority rights and benefits
>> Amnesty for all the strikers
>> A contract with no scabs.
>
> We have suffered for 18 months. . . . We know that the future of the whole community depends upon us, and today we will not accept just any contract. For the future of our children, we must fight![28]

Gill had been quoted in the media as saying he could not afford to pay as much as his competitors. This was a serious concern; the leaflet pointed out that if a deal was struck that was "lower than the other canneries, everyone's wages will go down." Sergio López made the same point at a meeting with strikers at the fairgrounds on February 28. Because of the "me, too" clauses in the Shaw and Crosetti contracts, López said, the union would be courting disaster if it settled for less than $5.85 an hour. True, the clauses referred specifically to pay scales at Watsonville Canning, so any attempt by either company to lower wages in response to a settlement at NorCal might be on shaky legal ground. But Richard Shaw had said publicly that if NorCal settled for less, he would have no choice but to lower his own workers' pay, even though he recognized that "$5.85 is a scavenger's living." (Shaw also told reporters that as far as he was concerned Gill was "in over his head.")[29]

Two other questions came up at the February 28 meeting that López could not answer. He did not know if the benefits strikers had earned under their old agreement with Watsonville Canning would be carried over under the new ownership. Nor could he say for certain whether the Teamsters would be willing to continue sanctioning the walkout, or for how long.

The meeting ended with the election of a rank-and-file bargaining committee made up of Gloria Betancourt, Chavelo Moreno, Cuca Lomeli, Carlos Hernández, and José Macias. All but Macias were active in the Strikers' Committee and had, for the past eighteen months, been immersed in the day-to-day conduct of the strike. Now they found themselves in a new and unfamiliar role. Realistically, it would be a largely passive one: their presence provided the trappings of rank-and-file representation, but Alex Ybarrolaza and Sergio López did the actual negotiating. Monday morning the five strikers traveled north to the Joint Council 7 offices near Candlestick Park in San Francisco, where the final phase of the struggle was to take place.

The negotiators' task seemed straightforward enough: it was just a matter of persuading Gill to accept the same terms that Richard Shaw had agreed to. And since the terms of the Shaw agreement were well-known, there should be no difficulty in explaining them to the strikers. By Tuesday afternoon, an agreement had been reached, and the rank-and-file negotiating committee was to report on it at the union hall at seven that evening. At a press conference in San Francisco that afternoon, an exhausted Gloria Betancourt told reporters, "We've been through hell, but I never lost hope. I hope the contract will be accepted."[30]

Back in Watsonville, Joe Fahey was exhausted as well, but he was also uneasy. He knew the Teamsters had already spent $6 million on the strike and were anxious to wrap it up. He found himself thinking, "This happened too quickly. If I were David Gill, I'd be driving a harder bargain. . . . There's got to be something missing in this deal." He wracked his brain and came up with a possible answer:

> It's got to be something so peculiar that if you don't mention it nobody would ever know.
>
> And I thought: health benefits. . . . You say it's a new company. You say, we're going to hire everybody back, and we'll respect seniority order, but we're going to pretend that your date of employ-

ment is March of 1987 instead of, say, September of 1961, when you actually started.

I knew the contract, and the contract said the seniority list gets made February 15 of every year. That's the only time you can be added to the seniority list . . . you have to work the previous fall, and work thirty days, to get on the seniority list. And you have to be on the seniority list three times in a row, if you're a seasonal worker, before you're entitled to health benefits. So a woman who's worked there for 25 years, and works nine months out of a year, was going to have to wait four years before she's covered by health insurance.[31]

Fahey may have overestimated Gill's bargaining leverage; the new owner needed a quick settlement even more than the Teamsters. But his assessment of the proposed settlement was otherwise on target. Fahey had put his finger on something everybody else seems to have missed. On the surface, having Gill sign on to the same contract as his competitors made perfect sense. But because NorCal was a new company, there was no way to protect the health benefits of the part-timers without adding new language, and it hadn't been done.

When Chavelo Moreno gave his report at the union hall that night, Fahey questioned him closely. The answers he got confirmed his fears and touched off a flood of uncertainty and anger in the strikers' ranks. As for Moreno, "I think he was troubled," Fahey recalled, but he kept his misgivings to himself. The Strikers' Committee had decided to make no formal recommendation one way or another on the proposed settlement; this, they reasoned, was a decision the rank and file had to make. Still, the members of the rank-and-file bargaining committee had all put their signatures to the tentative agreement, which could be taken as an endorsement—though Carlos Hernández took pains to point out that he signed on because he thought it should be submitted to the members for a vote, not because he necessarily intended to vote for it himself. Most likely, no one on the committee had realized the full implications of the contract language until they returned to Watsonville and Fahey started asking questions.

Fahey went home that night and did some math. He calculated that, taking the value of their health insurance into account, the part-timers would return to work making the equivalent of $5.05 an hour. Besides undercutting the new industry standard of $5.85, this was all too close to what they had been struggling against for months. He stressed this point in talking to strikers at the union hall the next day. But the most compelling arguments came from women who had waited a year and a half to take their children to the doctor. Asked why she was voting no, a pregnant striker named Elena Gonzalez simply pointed to her belly.[32]

Yet the decision was not an easy one. For the next two days—the ratification vote was scheduled for Friday—strikers debated it virtually around the clock. Rejecting the settlement carried real risks: the strikers could not count on continued union support; there was a danger that some of the mechanics and other full-time workers, whose benefits were protected in the settlement, might break ranks and return to work; David Gill might abandon his earlier decision to operate the plant as a union shop. For most of the winter, as Watsonville Canning careened towards insolvency, many strikers had resigned themselves to the possibility that they might never work in the plant again. Gloria Betancourt spoke for many when she described Gill's buyout as "a ray of hope."[33] By rejecting the contract, they could conceivably lose it all. And if they lost, Shaw and Crosetti would doubtless try to renegotiate their own contracts

The debate went on, in the union hall and on the picket line. Unless a meeting had been scheduled, the doors of the hall were now being locked promptly at 5 p.m., so people who came by in the evening would hold forth in the parking lot. Shiree Teng listened to the discussions and was moved not only by their intensity but by the way strikers "weighed the variables . . . Nobody saw things in terms of a pure solution." It was, she thought, "democracy in action."[34]

Two prominent nonstrikers weighed in with their own opinions. Cruz Gómez put out a leaflet headlined "MENTIRAS Y TRUCOS" (lies and tricks). It reiterated Fahey's arguments and charged, "The officials and the Strikers' Committee want you to lose what you've gained in 19 months of suffering."[35] Richard Shaw, coming from a very different place, likewise denounced the settlement. He accused the Teamsters of signing another "sweetheart agreement" with his largest competitor, just as they had done in 1982. He pointed out that he had to pay for health coverage for his own part-timers, and the NorCal agreement, if ratified, would give David Gill a labor cost advantage of $300,000 a year for the next several years.[36]

The Strikers' Committee called a mass meeting at the union hall on Thursday night where people could struggle things out in an organized way. The hall, Bob Johnson wrote, was "packed with anxious strikers. . . . The table in front of the picture of Our Lady of Guadalupe in the corner of the Teamsters Hall was covered with roses as 125 workers filled the room."[37]

The meeting was a long one. As the strikers pondered their options, it became clear that sentiment was turning against the settlement. Joe Fahey, who had confined himself to asking questions two days before, was applauded when he called the settlement "unjust" and urged the strikers to reject it. Esperanza Contreras said, "We went on strike to keep our medical insurance. That's what I've been fighting for. This is like an army that gives up its weapons and surrenders. We will not surrender, even if the union takes away our strike benefits." Her last words were characteristic: "Because God is not dead, we won't accept this contract."[38]

God, it turned out, was very much alive. Before the meeting adjourned, those in attendance had united around five demands. They wanted the medical benefits for part-timers restored. They wanted to postpone the ratification vote by one week, so strikers might better study the contract language and negotiators could correct any problems with it. To ensure maximum participation, they wanted the vote to be held on the weekend. They wanted the negotiations to take place in Watsonville, not San Francisco. Finally, they wanted the two-thirds rule thrown out; the contract had to be voted up or down by a simple majority.

Workers filing into the ratification meeting Friday morning were handed an orange leaflet headlined "¡SÍ, SE PUEDE!" (Yes, we can!) The leaflet listed the five demands agreed upon at the union hall the previous night. It explained, "After the negotiating committee informed union members about the proposed agreement with David Gill . . . we found out that the medical plan and benefits do not satisfy our interest." It concluded, "Our strike has lasted 19 months. We have fought for our future and one more week will not hurt the future of our kids and their health. Their future depends on us." The leaflet was signed "STRIKERS IN STRUGGLE."[39]

The ratification meeting, described in the press as "stormy," lasted four hours. Much of it was taken up with a wrangling argument over the two-thirds rule. Sergio López warned that a failure to ratify could cause the entire financial deal with Gill to collapse. Ybarrolaza reminded everyone that technically the strike had ended on March 2 and they should not expect any further benefit checks from the union. He praised the strikers' courage but added that the controversy over the settlement smacked of misplaced anger: "It breaks my heart to see you guys fighting among each other. We are not the enemy. Watsonville Canning is history."

The meeting finally voted, 283 to 193, to delay the ratification vote by one week. Asked why the Strikers' Committee had not supported the agreement after initially signing on to it, Gloria Betancourt told a reporter, "We are following what the strikers want. If the people don't like the settlement, it is not our position to come back and say, 'Take it.'"[40]

Since they had not actually voted on the contract itself, the argument over the two-thirds rule turned out to be moot. The real question was whether David Gill would be willing to go back to the bargaining table. The contract offer was good only until Monday morning.

A hastily issued press release from Joint Council 7 announced that the strikers had elected to "put off voting" on the tentative agreement: "There were some areas . . . that Teamsters Local 912 members had difficulty with and we will be attempting to address these concerns. . . . We will be requesting further negotiations . . . to extend the expiration date of the tentative agreement and afford our members the opportunity to vote on it." In a handwritten note dated Saturday, March 7, Ybarrolaza sought to reassure John Blake that the union could still negotiate a contract the workers would ratify.[41]

Years later David Gill recalled that, while he was "disappointed" in the March 6 vote, it did not alter his commitment to work with the Teamsters. He "understood that Sergio did not have complete control of his members," nor could he be expected to; this came with the territory. For the moment, however, the new owner opted to play hardball. He and attorney Dick Maltzman issued a press release of their own advising of NorCal's intention to "commence hiring Monday . . . on a non-discriminatory basis on the contract terms offered":

> If a majority of the personnel hired are former Watsonville Canning . . . personnel, NorCal will continue to recognize Local 912 as

the bargaining representative for its employees and will continue to work with the union to effect a fair contract for the workers. However, the contract proposal made was in essence an industry standard contract for start-up operation and represents NorCal's final offer.[42]

The press release indicated that NorCal's first priority would be to hire enough maintenance workers to have the plant up and running within two weeks. "The growers have crops in the ground and we can't tell them to stop growing," said Maltzman. "They're coming into market and we need to freeze it."[43]

Teamster officials representing Local 912, Joint Council 7, and the Western Conference made their own position clear in a letter to the strikers that weekend. It reiterated that the strike had formally ended when Watsonville Canning went out of business on March 2 and that no further strike benefits would be paid. Nevertheless, "we will continue to try to obtain a contract on your behalf with NorCal Frozen Foods. . . . We do not, however, have an authorized strike against NorCal and picketing and striking them with Teamster 912 signs is illegal and cannot be condoned." Their letter concluded, "Let us continue to pull together to make sure we get a contract that is the area standard, that guarantees first job rights to ALL the former Watsonville Canning workers. . . ."[44]

The last sentence notwithstanding, the strikers were now largely on their own. As soon as the Friday meeting adjourned, a group of the most active women met at Aurora Trujillo's house across the street from the plant. María Corralejo was there as well; she suggested that the workers dramatize their grievances with a hunger strike. She offered to join the fast herself and promised to secure help and advice from people in the community experienced in nonviolent direct action. Gloria Betancourt, Cuca Lomeli, Esperanza Contreras, Esperanza Torres, Margarita Ramos, and Saul Flores agreed to take part. Shiree Teng of the NCSSC soon joined them.

The union hall had been locked up for the weekend. However, Watsonville Canning was now out of business, so the court injunction designed to protect its property was no longer in effect. For now, at least, the strikers could congregate at the plant gate without police interference. A large tent was pitched on the sidewalk in front of the Trujillo house. David Monkawa, a graphic artist who worked with the NCSSC, produced a fifteen-foot banner reading, "Justicia, Dignidad,

Victoria." It was stretched across the top of the tent. Fortified with plenty of water, Gatorade, and a small charcoal stove for warmth, seven women and one man hunkered down in the tent for a fast that was to last nearly five days.

Sergio López was at home on Friday night mulling over the day's events when there was a knock at the door. It was Joe Fahey, probably the last person in the world he wanted to see. Fahey had been thinking about the Gill-Maltzman press release. He was concerned about NorCal's stated intent to assemble a maintenance crew starting Monday. Defections from the ranks of striking maintenance workers had effectively broken the strike at Richard Shaw, and Fahey worried that the same thing might happen again. Opposition to the proposed settlement had centered on an issue that did not involve maintenance personnel; being full-time employees, they would not have to wait to requalify for their health benefits.

Fahey had drawn up a statement on the union letterhead directing all strikers to remain out until an agreement had been reached that satisfactorily addressed everybody's needs. If López would sign it, he would get it reproduced and see that it was distributed to the strikers.

López had to struggle to keep his temper. As far as he was concerned Fahey was largely responsible for sabotaging the proposed settlement; now López was supposed to clean up the mess. He reminded Fahey of his role in the meeting: "I said, 'Joe, why did you do it?' and he said, 'Because I had confidence in you.'" Fahey, it seemed, expected him to be able to go back to the bargaining table and fix the problem.[45]

"Chickenshit asshole," López remembered thinking. But he signed the letter.

"I knew he would sign it," Fahey recalled, "the same way I knew [restoring health benefits for part-timers] was a winnable issue. . . . I never underestimated how furious with me he would be at that point, and how scared he must have been." Still, "I knew he was a decent person. . . . Angry as he was, I knew he wouldn't want the strike to end that way," with part-timers and full-timers pitted against each other.[46] And it didn't: when the plant reopened Monday morning none of the striking maintenance workers would apply for their old jobs.

On Saturday morning the hunger strikers issued a formal statement affirming the strikers' unity. "This is a non-violent demonstration to demand A UNION CONTRACT WITH FULL MEDICAL BENEFITS," they said. "We are committed to stay out on this hunger strike for as long as it takes to win this demand . . . the rest of the strikers from Local 912 will stay out on strike from work. As we camp here in front of the plant and as our fellow strikers continue to walk the picket line, we need your donations and your moral support."[47] Their tent became a de facto strike headquarters. Strikers used it to talk strategy, speak to the press, and keep an eye on the plant gate. Television crews, conspicuous in their absence for most of the strike, suddenly crowded around the tent.

Strikers in Struggle put out another leaflet Saturday and distributed it widely:

> What we have won so far is a tremendous victory . . . but it's not enough; our fight is not over. . . . We have won everything but our benefits. This is what we're demanding from the new owner, David Gill. We have stayed 1,000 strong; no one has crossed the picket line and this must continue. NO ONE SHOULD GO INTO WORK UNTIL EVERYBODY GOES TO WORK.

The leaflet urged people to "support the hunger strike," picket the plant gates at seven o'clock on Monday morning, and come to a scheduled meeting at the union hall Monday night. The last line read, "NO BENEFITS—NO CONTRACT!"[48]

Inside the tent, the hunger strikers continued their fast and kept their spirits up. They took turns standing guard. They said rosary every night. "Sometimes we were laughing, sometimes we were crying, sometimes we were singing," Esperanza Contreras recalled. Cuca Lomeli couldn't stop thinking about hamburgers. At one point Aurora Trujillo came out of her house and apologized to her compañeras in the tent: she was preparing dinner for her family, and the cooking smells wafting into the street were agony for those who had chosen to go without food.[49]

The real test came early Monday morning. NorCal had announced that it was hiring, and anyone who had not been following the news for the last few days might reasonably assume the strike was over. Esperanza Contreras was doing watch when she spotted a pickup truck approaching the plant gate.

She greeted it with a volley of insults: "¡Esquirol! ¡Esquirol! ¡Vendido la Raza! ¡Cucaracha!" Her daughter Salomé, who had helped support her family during the strike by babysitting and picking mushrooms, stepped directly in front of the truck and threw up her hands. The truck slammed on the brakes and Salomé pounded on the hood. The other hunger strikers surged out of the tent and surrounded it. For the next five minutes they harangued the driver; someone shoved a leaflet into his hands. The driver, embarrassed and angry, tried to argue and then gave up, threw the truck into reverse, and drove away. The women cheered.[50]

Soon a large, noisy crowd had gathered. Anyone trying to get into the plant had to run the gauntlet of several hundred angry, shouting pickets. That included David Gill; strikers pounded out a brisk tattoo on the fenders of his car as he drove past them. Police and county sheriff's deputies were billeted at St. Patrick's Church half a mile away, but they no longer had an injunction to enforce, and apparently nothing happening in front of the plant was deemed serious enough to require their intervention. Very few people went through the gate that day.

"Those would be our jobs they are applying for," Chavelo Moreno told the media, which finally seemed to have grasped that the strike was more than a "local story" and had turned out in force. "That is the plant our work built, and we have a right to keep our jobs. We are still united and we will be united until we have a settlement."[51]

The crowd that massed at the gate was also there for the hunger strikers encamped across the street. Esther Gonzalez took one look at them and began to weep. "It's one thing to be hungry when there's nothing to eat," she said. "To do it deliberately . . ." Her voice trailed off.[52]

Anita Contreras turned out to support her sister Esperanza. She also had a suggestion of her own to make: she proposed a *manda y peregrinación* (offering and pilgrimage) to enlist God's intervention on the strikers' behalf. A manda is a Mexican folk ritual, steeped in the Catholic doctrine of pentinence, which demonstrates one's humility and willingness to sacrifice in return for divine help. The peregrination involves approaching the place of sacrifice on one's knees. Anita Contreras wanted the strikers to proceed from the tent on Walker Street to St. Patrick's Church, half a mile away, on their knees.

Gloria Betancourt, whose entire public persona (one reporter described it as "flamboyant") could be interpreted as a repudiation of Catholic notions of female submissiveness, was not keen on the idea. "They've seen us on our knees enough already," she snapped. But after some earnest discussion, people decided to go ahead with it the follow-ing day. Gloria Betancourt agreed, though she insisted on remaining on her feet herself. "Some of those ladies are pretty religious," she would say years later. "If you're in leadership, you have to respect their wishes."[53]

As the television cameras jockeyed for position in front of the tent, María Corralejo told reporters what was about to happen. She introduced Anita Contreras, who wore a medallion of Jesus around her neck and had covered her head with a baseball cap. Anita Contreras explained in Spanish the religious significance of the ceremony; María Corralejo translated.[54]

At eleven o'clock the peregrination commenced. It would take about an hour to negotiate the five blocks to the church. The penitents included twenty women, one man, and an eight-year-old boy. Among them was Cuca Lomeli, who decided to join after concluding it was a show of faith and determination, not humility. "It felt good," she said later.[55]

A large crowd followed them toward the church. People ran ahead and spread blankets, bath mats, coats, and jackets on the ground so the procession would be less painful for the participants. People held up images of Christ and the Virgin of Guadalupe. Esperanza Contreras, weakened by four days of fasting, was supported by two other strik-ers as she struggled forward on her knees. Her sister Anita listed to one side—her right knee appeared to be bothering her—but forged on. Someone leaned over and mopped her brow.[56]

Gloria Betancourt and three other hunger strikers walked along-side holding a banner that read "Fe y Lucha" (faith and struggle). "Ev-eryone was crying," she said afterward. "I didn't want to cry. But when I looked back and saw one of our toughest macho men from the strike coming on his knees, I had to let go."[57]

Frank Bardacke, not a religious man, watched the group struggle toward the church on bloodied knees. He too found himself weep-ing. Years later, Joe Fahey's voice still shook as he described the scene: "So here come these women, and they're taller than they've ever been. They're more themselves." He paused and said, "It was a beautiful mo-ment, probably my favorite moment of the entire strike—when it was totally in the workers' hands."[58]

Children in the adjoining schoolyard cheered as the strikers ap-proached the church. The priest, though not unsympathetic, had never wanted to be perceived as taking sides; St. Patrick's had a number of growers in its congregation. But now the doors were unlocked and the pews filled up with strikers, along with families and supporters. Their voices resonated through the cavernous old church as the priest led them in mass. After the service, word came to report to the Veterans Hall at nine the next morning to vote on a new contract offer.

Union negotiators had found a way out of the impasse. The health benefits for part-time workers were restored. To help defray the extra cost to NorCal, the Teamsters agreed to modify the pension plan. "People can postpone their retirement for six months," said Sergio López. "But if you have a medical bill, you can't afford to wait. I think it was a good tradeoff."[59]

The strikers agreed. It took less than an hour to ratify the contract on Wednesday morning. The vote was 543 to 21. As John Blake announced the results, pandemonium broke out. Strikers shouted, chanted, hugged each other, and stood on chairs. The celebration went on and on. Amidst the chaos, Lydia Lerma, who had kept the food bank going since the very beginning of the strike eighteen months earlier, stood quietly off to one side by herself. Tears streamed down her face.

While the votes were being counted, Sergio López had slipped out to fetch David Gill at the union hall. Gill was asked to say a few words. Speaking in Spanish and English, he thanked the strikers and pledged to work with them: "This is a new company and a new beginning."

Gill was applauded warmly, but it was Carlos Hernández who probably best summed up the strikers' feelings: "We stayed united. It's our union, our plant, our victory."[60] As if to illustrate the point, everybody surged out of the Veterans Hall and marched on the plant, walking swiftly behind the banner that had adorned the hunger strikers' tent. Hernández led them in a call and response as they repeatedly spelled out the word, "V-I-C-T-O-R-I-A."

The crowd demonstrated briefly at the plant gate, then headed back downtown. They took over several blocks of Main Street as they moved toward the Pajaro River bridge chanting, "¡El pueblo . . . unido . . . jamás será vencido!" (The people united will never be defeated!) The police did not interfere. They crossed the bridge into the town of Pajaro and filed into the Assumption Church, where the strikers had always been welcome. There, Father Raúl Caraval led them in another mass.[61]

Only one thing remained to be done. Fidelia Carrisoza decided the strikers needed a *corrido* (ballad) to commemorate their victory, so she sat down and wrote one. Its last stanza:

> Here ends my telling of the story
> Of the struggle of the Watsonville one thousand
> We won our wages and benefits
> And we will never forget our unity and power.[62]

She called her corrido "The Song of the Stubborn One Thousand."

Epilogue

*"And if any dues-payer asks, 'When will it end? When can I knock off?'
the only answer is, 'Brother, not till we go all the way.'"*[1]

—Harry Bridges

The legendary longshore union leader Harry Bridges knew as well as anyone that nothing is permanently resolved when a strike is settled. It is a temporary truce in an ongoing struggle; its terms are no more than a representation of the balance of power between the contending parties at the time they signed off on them.

The field of "labor-management relations" is permeated with the jargon and mindset of the legal system. But there is a world of difference between a legal statute and a clause in a union contract. The former is supposed to lend our lives a measure of predictability, a set of shared expectations toward the civil authorities and each other. But a union contract, however vital it is to workers under its protection, is at heart a fragile and ephemeral thing, sensitive to any marked change in the economic and political climate. Its actual language is ultimately less important than what it says about the relative strength of workers and their employer.

A few days after the Watsonville settlement, I spoke on the phone with Jim Guyette, president of UFCW Local P-9, whose own strike against Hormel had ended when the UFCW placed the local in trusteeship. Upon learning that Watsonville workers would be earning significantly less than they made when they first walked out in 1985, Guyette wanted to know why their strike should be considered a victory.

Cesar Chavez saw it differently. Noting that Local 912 would be bargaining with the frozen food companies again in less than a year, he predicted that "next February and thereafter they're going to be able to get more." Chavez continued,

> When they went out on strike they were totally disorganized. There was no rank and file leadership. . . . [But] when they went back in there was strong leadership and a real union. . . .
>
> That union was revitalized. Remember, they went for thirty years without striking in that industry. These women in Watsonville have set a precedent. More than the money, more than the wages, is that they broke that long, long period of no strikes and no fight-back. . . . And the impact will be felt in the whole industry, by all the workers in the other canneries.[2]

Initially, Chavez's prediction was borne out by events. When Local 912 elections were held at the end of 1987, Joe Fahey was elected president, and while the personal tensions between him and Sergio López persisted, the two would work together effectively in the years to come. In the same election Gloria Betancourt and Chavelo Moreno ran for business agent; she lost and would not seek union office again, but he was elected and served until he retired. Cuca Lomeli was elected trustee; eventually she would serve as Local 912's vice president. And, just as Chavez predicted, the local won a forty-five-cent-an-hour raise in its 1988 contract, fighting off initial management demands for a wage cut.

The CWOP, now independent of TDU, saw its own work expand dramatically. Funded with a new grant from the Campaign for Human Development, it opened an office on Main Street in Watsonville. Over the next several years it held regular conferences that routinely drew several hundred workers from across the state. Reyna Guzmán and Chavelo Moreno served on its board of directors, along with activists from Local 890 in Salinas and two cannery locals in California's Central Valley. Oscar Ríos was its paid organizer. Much of its effort focused on the struggles in the Salinas Valley, where workers were battling the same kind of takeaways that Mort Console had tried to impose in Watsonville.

But it was in the political arena that Watsonville's cannery workers made their most visible and dramatic gains. In July 1988, the voting rights lawsuit brought by the Mexican American Legal Defense and Education Fund on behalf of Cruz Gómez and two others was upheld by the Ninth Circuit Court of Appeals. The city was ordered to elect its officials by district rather than at large. The US Supreme Court declined to hear the city's appeal, and elections for a new city council were scheduled for November 7, 1989. All eyes were on Districts 1 and 2, on the older and poorer south side of town, where Watsonville's Chicano and Mexicano population was concentrated. Oscar Ríos ran in District 2; Cruz Gómez sought to represent District 1.

On October 17, three weeks before the scheduled election, Northern California was hit by the Loma Prieta earthquake. Centered in the Santa Cruz Mountains some twenty miles from Watsonville, the quake did extensive damage throughout the Bay Area. Buildings in downtown Santa Cruz were reduced to rubble. A section of freeway collapsed in Oakland, killing dozens of people. Part of the lower deck of the San Francisco–Oakland Bay Bridge likewise gave way, terrorizing rush-hour commuters. San Francisco's Marina district, built on reclaimed land, saw a barrage of fires from ruptured gas lines. The quake hit just as baseball fans in Candlestick Park were preparing to watch a World Series game between the San Francisco Giants and the Oakland A's; the series had to be postponed.

So did Watsonville's city council vote, which was rescheduled for December 5. Paule Cruz Takash, a Berkeley graduate student researching the election, noted that while the delay "did provide candidates with more opportunities for exposure, it also provided them with a clearer notion of the enormous tasks before them if elected."[3] The earthquake destroyed 1,000 units of housing in the city and left some 2,500 people homeless. Districts 1 and 2, with older and more dilapidated housing, were particularly hard hit, and "a community of new homeless moved into temporary shelters or outdoors to makeshift tent cities at two local parks." The inadequate response of local and federal officials to the housing crisis became an issue in the campaign, particularly as Latino victims of the quake perceived that relief efforts had made them a low priority.[4]

Not surprisingly, both Ríos and Cruz Gómez threw themselves into the fight for more effective and equitable earthquake relief. The Gómez campaign appears to have suffered as a result: Jon Silver, who worked on her campaign, complained that the candidate was largely missing in action during efforts to mobilize District 1 voters.[5] Ríos was more successful in integrating his bid for office with the struggle over the city's earthquake response. He had the advantage of a large, effective campaign organization that tapped the energies of cannery workers and local Chicano high school and community college students; their dogged precinct work helped generate a threefold increase in Latino voter turnout in District 2.

Hopes for a united front of Latino voters were dashed by the lingering mistrust between Ríos and Cruz Gómez. Dan Dodge, a local activist of mixed anglo and Mexican stock, had initially supported Ríos until Gómez prevailed upon him to seek the District 2 seat himself. During the campaign the two of them made an issue of Ríos's association with the League and charged that his campaign workers were registering noncitizens to vote. "This charge," wrote Paule Cruz Takash, "was particularly ironic and disappointing to many, coming from a longtime champion" of immigrant rights.[6]

The attacks do not appear to have hurt Ríos, who won easily; he would go on to serve on the council for fifteen years, including four terms as mayor. Todd McFarren, an attorney who had worked with the Watsonville Strike Support Committee, won in District 4 and assumed the mayor's office; Ríos would serve under him as vice mayor. María Corralejo, who cochaired the Ríos campaign, was appointed to the city planning commission.

Over the next two years the city council had a four-member progressive majority. But Cruz Gómez was not a part of it. She lost her own race against a former part-owner of Richard Shaw by just thirty-eight votes. Frank Bardacke, for one, believed that the failure of herself and Ríos to resolve their differences may well have cost her the election.[7] The progressive bloc on the council consisted of Ríos and three white liberals.

The new council majority immediately passed a measure requiring bilingual translations of all council meetings, and began aggressively hiring bilingual staff for city departments. It curtailed city support for the INS. There was a 28 percent increase in Latino representation on local government commissions. Over time, Latinos would emerge as a force to be reckoned with in Watsonville politics; by 2004, three of the council's seven members would be children of cannery workers.[8]

But the gains reflected in a more inclusive city government were overshadowed by convulsive changes in the local economy. Citing the experience of African American mayors in cities like Newark and Detroit, historian David Levering Lewis has spoken of "the futility of political power without economic leverage."[9] "Futility" is perhaps too strong a word, but Lewis puts his finger on a problem, and Watsonville provides yet another manifestation. The frozen food industry, backbone of the local economy since the 1950s, was about to undergo a drastic downsizing.

In fall of 1987 the Crosetti family decided to get out of the business. Their company merged with NorCal Frozen Foods, and several hundred jobs were lost in the process. The following year, Richard Shaw was bought out by Dean Foods, an Illinois-based conglomerate that marketed under the Birdseye label. With the Shaw sale, NorCal became the only remaining locally owned plant producing frozen vegetables, and it had always been David Gill's intention to keep going only as long as it took him to recover his losses from the 1985 strike.

In 1995 Gill followed Shaw's lead and sold his operation to Dean Foods. NorCal's new owners "admitted at the time that they didn't need two facilities in Watsonville, they had clearly bought the plant in order to shut it down."[10] The NorCal plant was closed within three months.

Green Giant had moved its remaining local operations to Mexico the previous year. In 2005 Dean Foods followed Green Giant south of the border, and the old Richard Shaw facility—which had survived mainly because it was the newest and most efficient of Watsonville's frozen food plants—ceased production as well. The frozen food capital of the world was history.

The industry's decline is often attributed to growing consumer preference for fresh vegetables. This view has at least some merit in California, where the proximity of rich farmland and large population centers allows for a formidable market for fresh produce. But demand for frozen vegetables has not disappeared. Far from it: there remains a robust institutional market for frozen food, which is purchased in large quantities by the military, schools, hospitals, prisons, and chain restaurants. Supermarket freezer sections still feature elaborate concoctions of "prepared vegetables," whose share of the frozen vegetable market had already begun to increase dramatically in the 1980s. Watsonville's plant shutdowns are best explained not by a shrinking product market but by changes in the labor market, brought on by the violent currency fluctuations of a globalized economy.

To understand how this happened, it is necessary to go back to the onset of Mexico's debt crisis in the early 1980s. Traditionally, Mexico's food processing industry was relatively small and produced mainly for a domestic market. But in 1982, with the country's foreign debt spiraling out of control, the value of the peso fell by 80 percent. It suddenly became enormously profitable to sell north of the border; as Juan Borrego has noted, "the people who were in processing and exporting vegetables to the US became extremely wealthy overnight. . . . Other people saw the instant wealth that was generated at the time and they too wanted to get involved."[11]

New frozen food plants began cropping up throughout the Bajío region of Guanajuato province. Most operated under the umbrella of US-based transnationals like Green Giant, Birdseye, and United Foods. Mexican landowners who produced grain for the domestic market realized that by switching over to broccoli and cauliflower, both labor-intensive crops, they could take advantage of the yawning labor cost differential between Mexico and the United States. By the mid-1990s, Guanajuato had emerged as a "winter garden" for the United States. Green Giant, then the only transnational corporation with a plant in Watsonville, had begun importing frozen broccoli from Guanajuato in 1983; within ten years it was relying almost totally on its Mexican operations.[12]

Passage of the North American Trade Agreement (NAFTA) in 1994 all but finished off what was left of Watsonville's frozen food industry. President Bill Clinton pushed NAFTA through a Democratic-controlled Congress where his Republican predecessor had failed to do so—over the opposition of organized labor, whose failure to stop the treaty was seen as yet another example of its declining political influence. Union opposition to NAFTA was couched in terms that were often superficial and occasionally xenophobic, raising the specter of Mexicans "stealing American jobs."

Local 912, with its overwhelmingly Mexican membership, took a more sophisticated approach. Joe Fahey and Chavelo Moreno both travelled to the Guanajuato city of Irapuarto, where they observed conditions in the Mexican frozen food industry and discussed the possibility of cross-border organizing with representatives of El Frente Autentico del Trabajo, a Mexican opposition union.[13] Sergio López made the case against NAFTA to a group of undocumented workers in San Jose who had been organized by the Justice for Janitors campaign. At one point a member of the audience pointed out that he had been forced to come to the United States to find work; he wanted to know what was wrong with US corporations setting up shop in Mexico, if it brought new jobs to Mexico and made it possible for him to reunite with his family.

"I grew up in Mexico," López answered. "I went to school there, the same as you. I learned our country's history from the same textbooks. We all know what Standard Oil did to our country. Let me ask you, when has US investment ever brought Mexico anything but grief?"[14]

And, indeed, once NAFTA had passed, its impact proved equally disruptive on both sides of the border. Not only was there a flood of US manufacturing capital into Mexico's rural interior, but US–based agricultural conglomerates like Cargill and ConAgra were now able to dump their surplus corn on the Mexican market, driving prices down and forcing tens of thousands of Mexican small farmers off the land. The new army of the dispossessed drove Mexican wage levels down further and prompted a massive wave of emigration to the United States. Small plots were consolidated into giant corporate farms that serviced the frozen food plants in and around Irapuato, where the new regime of industrial agriculture and export-driven food processing drained the aquifers and polluted local rivers with untreated sewage.[15]

Watsonville was transformed as well. Pajaro Valley growers abandoned broccoli, cauliflower, and brussels sprouts and began concentrating on strawberries instead. Within a few years, half the US acreage devoted to strawberry cultivation was located in and around Watsonville. Most of this land was owned by a handful of anglo families, but by 1997 they were leasing their holdings out in small parcels to some five hundred local Latinos, who took responsibility for recruiting the work force and producing the crop. The strawberry fields required only modest capital but a great deal of labor, and both laid-off cannery workers and newly arrived immigrants from Mexico found work there.[16]

But it was nowhere near enough to counter the impact of deindustrialization on the town, whose population was growing thanks to a new wave of immigration. Plant shutdowns had crippled the local tax base, placed new burdens on city services, and pushed the local jobless rate to twice the countywide average. By the mid-nineties, more than one Watsonville worker in five was unemployed. As Patricia Zavella has noted, "Displaced workers who were often middle-aged competed with younger, more recent immigrants."[17] And the slow pace of rebuilding after the Loma Prieta earthquake led to an acute shortage of affordable housing.

City officials struggled to find solutions. Much of Oscar Ríos's tenure as mayor was absorbed with vexing conflicts over land use. Real estate developers were less interested in low income housing than in turning Watsonville into a bedroom community for the high-tech mecca of Silicon Valley, some thirty miles to the north. Vacant and underutilized land was at a premium, and there was constant pressure for the city to annex adjoining farmlands and rezone them for development. According to Kim Geron, a political scientist who made a close study of the city's evolving politics, Ríos's task was made more difficult by an increasingly fragmented constituency: "The Latino community, which mobilized as one voice for political empowerment, did not coalesce around land use issues. The complexity of the issues involved, the bureaucratic delays, and conflicting pulls to protect farmworker jobs, while also providing more jobs for families and the larger community, has resulted in disunity and confusion."[18]

Fights broke out over housing developments, a proposed retail center (opposed by Local 912 because it was expected to attract low-wage employers like Target), and even the construction of a badly needed high school campus to combat overcrowding at Watsonville High. An expanded retail sector promised to bring needed sales tax revenue into the city's coffers, but the jobs it offered were a far cry from the union pay and benefits of the old frozen food plants. Many in the Latino community who were primarily concerned with job creation found themselves at odds with the UFW, which was organizing in the strawberry fields and aligned with both environmentalists and growers to block city expansion into agricultural areas.[19]

Ríos dealt with land use issues on a case-by-case basis and managed to satisfy no one. An approach that linked immediate issues with a long-term political strategy would have been welcome, but the League was no longer around to provide it. Though League activists who had migrated to Watsonville during the strike remained active in the community, the League itself dissolved in 1990, having failed to navigate the difficult transition from revolutionary agitation to an ongoing role in the nation's political life. As for Ríos, he would eventually step down from the city council and devote himself full-time to his job as an organizer for Local 890 in Salinas.

Prospects for a transformed Teamsters union at the national level likewise failed to materialize as expected. Sergio López was one of those who pinned their hopes on Ron Carey, the reform candidate who was elected general president of the Teamsters in 1991 in a federally supervised vote. Carey was an outspoken and effective critic of NAFTA; he challenged the union's entrenched old guard and encouraged organizing efforts by Latino workers in the Pacific Northwest. His administration made the notion of cross-border organizing seem like at least a possibility. But it all came to an abrupt end in 1997 when three of Carey's top aides pleaded guilty to misappropriating union funds to pay for their boss's reelection campaign. Carey resigned in disgrace.

According to Dan LaBotz, "Carey's moral and political failure ... had a devastating impact," since it "discredited and ultimately destroyed ... one of the most important advances of the American labor movement in more than 50 years."[20] Nearly twenty years later, Sergio López would still speak of it as one of the great disappointments of his union career. TDU, which had supported Carey, regrouped around Tom Leedham, head of the Teamster Warehouse Division. Leedham ran a strong but ultimately unsuccessful campaign to succeed Carey for the union presidency in 1998; Joe Fahey served as his national campaign manager.

No assessment of the strike's impact is meaningful without some discussion of its impact on the strikers themselves, particularly the women. For many, it was a transformative experience.

Esperanza Torres became a paid organizer for the Teamsters and served for twelve years before being forced out in a union factional struggle.

Gloria Betancourt, who also applied for the organizing job but was passed over because "Sergio didn't like me," served as a Jesse Jackson delegate to the 1988 Democratic convention. After NorCal closed down, she clerked in a local chain drugstore until she retired. She remained close to Oscar Ríos and helped him out during several Local 890 campaigns.

Lydia Lerma's son Santos became president of Local 912 after Joe Fahey retired.

Though Cuca Lomeli went on to hold more than one union office after the strike, she steadfastly refused to see herself as a leader or "big shot." "I just represent the members," she told an interviewer. She felt the strike had changed her just as it had broadened the horizons of all the women who went through it together: "I'm proud because I'm grow-ing . . . in my mind, in everything. I travel to different conventions with the union. I learn everything in the conventions for the members—not for me, for the members. I share everything I learn with the workers."[21]

Delia Mendez spoke with pride of her students who did their best to help out their parents during the strike, then went on to college and professional careers.

Esperanza Contreras noted that many of the strikers "had no ed-ucation, no schooling—but they were the stronger ones." She came from the same village in Mexico as Chavelo Moreno, whose family there was as relatively prosperous as hers was poor. When the strike ended, she embraced him. "I was always embarrassed to talk to you before," she confessed, adding that their common struggle had "made us equals." When Moreno died of pneumonia in 2011, she wept, saying indignantly that the doctors had not taken proper care of him.

With Frank Bardacke's help, Fidelia Carrisoza honed her English language skills enough to land a job as an instructional assistant in the public schools, teaching special-needs children. It was demanding work, but it challenged and inspired her in ways that factory work never had.

Guillermina Ramírez, who played such a crucial role in the early months of the strike, was one of a handful who voted against the final settlement. Rather than return to work at lower wages, she went back to school, got a degree in social work, and wound up working for the county children's services department. In the middle of an interview for this book, she suddenly broke down sobbing.

"Too many memories," she explained through her tears. She did not elaborate, but perhaps it was her way of saying that much work remained to be done, and it would necessarily fall to others to do it.

Bibliography

ARCHIVAL COLLECTIONS

Agricultural History Project Collection. Santa Cruz County Fairgrounds, Watsonville, California.

Bardacke, Frank. Papers. Labor Archives and Research Center, San Francisco State University, San Francisco.

Beeson, Tayer & Bodine. Private collection.

Díaz, Manuel. Private collection.

Johnston, Michael. Private collection.

Morozumi, Steve. Private collection.

Teamsters Joint Council 7. Private collection.

Teamsters Local 70. Papers. Labor Archives and Research Center, San Francisco State University, San Francisco.

BOOKS

Amberg, Steven. "The CIO Political Strategy in Perspective." In *Organized Labor and American Politics, 1894–1994: The Labor-Liberal Alliance*. Edited by Kevin Boyle, 159–94. SUNY Series in American Labor History. Albany: State University of New York Press, 1998.

Apostolides, Paul. *Breaks in the Chain: What Immigrant Workers Can Teach America about Democracy*. Minneapolis: University of Minnesota Press, 2010.

Balderrama, Francisco and Raymond Rodríguez. *Decade of Betrayal: Mexican Repatriation in the 1930s*. Albuquerque: University of New Mexico Press, 1995.

Bardacke, Frank. *Tramping Out the Vintage: Cesar Chavez and the Two Souls of the United Farm Workers*. London: Verso, 2012.

———. "The United Farm Workers from the Ground Up." In *Rebel Rank and File: Labor Militancy and Revolt from Below During the Long 1970s*. Edited by Aaron Brenner, Robert Brenner, and Cal Winslow, 149–172. London: Verso, 2010.

Bluestone, Barry and Bennett Harrison. *The Deindustrialization of America: Plant Closings, Community Abandonment, and the Dismantling of Basic Industry*. New York: Basic Books, 1982.

Boyle, Kevin, ed. *Organized Labor and American Politics, 1894–1994: The Labor-Liberal Alliance*. SUNY Series on American Labor History. Albany: State University of New York Press, 1998.

Brenner, Aaron, Robert Brenner, and Cal Winslow, eds. *Rebel Rank and File: Labor Militancy and Revolt from Below During the Long 1970s*. London: Verso, 2010.

Davis, Mike. *Prisoners of the American Dream: Politics and Economy of the History of the US Working Class*. London: Verso, 1986.

Davis, Mike and Justin Akers Chacón. *No One Is Illegal: Fighting Racism and State Violence on the US–Mexico Border*. Chicago: Haymarket Books, 2006.

Dobbs, Farrell. *Teamster Power*. New York: Monad Press, 1973.

———. *Teamster Rebellion*. New York: Pathfinder Press, 2004.

Fisk, Milton. *Socialism from Below in the United States: The Origins of the International Socialist Organization*. Cleveland: Hera Press, 1977.

Foner, Eric. *Free Soil, Free Labor, Free Men: The Ideology of the Republican Party before the Civil War*. New York: Oxford University Press, 1995.

Flores, William V. and Rina Benmayor, eds. *Latino Cultural Citizenship: Claiming Identity, Space, and Rights*. Boston: Beacon Press, 1998.

Flores, William V. "Mujeres en Huelga: Cultural Citizenship and Gender Empowerment in a Cannery Strike." In *Latino Cultural Citizenship: Claiming Identity, Space, and Rights*. Edited by William V. Flores and Rina Benmajor, 210–254. Boston: Beacon Press, 1998.

Genoways, Ted. *The Chain: Farm, Factory, and the Fate of Our Food*. New York: Harper Collins, 2014.

Gitlin, Todd. *The Twilight of Common Dreams: Why America is Wracked by Culture Wars*. New York: Henry Holt, 1995.

Gregory, Charles. *Labor and the Law*, 2nd ed. New York: W. W. Norton, 1961.

Green, Hardy. *On Strike at Hormel: The Struggle for a Democratic Labor Movement*. Labor and Social Change Series. Philadelphia: Temple University Press, 1990.

Halpern, Rick. *Down on the Killing Floor: Black and White Workers in Chicago's Packinghouses, 1904–54*. Working Class in American History. Urbana: University of Illinois Press, 1997.

Heins, Marjorie. *Strictly Ghetto Property: The Story of Los Siete de la Raza*. San Francisco: Ramparts Press, 1972.

James, Ralph C. and Estelle Dinerstein James. *Hoffa and the Teamsters: A Study of Union Power*. Princeton: Van Nostrand Reinhold , 1965.

LaBotz, Dan. "Tumultuous Teamsters in the 1970s," in *Rebel Rank and File: Labor Militancy and Revolt from Below During the Long 1970s*. Edited by Aaron Brenner, Robert Brenner, and Cal Winslow, 199–228. London: Verso, 2010.

Levinson, Harold. *Determining Forces in Collective Wage Bargaining*. New York: John Wiley & Sons, 1966.

Lichtenstein, Nelson. *State of the Union: A Century of American Labor*. Revised and expanded ed. Politics and Society in Twentieth-Century America. Princeton: Princeton University Press, 2013. .

Massey, Douglas S., Jorge Durand, and Nolan J. Malone, *Beyond Smoke and Mirrors: Mexican Immigration in an Era of Economic Integration*. New York: Russell Sage Foundation, 2003.

McWilliams, Carey. *North from Mexico: The Spanish-Speaking People of the United States*. New York: J. B. Lippincott, 1948.

Moody, Kim. *An Injury to All: The Decline of American Unionism*. London: Verso, 1988.

———. *Workers in a Lean World: Unions in the International Economy*. London: Verso, 1997.

Nelson, Bruce. *Divided We Stand: American Workers and the Struggle for Black Equality*. Politics and Society in Twentieth-Century America. Princeton: Princeton University Press, 2001.

Ngai, Mae M. *Impossible Subjects: Illegal Aliens and the Making of Modern America*. Politics and Society in Twentieth-Century America. Princeton: Princeton University Press, 2004.

Rachleff, Peter. "The Failure of Minnesota Farmer-Laborism." In *Organized Labor and American Politics, 1894–1994: The Labor-Liberal Alliance*. Edited by Kevin Boyle, 103–120. SUNY Series in American Labor History. Albany: State University of New York Press, 1998.

———. *Hard-Pressed in the Heartland: The Hormel Strike and the Future of the Labor Movement*. Boston: South End Press, 1999.

Ruiz, Vicki L. *Cannery Women, Cannery Lives: Mexican Women, Unionization, and the California Food Processing Industry, 1930-1950*. Albuquerque: University of New Mexico Press, 1987.

Saxton, Alexander. *The Indispensable Enemy: Labor and the Anti-Chinese Movement in California*. Berkeley: University of California Press, 1997.

Schlosser, Eric. *Fast Food Nation: The Dark Side of the All-American Meal*. New York: Harper Perennial, 2002.

Shaiken, Harley. *Mexico in the Global Economy: High Technology and Work Organization in Export Industries*. Mimeograph ser. 33. San Diego: Center for US–Mexican Studies, 1989.

Stein, Judith. "Conflict, Change, and Economic Policy in the Long 1970s." In *Rebel Rank and File: Labor Militancy and Revolt from Below During the Long 1970s*. Edited by Aaron Brenner, Robert Brenner, and Cal Winslow, 77–102. London: Verso, 2010.

US League of Revolutionary Struggle. *Peace, Justice, Equality and Socialism: Program of the US League of Revolutionary Struggle*. Oakland, CA: Getting Together Publications, 1984.

Weir, Robert E and James P. Hanlan, eds. *Historical Encyclopedia of American Labor*. 2 vols. Westport, CT: Greenwood Press, 2004.

Wolman, William and Anne Colamosca. *The Judas Economy: The Triumph of Capital and the Betrayal of Work*. New York: Addison-Wesley Publishing 1997.

Woodward, C. Vann. *Tom Watson: Agrarian Rebel*. London: Oxford University Press, 1955.

————. *Origins of the New South, 1871–1913: A History of the South*. Baton Rouge: Louisiana State University Press, 1951.

Zavella, Patricia. *I'm Neither Here nor There: Mexicans' Quotidian Struggles with Migration and Poverty*. Durham: Duke University Press, 2011.

————. *Women's Work and Chicano Families: Cannery Workers of the Santa Clara Valley*. Anthropology of Contemporary Issues, 8. Ithaca: Cornell University Press, 1987.

PERIODICALS

Balanoff, Tom. "In-Plant Strategies: The Cement Workers' Experience." *Labor Research Review* 1, no. 7 (1985): 5–32.

Bardacke, Frank. "Watsonville: How the Strikers Won." *Against the Current* (May–June 1987): 15–21.

Barr, Nancy. "The People Whose Labor Makes the Plants Run." *Watsonville Register-Pajaronian*, September 3, 1984.

Benson, Jackson L. "John Steinbeck and Farm Labor Unionization: The Background of *In Dubious Battle*." *American Literature* 5, no. 2 (May 1980): 194–223.

Betancourt, Gloria. "Our Eyes Have Been Opened." *Forward* 7, no. 7 (Summer 1987): 47–57.

Betancourt, Gloria, et al. "Round-Table Discussion with Watsonville Workers." *Forward* 7, no. 1 (January 1987): 3–23.

Bluestone, Barry. "Goodbye to the Management Rights Clause." *Labor Research Review* 14 (Fall 1989): 66–72.

Bock, Richard A. "Secondary Boycotts: Understanding NLRB Interpretation of Section 8(b)(4)(b) of the National Labor Relations Act." *University of Pennsylvania Journal of Labor and Employment Law* 7, no. 4 (2005): 905–969.

Brough, Jim. Opinion. *Santa Cruz Sun*. November 26, 1986.

Budd, John W. "The Internal Political Imperative for UAW Pattern Bargaining," *Journal of Labor Research* 16, no. 1 (Winter 1995): 431–457.

Castillo, Alfredo. "Cannery Strike Grows Stronger." *Unity*. November 8, 1985.

Cruz Takash, Paule. "Remedying Racial and Ethnic Inequality in California Politics: Watsonville Before and After District Elections." Chicano/Latino Policy Project. *CLPP Policy Report* 1, no. 4 (June 1999).

Dickey, Jim. "4,000 March in Support of Watsonville Strike." *San Jose Mercury News*. November 4, 1985.

————. "'La Familia' on Strike." *San Jose Mercury News*. November 7, 1985.

————. "Misery in Watsonville Strike," *San Jose Mercury News*. February 11, 1986.

Draper, Bobsy. "The Mouse That Roared." *Matrix* (November 1986).

Erickson, Christopher. "A Reinterpretation of Pattern Bargaining." *Industrial and Labor Relations Review* 46 no. 4 (July 1996): 615–634.

Fahey, Joe. "Casualties of Free Trade: Workers' Loss in Watsonville." *Multinational Monitor* (May 1993).

Flores, Roberto. "Labor in Reagan's USA." *Forward* 7, no. 1 (January 1987):

53–67.

Freedman, Audrey and William E. Fulmer. "Last Rites for Pattern Bargaining." *Harvard Business Review* 61, no. 2 (1982):30-48.

Gallegos, Bill. "The 'Sunbelt Strategy' and Chicano Liberation." *Forward* 5 (Spring 1986): 1–31.

Heckman, Susanna. "Wage Wars." *City on a Hill*. February 20, 1986.

Jarley, Paul and Cheryl L. Maranto. "Union Corporate Campaigns: An Assessment." *Industrial and Labor Relations Review* 43, no. 5 (July 1990): 505–524.

Johnson, Bob. "1,500 March for Strikers." *San Jose Mercury News*. October 7, 1985.

———. "New Owners at Watsonville Canning." *San Jose Mercury News*. February 12, 1987.

———. "Pay Cuts Spread in Watsonville Frozen Food Strike." *San Jose Mercury News*. March 9, 1986.

———. "Strikers Take Compensation Issue to Court." *San Jose Mercury News*. February 10, 1986.

———. "Tale of Two Tongues: The Case of *Juan Manuel Parra vs. Watsonville Canning Company*." *Santa Cruz Express*. December 12, 1985.

———. "Teamsters Fight for Survival as Canning Season Begins." *San Jose Mercury News*. March 20, 1986.

———. "Unity and Victory: The Strikers' Story." *Santa Cruz Sun*. March 26, 1987.

Johnson, Bob and Geoffrey Dunn. "Legal Terrorism: The Border Patrol in the Local Hispanic Community." *Santa Cruz Express*. November 19, 1984.

Johnston, Michael [Mark Johnson, pseud.]. "The Fight to Save the Teamsters Union." *Unity*. May 18, 1986.

LaBotz, Dan. "Rank and File Teamsters Fight for Labor's Future." *Dollars and Sense*. September–October 1998.

Lewis, David Levering. "The Segregated North." *New York Times Book Review*, January 11, 2015.

Lindley, Robert. "New Food Patterns Affect Strike in West." *New York Times*. January 1, 1986.

Logan, John. "Permanent Replacements and the End of 'Labor's Only True Weapon.'" *International Labor and Working Class History* 78 (September 2008): 171–92.

Lustig, Nora. "The Impact of the Economic Crisis on Living Conditions in Mexico, 1982–1985." *Brookings Discussion Papers in International Economics* 75 (July 1989).

Lynd, Staughton. "The Genesis of the Idea of a Community Right to Industrial Property in Youngstown and Pittsburgh." *Journal of American History* 74, no. 3 (December 1987): 926–958.

Marks, Jamie and Donald Miller. "Profile of a Community." *Santa Cruz Sentinel*. May 10, 1989.

Marshall, Jonathan. "Law Firm Cashes In by Aiding Employers." *San Francisco Chronicle*. June 5, 1996.

McIntosh, Barbara. "That Mess at Watsonville Canning." *San Jose Mercury News.* September 28, 1986, 5–24.

McIntosh, Don. "Labor Still Reeling from 1981 PATCO Strike." *Northwest Labor Press.* June 1, 2007.

Midwest Center for Labor Research. "Labor Community Unity: The Morse Strike against Disinvestment and Concession." Special issue, *Labor Research Review* 1, no. 1 (Winter 1982).

Miller, Donald. "The Strike/How It Happened." *Santa Cruz Sentinel*, November 15, 1985.

Miller, Donald and Steve Shender. "Production Manager Has Had an Eventful Year." *Santa Cruz Sentinel.* November 13, 1986.

Miller, Donald and Steve Shender. "Produce Kickback Scheme Described, Denied." *Santa Cruz Sentinel.* November 16, 1986.

Montgomery, David. "The Shuttle and the Cross: Weavers and Artisans in the Kensington Riots of 1844." *Journal of Social History* 5, no. 4 (Summer 1972): 413–446.

Moody, Kim. "A Pattern of Retreat: The Decline of Pattern Bargaining." *Labor Notes* 371 (February 2010).

Rannels, Jack. "Birdseye Celebrating Its 30th Anniversary." *Santa Cruz Sentinel.* March 25, 1959.

Ríos, Oscar, "Strikers Stronger by the Day." *Unity.* October 25, 1985.

Ross, John and Joe Blum. "For Watsonville Women, '*Huelga*' Means More Than Strike." *Fresno Bee.* January 12, 1986.

Schoenberg, Amanda. "A View in to Birdseye." *Watsonville Register-Pajaronian.* December 15, 2006.

Segal, William. "Watsonville: A Fight that Labor Can Win." *Labor Center Reporter* 198 (November 1986).

Sheerin, Howard. "Watsonville Canning Co.'s Annual Production Is Valued at $2.5 Million." *Watsonville Register-Pajaronian.* November 30, 1946.

Shinoff, Paul. "Troubles within the Teamsters." *San Francisco Sunday Examiner.* June 1, 1986.

Turner, Steve. "Strike Town USA." *San Francisco Examiner.* June 7, 1987, 23–35.

Walsh, Joan. "Veggie Barons Try Union Freeze-Out." *In These Times.* December 18, 1985.

Wollenberg, Charles. "Working on *El Traque.*" *Pacific Historical Review* 42, no. 3 (August 1973): 358–369.

DISSERTATIONS, THESES, AND UNPUBLISHED PAPERS

Borrego, Juan. "The Restructuring of Frozen Food Production in North America and its Impact on Daily Life in Two Communities." University of California–Santa Cruz Chicano/Latino Research Center, Working Paper #21, October 1988.

Cruz Takash, Paule. "A Crisis of Democracy: Community Responses to the

Latinization of a California Town Dependent on Immigrant Labor." PhD diss., University of California–Berkeley, 1992.

DeLoitte and Touche, Inc. "The Frozen Food Processing Industry in South Santa Cruz County." April 1991.

Geron, Kim. "The Struggle to Achieve Political Representation in Watsonville, California," PhD diss., University of California–Riverside, 1998; updated 2002.

Johnson, Brooke Elise. "From Strike to Social Movement: Economic Restructuring, Latino Organizing, and Political Mobilization in Watsonville, California." MS thesis, University of California–Davis, 2004.

Michael Johnston [Mark Johnson, pseud.], "Cannery Workers History Draft," prepared for the Labor Commission of the League of Revolutionary Struggle, December 8, 1987.

Segal, William. "Economic Dualism and Collective Bargaining Structures in Food Manufacturing Industries." PhD diss., University of California–Berkeley, 1988.

Thomson, Heather. "A Look at the Watsonville Strike." Thesis, University of California–Santa Cruz, 1987.

FILMS

Silver, Jon. *Watsonville on Strike*. Migrant Media Productions, 1989.

Wong, Eddie. *¡Sí, Se Puede!* Unfinished rough cut of film. Cannery Workers Organizing Project, 1987.

INTERVIEWS

Hermilo Alamillo, interview with the author, July 6, 2012.

Elisa Moreno Alvarado, interview with the author, January 29, 2012.

Frank Bardacke, interviews with the author, March 25, 2010; May 6, 2014.

Duane Beeson, interview with the author, March 9, 2012.

Gloria Betancourt, interviews with the author, January 25, 2010; November 17, 2010.

Jim Brough, interviews with the author, June 20, 2014; August 28, 2015.

Fidelia Carrisoza, interviews with the author, November 18, 2010; November 4, 2014.

Anita Contreras, interview with the author, November 20, 2010.

Esperanza Contreras, interview with the author, November 28, 2012.

Manuel Díaz, interviews with the author, November 13, 2013; February 7 and 25, 2014.

Joe Fahey, interviews with the author, July 18, 2009; April 9 and 23, 2014; December 9, 2014.

David Gill, interview with the author, June 30, 2010.

Cruz Gómez, interview with the author, December 2, 2014.

Esther Gonzalez, interview with the author, January 29, 2012.

Jesus Hermosa, interview with the author, July 6, 2012.

Emma Jiménez, interview with the author, November 19, 2010.

Michael Johnston, interview with the author, July 16, 2009.

Lydia Lerma, interview with the author, November 18, 2010.

Cuca Lomeli, interview with the author, November 17, 2010.

Sergio López, interviews with the author, July 16 and 19, 2009; March 31, 2011; March 8, 2013; September 27, 2014; December 4 and 9, 2014.

Chuck Mack, interviews with the author, February 23, 2009; November 24, 2010.

Richard Maltzman, interview with the author, April 23, 2010.

Carolina Martínez, interview with the author, June 4, 2014.

Delia Mendez, interview with the author, November 18, 2010.

David Moore, interview by Pat Johns, December 20, 2004. Agricultural History Project Collection, Santa Cruz County Fairgrounds, Watsonville, California.

Chavelo Moreno, interviews with the author, March 25, 2010; July 5, 2010.

Steve Morozumi, interview with the author, January 30, 2012.

Karen Osmundson, interview with the author, September 3, 2014.

Margarita Paramo, interview with the author, November 19, 2010.

Socorro Parra, interview with the author, July 6, 2012.

Guillermina Ramírez, interview with the author, February 9, 2013.

Oscar Ríos, interviews with the author, July 5, 2010; November 21, 2010; June 17, 2014.

Tom Ryan, interviews with the author, November 21, 2010; May 29, 2014; September 14, 2014; February 5, 2015.

Francisco Sánchez, interview with the author, November 19, 2010.

Jon Silver, interview with the author, June 17, 2014.

Shiree Teng, interviews with the author, July 8, 2010; October 3, 2014; February 18, 2015.

Esperanza Torres, interview with the author, December 27, 2014.

David Werlin, interview with the author, June 1, 2014.

Alex Ybarrolaza, interview with the author, February 25, 2009

Notes

Preface

1   Eric Hobsbawm (with George Rude), *Captain Swing* (Harmondsworth: Penguin Books, 1973), xxv.

Introduction

1   Anita Contreras, interview.
2   She can be seen doing just that in Jon Silver's documentary film *Watsonville on Strike*, which provides a powerful visual record of the struggle despite a somewhat schematic (and occasionally misleading) analysis.
3   Davis, *Prisoners of the American Dream*, 103.
4   Bluestone and Harrison, *Deindustrialization of America*, 18, 116.
5   Laid-off steelworkers in the Pittsburgh area proposed the most radical demand. They argued that workers and community had made a large tangible investment in a plant and had as much of a stake in its future as shareholders did. Accordingly, they had a right to run it themselves if its owners were no longer interested in doing so. Their claim was buttressed by a legal theory developed by local labor lawyer and historian Staughton Lynd, who argued that, under eminent domain powers implicitly sanctioned in the Constitution, public authorities could take possession of a plant slated for closing and continue to operate it under worker and community control. Lynd likened the strategy to "throwing bricks at a tank," but its agitational value was undeniable, and it was actually used successfully on a smaller scale at Morse Tool in New Bedford, Connecticut. See Lynd, "Genesis of the Idea," 926–958, and Midwest Center for Labor Research, "Labor Community Control."
6   Bluestone, "Goodbye to Management," 65.
7   Lichtenstein, *State of the Union*, 99.
8   Ibid., 99, 129–30, and chapter 3, passim.
9   Quoted in ibid., 25.
10 For a detailed account of the evolution of federal economic policy during this period see Stein, "Conflict, Change," 77–102.
11 Moody, *An Injury to All*, 97, 103, and chapter 5, passim.

12   See Wolman and Colamosca, *The Judas Economy*, 186. Wolman was an editor of *Business Week* during the 1980s.

13   Massey and Malone, *Beyond Smoke and Mirrors*, 74–83; Shaiken, *Mexico in the Global Economy*, 9; and Lustig, "Impact of the Economic Crisis."

14   Moody, *Workers in a Lean World*, 131.

15   This strategy, and its use by growing numbers of employers, was analyzed by Joseph McCartin in a paper delivered at the annual meeting of the Pacific Northwest Labor History Association, May 12, 2007. For a good summary of his presentation see McIntosh, "Labor Still Reeling."

16   Robert E. Weir writes, "By the 1980s, for every three new union members gained, one was lost in a decertification drive." *Historical Encyclopedia of American Labor*, 130.

17   Ríos, interview, November 21, 2010.

18   For a discussion of the novel's sources see Benson, "John Steinbeck and Farm Labor Unionization."

19   Betancourt, "Our Eyes Have Been Opened," 48.

20   Green, *On Strike at Hormel.*

Chapter 1

1   Rannels, "Birdseye Celebrating its 30th Anniversary"; Schoenberg, "A View in to Birdseye."

2   Sheerin, "Watsonville Canning Co's Annual Production."

3   Barr, "Fifteen Minutes in the Life of a Spinach Green," *Watsonville Register-Pajaronian* undated clipping, Agricultural History Project Collection, Santa Cruz County Fairgrounds, Watsonville, California.

4   Moore, interview.

5   Ibid.

6   Schoenberg, "A View into Birdseye"; display, Agricultural History Project.

7   Moore, interview.

8   Ibid.

9   Deloitte and Touche, Inc., "The Frozen Food Processing Industry."

10   Richard Shaw, quoted in *Watsonville Register-Pajaronian*, March 20, 1985.

11   López, interview, March 31, 2011.

12   Betancourt, interview, January 25, 2010.

13   Ngai, *Impossible Subjects*, 129.

14   Wollenberg, "Working on *El Traque*," 362–63.

15   Ngai, *Impossible Subjects*, 131.

16   McWilliams, *North from Mexico*, 55–58.

17   Balderrama and Rodríguez, *Decade of Betrayal*, 6, 19–20; Ngai, *Impossible Subjects*, 132.

18   McWilliams, *North from Mexico*, 163.

19   Balderrama and Rodríguez, *Decade of Betrayal*, 11, 16; McWilliams, *North from Mexico*, 176–77.

20 Davis and Chacón, *No One is Illegal*, 126.
21 Balderrama and Rodríguez, *Decade of Betrayal*, 19; Ngai, *Impossible Subjects*, 131.
22 Balderrama and Rodríguez, *Decade of Betrayal*, 9; Ngai, *Impossible Subjects*, 68.
23 Balderrama and Rodríguez, *Decade of Betrayal*, 113.
24 Ngai, *Impossible Subjects*, 138–47.
25 Ngai, *Impossible Subjects*, 147.
26 Davis and Chacón, *No One is Illegal*, 137, 145–146.
27 Zavella, *I'm Neither Here Nor There*, 63; Johnson, "From Strike to Social Movement," 66.
28 Betancourt, interview, January 25, 2010.
29 Lomeli, interview.
30 Moreno, interview, March 25, 2010.
31 Torres, interview.
32 Marks and Miller, "Profile of a Community"; Zavella, *I'm Neither Here nor There*, 101.

Chapter 2

1 Levinson, *Determining Forces in Collective Wage Bargaining*, 222–23.
2 Dobbs, *Teamster Rebellion*; Dobbs, *Teamster Power*; James and James, *Hoffa and the Teamsters*, 89–92.
3 Levinson, *Determining Forces in Collective Wage Bargaining*, 223; James and James, *Hoffa and the Teamsters*, 96–101; see also chapter 10.
4 Levinson, *Determining Forces in Collective Wage Bargaining*, 224.
5 James and James, *Hoffa and the Teamsters*, 95–96.
6 Ibid., 68.
7 Ibid., 116.
8 LaBotz, "Tumultuous Teamsters," 201; James and James, *Hoffa and the Teamsters*, chapter 11.
9 LaBotz, "Tumultuous Teamsters," 202.
10 James and James, *Hoffa and the Teamsters*, 143–44.
11 For a detailed account see Ruiz, *Cannery Women, Cannery Lives*, chapter 6.
12 LaBotz, "Tumultuous Teamsters," 205.
13 Johnston [Mark Johnson, pseud.], "Fight to Save Teamsters Union."
14 LaBotz, "Tumultuous Teamsters," 209–213.
15 Ibid., 215; Fisk, *Socialism from Below*. On the concept of "business unionism," see Moody, *An Injury to All*.
16 LaBotz, "Tumultuous Teamsters," 219.
17 Fisk, *Socialism from Below*, part VI.
18 Johnston, interview. For a good summary of the history of the cannery workers' movement, see Zavella, *Women's Work and Chicano Families*, 62–69.
19 Johnston, "Cannery Workers History Draft."
20 Ibid.
21 Díaz, interview, November 13, 2013; Michael Johnston to Ken Paff, February

27, 1985, Michael Johnston papers.

22 US League of Revolutionary Struggle, *Peace, Justice, Equality and Socialism*, 90.

23 Gallegos, "The 'Sunbelt Strategy' and Chicano Liberation."

24 Flores, "Labor in Reagan's USA."

25 For a sophisticated version of the latter position see Gitlin, *Twilight of Common Dreams*. For a scholarly rebuttal by a labor historian see Nelson, *Divided We Stand*.

26 Some superb historians have devoted their attention to this issue. See Montgomery, "The Shuttle and the Cross"; Foner, *Free Soil, Free Labor*; Saxton, *The Indispensible Enemy*; Woodward, *Tom Watson: Agrarian Rebel* and *Origins of the New South*, chap. IX.

Chapter 3

1 *Watsonville Register-Pajaronian*, May 8–11, 1950, and July 28, 1987.

2 Sergio López, interview, March 31, 2011; International Brotherhood of Teamsters archives (courtesy Jim Kimball).

3 Moreno, interview, July 5, 2010.

4 Sergio López, interview, March 31, 2011; *Watsonville Register-Pajaronian*, December 28, 1985.

5 *Watsonville Register-Pajaronian*, December 28, 1985; Mack, interview, February 23, 2009.

6 Paramo, interview.

7 Gonzalez, interview; Guillermina Ramírez, quoted in Ríos, "Strikers Stronger by the Day."

8 Gonzalez, interview; *Watsonville Register-Pajaronian*, September 9, 1984.

9 Jiménez, interview; Reina Lagusman and Gloria Betancourt, quoted by Ross and Blum in "'Huelga' Means More Than Strike."

10 Carrisoza, interview, November 18, 2010.

11 *Watsonville Register-Pajaronian*, September 3, 1984.

12 Jiménez, interview.

13 Gonzalez, interview, and Betancourt, interview, January 25, 2010. Guillermina Ramírez, quoted in Ross and Blum, "'Huelga' Means More Than Strike."

14 Sergio López, interview, July 19, 2009.

15 Bardacke, interview, March 25, 2010.

16 Bardacke, *Tramping Out the Vintage*.

17 Bardacke, interview, March 25, 2010; Bardacke, *Tramping Out the Vintage*, 13–17 and passim; "Do You Remember the TDU Program??" undated flier, Bardacke Papers, Box 1, File 7.

18 Fahey, interview, July 18, 2009.

19 Interviews with Bardacke, Jiménez, and Betancourt.

20 Anita Contreras, interview; Parra, interview; and Bardacke, interview, March 25, 2010. For an account of the Juan Parra case, see Johnson, "Tale of Two Tongues."

21 Bardacke, interview, March 25, 2010. See also Johnson and Dunn, "Legal

Terrorism: the Border Patrol in the Local Hispanic Community."

22   Sergio López, interview, July 19, 2009.

23   Richard Shaw, interview, oral history, Agricultural History Project Collection.

24   Many workers came to believe that Verduzco was exploiting his Mexican heritage to further management's agenda, and regarded him as a *vendido* (sellout). "Even though he was born here, the cactus is clearly imprinted on his forehead," *Unity*, October 25, 1985.

25   Sergio López, interview, July 16, 2009.

26   As the figures suggest, only two thousand ballots were counted. Low turnout was at least partly due to the local's decision to send the ballots out by bulk mail, meaning they could not be forwarded. Members who had changed their address were thus effectively prevented from voting. Bardacke raised this issue in his unsuccessful challenge to the election.

27   Fahey, interviews July 18, 2009 and April 9, 2014.

Chapter 4

1   Betancourt, interview, January 25, 2010.

2   *Watsonville Register-Pajaronian*, June 18, 1986; Sergio López, interview, July 19, 2009.

3   Beeson, interview.

4   Miller, "The Strike/How It Happened"; Gill, interview.

5   *Watsonville Register-Pajaronian*, October 10, 1986.

6   Marshall, "Law Firm Cashes In"; Beeson, interview.

7   Logan, "Permanent Replacements."

8   McIntosh, "Labor Still Reeling."

9   Sergio López, interview, March 8, 2013.

10 "Threat of Strike at Shaw's," *Watsonville Register-Pajaronian*, July 5, 1985.

11 *Watsonville Register-Pajaronian*, July 8, 1985.

12 Sergio López, interview, March 8, 2013.

13 Gonzalez, interview.

14 Esperanza Contreras, interview.

15 Jiménez, interview.

16 Quoted in Turner, "Strike Town USA," 25.

17 *Watsonville Register-Pajaronian*, August 30, 1985.

18 McIntosh, "That Mess at Watsonville Canning," 13.

19 Paramo, interview.

20 López, interview, March 8, 2013.

21 *Watsonville Register-Pajaronian*, August 14, 1985.

22 López, interview, July 19, 2009, and Mack, interview, February 23, 2009.

23 *Watsonville Register-Pajarionian*, August 13 and 15, 1985.

24 *Watsonville Register-Pajaronian*, August 19, 1985.

25 Fahey, interview, April 9, 2014; Local 912 minutes, Teamster Joint Council 7 papers.

26   López, interview, July 16, 2009; King quoted in *Watsonville Register-Pajaronian*, August 14, 1985.

27   *Watsonville Register-Pajaronian*, August 14, 1985.

28   Bardacke Papers, Box 1 File 1. For an account of the meeting, see *Watsonville Register-Pajaronian* August 19, 1985.

29   Richard King quoted in *Watsonville Register-Pajaronian*, August 30, 1985.

30   *Watsonville Register-Pajaronian*, September 2 and 7, 1985.

31   *Watsonville Register-Pajaronian*, September 7, 1985.

32   *Watsonville Register-Pajaronian*, September 9, 1985.

33   Order and Preliminary Injunction No. 95156, Santa Cruz County Superior Court, Watsonville Canning and Frozen Food Co., Inc. vs. Local 912, International Brotherhood of Teamsters, September 20, 1985, Beeson, Tayer & Bodine collection. This injunction formalized the terms of the temporary restraining order issued ten days earlier. See also *Watsonville Register-Pajaronian*, September 10, 1985.

34   *Watsonville Register-Pajaronian*, September 12 and 18, 1985.

35   Bardacke, interview, May 6, 2014.

36   Esperanza Contreras, interview.

37   *Watsonville Register-Pajaronian*, September 21, 1985.

38   Betancourt, interview, November 17, 2010; Esperanza Contreras, interview.

39   *Watsonville Register-Pajaronian*, September 12, 1985.

40   *Watsonville Register-Pajaronian*, September 25, 1985.

41   *Watsonville Register-Pajaronian*, September 17 and 21, 1985.

42   *Watsonville Register-Pajaronian*, October 18, 1985.

43   *Santa Cruz Sentinel*, September 25, 1985; *Watsonville Register-Pajaronian*, November 19, 1985.

44   Mendez, interview, November 18, 2010.

45   *Watsonville Register-Pajaronian*, September 25, 1985.

46   Local 912 minutes, Joint Council 7 papers.

47   Mack, interview, February 23, 2009.

48   Ibid.

49   Ybarrrolaza, interview.

50   Alex Ybarrolaza to Chuck Mack, October 4, 1985, Local 70 papers, Box 45.

51   Ibid.

52   Fahey, interview, April 9, 2014.

53   Alex Ybarrolaza to Check Mack, October 4, 1985.

54   Chuck Mack to Arnie Weinmeister, October 7, 1985, Joint Council 7 papers.

Chapter 5

1   Díaz, interviews, November 13, 2013; February 7 and 25, 2014.

2   Manuel Díaz to Teamsters Democratic Union national office, n.d., probably early February 1985; Díaz, interview, February 7, 2014.

3 Díaz, interview, November 13, 2013; Ken Paff to Michael Johnston, February 18, 1985, Michael Johnston papers.

4 Díaz interview, February 7, 2014.

5 Fahey, interview, April 9, 2014.

6 Teamsters for a Democratic Union, "Strike Report #1," Bardacke Papers, Box 1, File 6; Bardacke, interview, May 6, 2014.

7 Díaz, interview, February 7, 2014.

8 Fahey, interview, April 9, 2014.

9 Bardacke, "Watsonville: How the Strikers Won"; undated draft of leaflet, Bardacke Papers, Box 1, File 1.

10 Díaz, interview, February 7, 2014.

11 *Santa Cruz Sentinel*, November 7, 1985.

12 Leaflet, "Solidarity Day—End Martial Law in Watsonville," Bardacke Papers, Box 1, File 1.

13 Brough, interview, August 28, 2015.

14 Cruz Takash, "Remedying Racial and Ethnic Inequality."

15 Johnson, "Tale of Two Tongues."

16 Fahey, interview, April 9, 2014.

17 Ríos, interview, July 5, 2010.

18 Quoted in Ríos, "Strikers Stronger by the Day."

19 Ríos, interview, July 5, 2010.

20 Fahey, interview, July 18, 2009.

21 Johnson, "Tale of Two Tongues"; *Rank and File Voice: News for Northern California Food Industry Teamsters* (Teamsters for a Democratic Union): Fall 1985.

22 This account of the rally and its aftermath is based on interviews with Oscar Ríos, Joe Fahey, and Manuel Díaz. Guillermina Ramírez's characterization of Fahey after the rally is based on his recollection, not hers, but she was not the only striker to take offense at the way the rally was handled.

23 Bardacke, interview, May 6, 2014 and Betancourt, interview, January 25, 2010.

24 Fahey, interview, July 18, 2009.

25 "Reunion General de Huelgistas/Strikers' Meeting," Bardacke Papers, Box 1, File 1.

26 *Strikers' Voice*, November 9, 1985, Bardacke Papers, Box 1, File 1.

27 Quoted in Flores, "Mujeres en Huelga," 241.

28 This was the image of the Strikers' Committee conveyed in Jon Silver's award-winning documentary *Watsonville on Strike*. The film's narration describes the Strikers' Committee as an alliance between "the Teamster officials and the more moderate strikers."

29 Quoted in Heather Thomson, "A Look at the Watsonville Strike," 76, 78. The author obtained a copy from Steve Morozumi. Brough would recall years later that the Strikers' Committee "did damned good work." Brough, interview, August 28, 2015.

30 Ríos, "Strikers Stronger by the Day."

31 Carrisoza, interview, November 18, 2010; Gonzalez, interview; Moreno,

interviews, March 25 and July 5, 2010.

32   Betancourt, interview, January 25, 2010; Ross and Blum, "'*Huelga*' Means More Than Strike."

33   Betancourt, interview, January 25, 2010, and Ybarrolaza, interview.

34   Fahey, interview, July 18, 2009.   ·

35   Ríos, interview, June 17, 2014; Fahey quoted in Joan Walsh, "Veggie Barons Try Union Freeze-Out."

36   Osmundson, interview. Sergio López made the same charge but applied it to TDU as well. Sergio López, interview, July 16, 2009.

37   Brough, interviews, June 20, 2014, and August 28, 2015.

38   Bardacke, "Watsonville: How the Strikers Won."

39   Ríos, interview, June 17, 2014. For an account of the Los Siete trial, see Heins, *Strictly Ghetto Property*.

40   Betancourt, interview, January 25, 2010.

41   Ríos, "Strikers Stronger by the Day."

42   Interviewed in Wong, *¡Sí, Se Puede.*

43   Betancourt, interview, January 25, 2010; Betancourt, "Our Eyes Have Been Opened."

44   Bardacke, "Watsonville: How the Strikers Won."

45   Quoted in Flores, "Mujeres en Huelga," 241.

46   Teng, interviews, July 8, 2010, and October 3, 2014.

47   Ríos, interview, June 17, 2014.

48   Gonzalez, interview, and Teng, interview, October 3, 2014.

49   "Summation of the League's Work in Watsonville, 1985–1987," League of Revolutionary Struggle, Watsonville Unit, Labor Commission/Secretariat, January 1988; copy in author's possession.

50   Castillo, "Cannery Strike Grows Stronger."

Chapter 6

1   Ríos, "Strikers Stronger by the Day."

2   Johnson, "1,500 March for Strikers."

3   *Watsonville Register-Pajaronian,* December 21, 1985.

4   Dickey, "4,000 March in Support of Watsonville Strike."

5   Castillo, "Cannery Strike Grows Stronger."

6   Dickey, "'La Familia' on Strike."

7   Joint Council 7 papers.

8   López, interview, July 16, 2009.

9   *Watsonville Register-Pajaronian*, November 25, 1985.

10   Fahey, interview, April 23, 2014.

11   *San Jose Mercury News*, January 1, 1986.

12   Díaz, interview, November 13, 2013. For detailed coverage of the November 24 nomination meeting, see *Watsonville Register-Pajaronian*, November 25, 1986.

13 Fahey, interview, April 9, 2014.

14 Díaz, interview, November 13, 2013, and Ybarrolaza, interview, February 25, 2009.

15 Ybarrolaza, interview.

16 López, interview, July 19, 2009.

17 Bardacke Papers, Box 1, File 7; copies of the leaflet "La Planillo del Pueblo" obtained from Steve Morozumi.

18 *Watsonville Register-Pajaronian*, November 25, 1985; copies of the People's Slate tabloid obtained from Steve Morozumi.

19 Bardacke Papers, Box 7, File 1.

20 Bardacke Papers, Box 7, File 1; Fahey, interview, April 9, 2014.

21 Díaz, interview, February 25, 2014.

22 Bardacke, interview, May 6, 2014.

23 Walsh, "Veggie Barons Try Union Freeze-Out." Frank Bardacke believed there were genuine political differences, but "they were about strike strategy. They weren't about somebody's line on China." Bardacke, interview, May 6, 2014.

24 *In These Times*, January 1, 1986; "Summation of the League's Work in Watsonville," 5.

25 *Convoy Dispatch*, February 1986; Michael Johnston to Ken Paff (n.d.), Michael Johnston papers.

26 Quoted in Flores, "Mujeres en Huelga," 238.

27 Díaz, interview, February 7, 2014, and Ríos, interview, November 21, 2010.

28 Carrisoza, interview, November 18, 2010.

29 McIntosh, "That Mess at Watsonville Canning," 22; *National Alliance*, March 13, 1987, Bardacke Papers, Box 1, File 35.

30 Ross and Blum, "'*Huelga*' Means More Than Strike."

31 Flores, "Mujeres en Huelga," 237.

32 Flores, "Mujeres en Huelga," 237; Jiménez, interview. Aurora Trujillo's appearance before the city council is recorded in Silver, *Watsonville on Strike*.

33 Paramo, interview, November 19, 2010; McIntosh, "That Mess at Watsonville Canning," 20. The story of the Torres family is vividly told in *Watsonville on Strike*.

34 Dickey, "Misery in Watsonville Strike"; Flores, "Mujeres en Huelga," 235.

35 *Watsonville Register-Pajaronian*, November 6 and 15, 1985.

36 Duane Beeson to Teamsters Joint Council 7 executive board, October 21, 1985, Beeson, Tayer & Bodine collection.

37 Dickey, "Misery in Watsonville Strike."

38 *Watsonville Register-Pajaronian*, December 18, 1985.

39 Dickey, "Misery in Watsonville Strike."

40 Watsonville Strike Support Committee, "Dear Community Members," Bardacke Papers, Box 1, Folder 9.

41 Watsonville Strike Support Committee, "No Evictions Because of Strike," Bardacke Papers, Box 1, Folder 9.

42 Watsonville Strike Support Committee, "Dear Community Members,"

Bardacke Papers, Box 1, File 31; Draper, "The Mouse that Roared"; Mendez, interview.

43 Díaz, interview, February 7, 2014; Silver, interview; and Osmundson, interview.

44 Gómez, interview.

45 Thomson, "A Look at the Watsonville Strike," 69, 76.

46 Quoted by Flores, "Mujeres en Huelga," 235–36.

47 Díaz, interview, February 25, 2014.

48 Walsh, "Veggie Barons Try Union Freeze-Out."

49 Quoted by Flores, "Mujeres en Huelga," 239.

50 Diaz, interview, February 25, 2014.

51 Carrisoza, interview, November 4, 2014, and Torres, interview.

52 Quoted by Flores, "Mujeres en Huelga," 240.

53 Flores, "Mujeres en Huelga," 242.

54 *Watsonville Register-Pajaronian*, December 21, 1985.

55 *Watsonville Register-Pajaronian*, November 25, 1985.

56 The vote tally can be found in the file, Local 912, in Box 45 of the Teamsters Local 70 papers.

Chapter 7

1 For scholarly perspectives, see Freedman and Fulmer, "Last Rites for Pattern Bargaining"; Erickson, "A Reinterpretation," 615–34; Budd, "The Internal Political Imperative"; and Segal, "Economic Dualism." See also James and James, *Hoffa and the Teamsters,* 138–40.

2 Moody, "A Pattern of Retreat."

3 Green, *On Strike at Hormel,* 11, 300–301, and passim.

4 Ybarrolaza, interview; Alex Ybarrolaza to William Segal, November 19, 1986, Local 70 papers, Box 45, File "Letters: Draft"; Alex Ybarrolaza to Chuck Mack, September 8, 1986, Local 70 papers, Box 45, File "Economic Boycott: Correspondence."

5 Duane Beeson to George Tichy, November 26, 1985, Local 70 papers, Box 45, File "Watsonville Canning Financial Records Disc." Copies of Watsonville Canning's disclosure terms are in the Joint Council 7 papers.

6 Ybarrolaza, interview.

7 Richard A. Shaw, Inc. and Teamsters Local 912, "Fact Finding Report," January 23, 1986, Beeson, Tayer & Bodine collection.

8 Verduzco quoted in *Watsonville Register-Pajaronian*, June 21, 1986, and Lindley, "New Food Patterns." Richard Shaw told the *Watsonville Register-Pajaronian* (September 23, 1986), "I'll be damned if I'm going to roll over and play dead and let these foreigners take away my business," Bardacke Papers, Box 1, File 29).

9 Miller, "The Strike/How It Happened."

10 Ibid.

11 Ybarrolaza, interview; *Register-Pajaronian*, May 9, 1986, Bardacke Papers, Box 1, File 25. In his internal communications with Teamsters officials, Ybarrolaza

remarked as well on the use of undocumented workers as strikebreakers. (See his report to Chuck Mack, October 6, 1985, Teamsters Local 70 papers, Box 45, File "912.") It is doubtful that so keen an observer would not have known that many strikers were undocumented as well.

12 Chuck Mack to Jackie Presser and Arnie Weinmeister, December 2, 1985, Joint Council 7 papers.

13 Two such instances occurred within a four-day period: see *Watsonville Register-Pajaronian*, January 24 and 28, 1986.

14 *Watsonville Register-Pajaronian*, June 7, 1986; January 24, 1986; August 1, 1986, Bardacke Papers, Box 1, Files 21, 26, and 28.

15 *San Jose Mercury News*, November 12, 1985, Bardacke Papers, Box 1, File 19.

16 *Watsonville Register-Pajaronian*, November 8, 1985, Bardacke Papers, Box 1, File 19.

17 Esperanza Contreras, interview.

18 Díaz, interview, February 7, 2014.

19 López, interview, September 27, 2014; *San Jose Mercury News*, "Violence Continues in Watsonville," January 19, 1986.

20 McIntosh, "That Mess at Watsonville Canning."

21 *Watsonville Register-Pajaronian*, January 28, 1986, March 7 and 12, 1986, Bardacke Papers, Box 1, Files 21 and 23; Ryan, interview, September 14, 2014; Díaz, interview, February 25, 2014.

22 *Watsonville Register-Pajaronian*, November 27, 1985, and March 13, 1986, Bardacke Papers, Box 1, Files 19 and 23.

23 *Santa Cruz Sentinel*, November 14, 1986. On January 29 of the following year, the *Watsonville Register-Pajaronian* reported that the district attorney's office was investigating the company for possible insurance fraud in connection with the fire.

24 *Watsonville Register-Pajaronian*, January 10 and 20, 1986, Bardacke Papers, Box 1, File 21.

25 Brough, interview, August 28, 2015.

26 *Watsonville Register-Pajaronian*, October 15, 1985, Bardacke Papers, Box 1, File 18.

27 Martínez, interview, June 4, 2014. The students' encounter with police appears in Silver, *Watsonville on Strike*. Silver's film devotes much of its attention to police confrontations.

28 Santa Cruz County Superior Court, "Complaint for Damages," Watsonville Canning, plaintiff, vs. Teamsters Local 912, filed September 15, 1986, 2, 4–5 (copy in Beeson papers).

29 López, interview, July 16, 2009, and Beeson, interview; Duane Beeson to Joint Council 7 executive board, October 21, 1985, Teamsters Local 70 Papers, Box 45, File "912".

30 Silver, interview.

31 Torres, interview.

32 Fahey, interview, April 23, 2014.

33   "UNITE to win the strike," Bardacke Papers, Box 1, File 8; "In the matter of the majority of the Executive Board of IBT Local 912 vs. Joe Fahey, June 4, 1986," 27 (Joint Council 7 papers).

34   "Local 912 Executive Board vs. Joe Fahey," 61–62.

35   Bardacke Papers, Box 1, File 1.

36   "Local 912 Executive Board vs. Joe Fahey," 59.

37   Ibid., 4–6, 12–13, 59, and passim.

38   "We didn't realize it at the time," Frank Bardacke would recall, "but the Shaw strike was already lost." Bardacke, interview, September 11, 2014.

39   Ybarrolaza, interview; López, interview, September 27, 2014.

40   Bardacke Papers, Box 1, File 1.

41   *Santa Cruz Sentinel*, February 14, 1986; *Watsonville Register–Pajaronian*, February 13, 1986; *San Jose Mercury News*, February 15, 1986. A bilingual summary of the agreement, minus the critical component of wage rates, was distributed at the meeting; a copy can be found in Bardacke Papers, Box 1, File 3.

42   *Watsonville Register–Pajaronian*, February 14, 1986; Fahey, interview, April 23, 2014. Footage of the meeting can be seen in *Watsonville on Strike*.

43   *Unity*, February 21, 1986; "Watsonville Firm Wins Strike Battle," *San Francisco Chronicle*, February 15, 1986; "Strike against One Watsonville Food Packer Ends with Wage Cut," *San Francisco Examiner*, February 15, 1986.

44   Bart J. Curto to Jackie Presser, February 27, 1986, Joint Council 7 papers.

45   Gloria Betancourt quoted in Heckman, "Wage Wars"; Sandra Perez quoted by Donald Miller in *Santa Cruz Sentinel*, March 12, 1986; López, interview, September 27, 2014.

46   Torres, interview.

47   This is Joe Fahey's analysis, Fahey, interview, July 18, 2009.

48   Bardacke, "Watsonville: How the Strikers Won," 18.

49   Terry Medina to Sergio López, January 28, 1986, Joint Council 7 papers; *Watsonville Register–Pajaronian*, January 31, 1986.

50   Johnson, "Strikers Take Compensation Issue to Court."

51   "Local 912 Executive Board vs. Joe Fahey," 32.

52   The fullest accounts of the February 17 events are the front-page story in the *Watsonville Register–Pajaronian*, February 18, 1986, and Heckman, "Wage Wars." See also *Unity*, February 21, 1986, and Silver, *Watsonville on Strike*.

53   Brough, interview, June 20, 2014; *Watsonville Register–Pajaronian*, February 18, 1986.

54   Heckman, "Wage Wars"; Bardacke, interview, May 6, 2014.

55   "Organizers Didn't Plan Violence," *Watsonville Register–Pajaronian*, February 18, 1986.

56   López, interview, July 16, 2009.

57   Copies of Sergio López's letter to the *Watsonville Register–Pajaronian*, February 21, 1986, and Chuck Mack's letter to Sergio López, February 20, 1986, are included in the transcript of Joe Fahey's June 4 hearing in the Joint

Council 7 papers.

58 *Watsonville Register-Pajaronian*, February 26, 1986.

Chapter 8

1   Bardacke Papers, Box 1, File 10; *Watsonville Register-Pajaronian*, March 10, 1986; *Unity*, March 21, 1986.

2   Rachleff, "The Failure of Minnesota," 103–120; Halpern, *Down on the Killing Floor*, 191, 195, 199.

3   Green, *On Strike at Hormel*, 3.

4   By the end of the century Mexican and Central American immigrants, many of them undocumented, would make up a large portion of the industry work force, laboring under conditions that flouted federal labor and workplace safety laws. See Genoways, *The Chain*, 3–93; Schlosser, *Fast Food Nation*, chapters 7–8, and Apostolides, *Breaks in the Chain*.

5   Green, *On Strike at Hormel*, passim; Betancourt, et al., "Round-Table Discussion." For a useful chronology, see the appendix of Ratchleff, *Hard-Pressed in the Heartland*, the author's polemic in defense of the Hormel strikers. Rachleff's book is a rejoinder to Barbara Koppel's Academy Award–winning documentary *American Dream* (Cabin Creek, 1990), whose portrayal of the strike is downbeat and essentially critical.

6   Green, *On Strike at Hormel*, 15–19.

7   Jarley and Maranto, "Union Corporate Campaigns."

8   Bardacke, "The United Farmworkers from the Ground Up," in Brenner, Brenner, and Winslow, eds., *Rebel Rank and File*. See also "Behind FLOC's Victory over Campbell: *Unity* interviews Baldemar Velasquez," *Unity*, April 25, 1986; FLOC won union recognition from Midwest growers through a consumer boycott of their biggest customer, Campbell's Soup. For a detailed account of the UFW boycott strategy and its impact on the evolution of the union, see Bardacke, *Tramping Out the Vintage*.

9   The speech is recorded, along with a follow-up interview, in *Watsonville on Strike*. Filmmaker Jon Silver acknowledged years later that Chavez likely could not have done much to disrupt the flow of produce into the struck plants and was understandably reluctant to admit it on camera. (Silver, interview, June 17, 2014.)

10 Brough, interview, August 28, 2015 and "Summation of the League's Work in Watsonville," 7.

11 Silver, interview. The *Watsonville Register-Pajaronian* provided ongoing coverage of the trials in April and May 1986. See also Bardacke Papers, Box 1, File 9.

12 June 3, 1986.

13 Teng, interview, October 3, 2014. She remarked that she'd had no inkling that the document had gotten this kind of attention from the union.

14 Local 70 papers, Box 45, File "Shiree Teng."

15 Ybarrolaza, interview.

16   Local 912 executive board to Chuck Mack, April 17, 1986, Local 70 papers, Box 45, File "5 PT Plan."

17   Amberg, "The CIO Political Strategy." The anticommunist clause was eventually thrown out by the Supreme Court, but not before it had provoked a damaging wave of expulsions and internal divisions within the labor movement's ranks.

18   Gregory, *Labor and the Law*, 421, 426–27. For a fuller discussion see Bock, "Secondary Boycotts."

19   "Watsonville Canning Strike and Economic Sanctions," April 7, 1986, Local 70 papers, Box 45, File "5 PT Plan."

20   Duane Beeson to Walter Englebert, Western Conference of Teamsters, April 10, 1986, Beeson, Tayer & Bodine collection.

21   The possibility of decertification was discussed in the Local 912 *Weekly Bulletin,* no. 15 (March 18, 1986), Bardacke Papers, Box 1, File 2.

22   "Watsonville Canning Strike and Economic Sanctions"; Local 912 *Weekly Bulletin,* no. 18 (April 8, 1986), Bardacke Papers, Box 1, File 2.

23   Local 912 *Weekly Bulletin,* no. 19 (April 15, 1986), Bardacke Papers, Box 1, File 2; *Watsonville Register-Pajaronian*, April 14, 1986; Ralph J. Torelli to Sergio López, April 22, 1986, Local 70 papers, Box 45, File "5 PT Plan"; Ybarrolaza, interview.

24   Johnson. "Pay Cuts Spread."

25   Bardacke Papers, Box 1, File 1.

26   *Watsonville Register-Pajaronian*, March 7, 1986.

27   *Watsonville Register-Pajaronian*, March 10, 1986.

28   *Watsonville Register-Pajaronian*, March 13, 1986.

29   Johnson, "Teamsters Fight for Survival."

30   Watsonville Strikers' Committee and Northern California Strike Support Committee to Reverend Jesse Jackson, n.d., Steve Morozumi papers.

31   Quoted in *Unity*, July 25, 1986.

32   Lerma, interview, November 18, 2010.

33   Johnston, "The Fight to Save the Teamsters Union."

34   Shinoff, "Troubles within the Teamsters."

35   Ybarrolaza, interview.

36   *Northern California Teamster*, August 1986; Ybarrolaza, interview; Moreno, interview, July 5, 2010.

37   Ybarrolaza, interview, and López, interview, July 16, 2009.

38   John Blake to Arnie Weinmeister, July 24, 1986, Local 70 papers, Box 45, File "Economic Boycott Campaign." See also Alex Ybarrolaza to Chuck Mack, September 8, 1986, Local 70 papers, Box 45, File "Economic Boycott: Correspondence."

39   *Watsonville Register-Pajaronian*, May 15, 1986, and June 5, 1986; Crosetti Workers for a Fair Contract, "We need more time," n.d., copies in Steve Morozumi papers.

40   *San Jose Mercury News*, July 3, 1986; footage of workers' meeting in Silver,

Watsonville on Strike.

41   Local 912 *Weekly Bulletin*, no. 26 (June 17, 1986).

42   "Open letter to Watsonville strikers," Bardacke Papers, Box 1, File 9; *Santa Cruz Sentinel*, July 13, 1986.

43   Gómez, interview.

44   Brough, interview, August 28, 2015.

45   *Watsonville Register-Pajaronian*, June 30, 2014; *San Jose Mercury News*, June 30, 1986; Betancourt, interview, November 17, 2010.

46   *Watsonville Register-Pajaronian*, July 3, 1986; Crosetti Workers for a Fair Contract, "We need more time" and "Vote no on this contract," n.d., copies in Steve Morozumi papers; Richard Allen to Sergio López, June 30, 1986, Bardacke Papers, Box 1, File 42.

47   Local 70 papers, Box 45, File "Economic Boycott Campaign."

48   López, interview, December 4 and 9, 2014. Shown the memo nearly thirty years later, López reacted with what appeared to be genuine shock and dismay.

49   *Santa Cruz Sentinel*, January 26, 1986, and July 13, 1986; *Watsonville Register-Pajaronian*, July 3, 1986; López, interview, September 27, 2014; Sergio López to Frank Bardacke, July 17, 1986, Bardacke Papers, Box 1, File 42.

50   Local 912 *Weekly Bulletin*, no. 31 (July 22, 1986).

51   *Watsonville Register-Pajaronian*, July 16 and 17, 1986.

52   Fahey, interview, December 9, 2014; Balanoff, "In-Plant Strategies." According to Fahey, Esperanza Contreras was particularly incensed at the idea; he attributed her reaction to the belief of many observant Catholic strikers that the hardships of the struggle were a test of their faith and a tactical retreat would reflect a lack of trust in God.

53   Beeson, interview; Local 912 *Weekly Bulletin*, no. 31 (July 22, 1986) and no. 32 (August 5, 1986).

Chapter 9

1   Ron Trine, "Facts about Teamsters union" n.d., copy in Steve Morozumi papers.

2   Moreno, interview, July 5, 2010. Copies of Strikers' Committee contact list in Steve Morozumi papers.

3   Ybarrolaza, interview; *Unity*, August 29, 1986; copies of thank-you letters to election observers in Local 70 papers, Box 45, File "Economic Boycott: Correspondence."

4   John Blake to Arnie Weinmeister, July 24, 1986, Local 70 papers, Box 45, File "Economic Boycott Campaign."

5   Betancourt, interview, January 25, 2010; Torres, interview; Lerma, interview, November 18, 2010.

6   Copy of the leaflet in Steve Morozumi papers.

7   Fahey, interview, July 18, 2009.

8   *Santa Cruz Sentinel*, August 13, 1986; *Unity*, August 29, 1986; Ybarrolaza,

interview.

9　*Watsonville Register-Pajaronian*, August 15, 1986; Local 912 *Weekly Bulletin*, no. 34 (August 26, 1986), in Bardacke Papers, Box 1, File 2.

10　*Unity*, August 29, 1986.

11　Ybarrolaza, interview; *Santa Cruz Sentinel*, September 4, 1986. After the strike Dan Siegel speculated that the law firm had collected over $1 million in fees from Mort Console.

12　The *Watsonville Register-Pajaronian* confirmed on October 8 that the credit line was completely exhausted.

13　October 8, 1986; *Watsonville Register-Pajaronian*, October 4, 1986.

14　*Watsonville Register-Pajaronian*, October 8, 1986.

15　*Santa Cruz Sentinel*, October 8, 1986.

16　*Santa Cruz Sentinel*, October 9, 1986; *Watsonville Register-Pajaronian*, October 11, 1986.

17　All three letters in Local 70 papers, Box 45, File "Growers."

18　*Santa Cruz Sentinel*, September 26 and October 9, 1986.

19　*Watsonville Register-Pajaronian*, September 26, 1986.

20　*Watsonville Register-Pajaronian*, September 27 and October 11, 1986.

21　*Watsonville Register-Pajaronian*, June 18, 1986 and February 26, 1987.

22　Alex Ybarrolaza to Arnie Weinmeister, October 30, 1986; Arnie Weinmeister to Alex Ybarrolaza, November 4, 1986; Alex Ybarrolaza to Chuck Mack, December 16, 1986, all in Local 70 papers, Box 45, File "Wells Fargo."

23　Local 70 papers, Box 45, File "Wells Fargo."

24　Ybarrolaza, interview.

25　*Santa Cruz Sentinel*, October 22, 1986; *Los Angeles Times*, September 10, 1986.

26　Joint Council 7 papers, "Local 912 Watsonville Canning strike—Media Coverage."

27　Ybarrolaza, interview; Duane Beeson to Gary Witlen, Esq., October 29, 1986, Beeson, Tayer & Bodine collection; Chuck Mack to union trustees, Western Conference of Teamsters Trust Fund, November 28, 1986, Beeson, Tayer & Bodine collection.

28　*Unity*, August 29, 1986.

29　Alex Ybarrolaza to Bill Segal, November 19, 1986; Ybarrolaza to Robert Chacanaca, March 5, 1987; *Santa Cruz Sentinel*, November 10, 1986; "Report on Watsonville Canning and Frozen Food (WC&FF) Strike," Ybarrolaza to Joint Council 7 Executive Board, December 16, 1986, in Joint Council 7 papers. *Strikers' Committee Bulletin* in Frank Bardacke Papers, Box 1, File 1.

30　Alex Ybarrolaza to Sergio López, December 19, 1986, Joint Council 7 papers.

31　Bill Segal, "Watsonville: A Fight that Labor Can Win," copy in Local 70 papers, Box 45, File "Wells Fargo"; Carrisoza, interview, November 4, 2014; Alex Ybarrolaza to Duane Beeson, November 6, 1986, Local 70 papers, Box 45, File "Job Placement."

32　Bardacke Papers, Box 1, File 1.

33　Local 912 *Weekly Bulletin* (December 23, 1985); López, interview, September

27, 2014.

34   *Santa Cruz Sentinel*, November 14, 1986; *Watsonville Register-Pajaronian*,
     January 29, 1987. The disputed claim was first reported in the *Watsonville
     Register-Pajaronian* on June 20, but the *Sentinel* coverage lent new credibility
     to the insurer's position.

35   *Santa Cruz Sentinel*, November 13 and 16, 1986.

36   *Santa Cruz Sentinel*, November 16, 1986. The jailing of the two company
     officials was reported in the *Watsonville Register-Pajaronian* on January 22,
     1986.

37   *Santa Cruz Sentinel*, October 29, 1986.

38   *Santa Cruz Sentinel*, November 21, 1986.

39   John Blake to "All Area Offices," Economic Boycott Campaign, Decem-
     ber 16, 1986, Local 70 papers, Box 45, unlabeled file.

40   *Watsonville Register-Pajaronian*, October 7 and 8, 1986.

41   *San Jose Mercury News*, October 10, 1986.

42   "Watsonville Frozen Food Strike Status Report—November 1986," Local 70
     papers, Box 45, File "Status Reports"; Arnold Highbarger quoted in *Santa
     Cruz Sentinel*, September 26, 1986.

43   "Status Report—November 1986"; Alex Ybarrolaza to Chuck Mack, October
     21, 1986, Beeson, Tayer & Bodine collection.

44   Copy of the November 25 Strikers' Committee bulletin and Steve Morozu-
     mi's handwritten notes on the November 25 meeting of Local 912 in Steve
     Morozumi papers.

45   *Santa Cruz Sun*, November 26, 1986; *Unity*, November 10, 1986. Brough was
     proposing a strategy first advanced by labor lawyer Staughton Lynd on behalf
     of workers battling steel mill shutdowns in Youngstown, Ohio, and Home-
     stead, Pennsylvania. (See Introduction, note 5.) David Gill, largest of the
     Salinas Valley growers, pointed out that the bank was far too heavily invested
     in its farm loan business to pursue the strategy suggested in the *Unity* article.
     (Gill, interview, June 30, 2010.)

Chapter 10

1   Gill, interview.

2   López, interview, July 16, 2009.

3   Johnson, "New Owners at Watsonville Canning."

4   *Santa Cruz Sentinel*, February 20, 1987.

5   Teng, interview, February 18, 2015. See also Strikers' Committee, "Important
     Notice to Strikers," Bardacke Papers, Box 1, File 1.

6   Quoted in Johnson, "New Owners at Watsonville Canning."

7   *Santa Cruz Sun*, February 19, 1987.

8   Copy in Beeson, Tayer & Bodine collection.

9   "Summation of the League's Work in Watsonville," 9.

10   Chuck Mack to Sergio López, February 5, 1987, Local 70 papers, Box 45,

File "Economic Boycott: Correspondence."

11   Chuck Mack to Sergio López, January 20, 1987, Joint Council 7 papers; Duane Beeson to Sergio López, March 12, 1986, Beeson, Tayer & Bodine collection; Fahey, interview, April 9, 2014.

12   Betancount, et al., "Round-Table Discussion," 14–15.

13   Ibid., 14.

14   *Watsonville Register-Pajaronian*, January 16 and 30, 1987; *Santa Cruz Sentinel*, January 16 and 22, 1987.

15   Chuck Mack to Sergio López, January 20, 1987, Joint Council 7 papers, January 20, 1987.

16   Ryan, interview, February 5, 2015.

17   Bardacke, "Watsonville: How the Strikers Won," 20.

18   *Santa Cruz Sentinel*, February 1, 1987.

19   Chuck Mack's copy of the Sergio López letter is in the Joint Council 7 files. Mack's letter is in the Local 70 papers, Box 45, File "Wells Fargo."

20   Alex Ybarrolaza to Duane Beeson, February 3, 1987, Local 70 papers, Box 45, File "Wells Fargo."

21   This and earlier correspondence with the bank in Local 70 papers, Box 45, File "Wells Fargo."

22   Mack, interview, February 23, 2009.

23   *Santa Cruz Sentinel*, February 18, 1987; *Watsonville Register-Pajaronian*, February 18, 1987; Teng, interview, February 18, 2015. Margarita Paramo quoted in Flores, "Mujeres en Huelga," 245.

24   Chuck Mack to Jackie Presser, February 20, 1987, Joint Council 7 papers.

25   Mack, interview, November 24, 2010; Sergio López to Chuck Mack, February 20, 1987, Joint Council 7 papers.

26   Gill, interview.

27   *Santa Cruz Sentinel*, March 2, 1987; Maltzman, interview.

28   "*Hoy es tiempo de decider tu futuro*," Bardacke Papers, Box 1, File 1.

29   *Santa Cruz Sentinel*, March 1 and 2, 1987.

30   *San Jose Mercury News*, March 4, 1987.

31   Fahey, interview, July 18, 2009.

32   Ibid., *Watsonville Register-Pajaronian*, March 4, 1987; *Santa Cruz Sentinel*, March 5, 1987.

33   Betancourt, interview, January 25, 2010.

34   Teng, interview, February 18, 2015.

35   Bardacke Papers, Box 1, File 6.

36   *San Jose Mercury News*, March 5, 1987; *Santa Cruz Sentinel*, March 8, 1987.

37   Johnson, "Unity and Victory: The Strikers' Story."

38   Footage of Fahey and Esperanza Contreras addressing the meeting in Silver, *Watsonville on Strike*.

39   Bardacke Papers, Box 1, File 1; *San Jose Mercury News*, March 7, 1987; Silver, *Watsonville on Strike*.

40   *Watsonville Register-Pajaronian*, March 7, 1987.

41 Both documents in Local 70 papers, Box 45, File "EBC Area Offices."

42 "News Release, March 6, 1987," Agricultural History Project Collection.

43 *Watsonville Register-Pajaronian*, March 7, 1987.

44 Bardacke Papers, Box 1, File 1.

45 López, interview, July 16, 2009.

46 Fahey, interview, July 18, 2009.

47 "Dear Supporters," Bardacke Papers, Box 1, File 1.

48 *"Huelgistas: La huelga no ha terminado!"* copy in Morozumi papers.

49 Esperanza Contreras, interview; Lomeli, interview, November 17, 2010.

50 The incident is recorded in a single extended take from the footage for Wong, *¡Sí, Se Puede!* Except where otherwise indicated, the account that follows is drawn from this footage: from Silver, *Watsonville on Strike*; from Johnson, "Unity and Victory: The Strikers' Story"; and from Turner, "Strike Town USA."

51 *Watsonville Register-Pajaronian*, March 9, 1987.

52 Gonzalez, interview.

53 Betancourt, interview, January 25, 2010; see also Turner, "Strike Town USA," 26–27.

54 Wong, *¡Sí, Se Puede!*

55 Quoted by Turner, "Strike Town USA," 27. See Johnson, "Unity and Victory."

56 Wong, *¡Sí, Se Puede!* and Silver, *Watsonville on Strike*.

57 Turner, "Strike Town USA," 27.

58 Fahey, interview, July 18, 2009.

59 Quoted by Johnson, "Unity and Victory," 13.

60 Quoted in *Unity*, March 16, 1987.

61 Johnson, "Unity and Victory," 13–14; Wong, *¡Sí, Se Puede!*

62 Quoted in Turner, "Strike Town USA," 23–24.

Epilogue

1 Postscript to Mike Quin, *The Big Strike* (Olema, CA: Olema Publishing Co., 1949), 238. Available online at https://archive.org/stream/bigstrike00quinrich #page/238/mode/2up.

2 *Unity*, March 30, 1987.

3 Cruz Takash, "Crisis of Democracy," 349.

4 Geron, "The Struggle to Achieve Political Representation in Watsonville, California," 6.

5 Silver, interview, June 17, 2014.

6 Cruz Takash, "Crisis of Democracy," 353.

7 Interview, June 25, 2010.

8 Geron, "The Struggle to Achieve," 11.

9 Lewis, "The Segregated North," 13.

10 Borrego, "The Restructuring of Frozen Food," 12.

11 Ibid., 2–3 and passim.

12   Ibid., 7–8 and 36–37.

13   Zavella, *I'm Neither Here Nor There,* 102–3.

14   The author was present at this event and retains a vivid recollection of López's words after more than twenty years.

15   Fahey, "Casualties of Free Trade"; Zavella, *I'm Neither Here Nor There,* 102.

16   Borrego, "The Restructuring of Frozen Food," 17; Zavella, *I'm Neither Here Nor There,* 108.

17   Zavella, *I'm Neither Here nor There,* 102.

18   Geron, "The Struggle to Achieve," 30.

19   Ibid. and passim; Zavella, *I'm Neither Here Nor There,* 107; Borrego, "The Restructuring of Frozen Food," 15–16.

20   LaBotz, "Rank and File Teamsters Fight for Labor's Future."

21   Johnson, "From Strike to Social Movement," 90.

INDEX

AFL-CIO, 27

air traffic controllers, xi, 3, 5, 55

Akers Chacón, Justin, 24

Alaniz v. California Processors, Inc., 36

Alinsky, Saul, 12

Álvarez, Elva, 58

Aloise, Vince, 144, 153

American Federation of Labor (AFL), 30

Anderson, Andy, 158–59

arrests, 86, 113, 112–16, 123, 124, 125, 135, 175

Assumption Church, 80, 91, 145, 147, 190

Baca, Richard, 83

Balanoff, Tom, 149

Balderrama, Francisco, 20, 22

Bardacke, Frank, xii, xiii, xiv, 45, 50, 62, 84, 188, 200, 217n; founds Watsonville TDU, 46–49; runs against Richard King, 51, 213n; steps down from TDU leadership, 52; and CWOP, 62, 71–73; and Strikers' Committee, 74, 79–80, 88–89; and Solidarity Day, 79; views on strike strategy 74, 76, 133, 172–73; and Watsonville Strike Support Committee, 102, 121, 156; and Local 912 election, 96–97, 106;

February 17 demonstration, 117, 126; and Crosetti contract, 148; barred from union hall, 152

Beeson, Duane, xiv, 53, 54, 110, 161, 171, 174; legal strategy, 116; economic boycott campaign, 135; certification vote, 149–151

Belgard, Ray, 62–4, 125

Benevidez, Victoria, 94

Bernstein, Harry, 159

Betancourt, Amador, 99, 114

Betancourt, Gloria, xvi, 11, 18, 25, 43, 44, 47, 53, 63, 66, 72, 78, 87, 147, 152, 192, 199; Strikers' Committee, 79–82; and Local 912 election, 93–98, 104–06; reacts to Shaw settlement, 121; and February 17 demonstration, 117, 124–26; attitude toward Teamsters, 171; pickets Wells Fargo Bank, 173; rally at police station, 176; rank-and-file bargaining committee, 179–83; hunger strike, 184–88

Birdseye, Clarence, 16

Black Panther Party, 38, 86

Blake, John, 152, 158, 183, 189; at Teamster Convention, 143; Western Conference Task Force, 144–49; certification vote, 151–53; Economic Boycott

Campaign, 144, 159–63; trusteeship threat, 177

Bluestone, Barry, 3–4

Border Patrol (*la Migra*) 21, 22, 48–49, 77, 102. *See also* Bureau of Immigration (BOI), Immigration and Naturalization Service (INS)

Borrego, Juan, 196

boycott, 133–44, 148, 159–61, 176, 221n. *See also* secondary boycotts

bracero program, 18, 23–25

Bridges, Harry, 191

Brill, Steven, 46

Brough, Jim, 76, 81, 84, 126, 134, 146, 185, 216, 225n

Bubich, John, 42, 95

Bureau of Immigration (BOI), 21–22

California Department of Food and Agriculture, 157

California Processors and Growers, 31

Calvo, Tony, 68

Camarata, Pete, 35

Campaign for Human Development, 37, 192

canneries and cannery workers, xii, 15–16, 30–31, 35–37, 41, 71, 77, 84, 143, 178, 192, 194, 197

Cannery Workers Committee (CWC), 36–37, 51

Cannery Workers Organizing Project (CWOP), 37, 71, 72, 78, 192.

Carey, Ron, 199

Cargill, 130, 197

Carrisoza, Fidelia, 48, 49, 104, 161, 190, 200

Catholicism, 1–3, 46, 88, 182, 187, 224n

Celis, Henry, 63, 72, 81, 94

Cervantes, Juan, 75–76

certification vote, 150–51, 154, 158, 172

Chavez, Cesar, 18, 30, 35, 43, 45, 75, 133, 135, 141, 191–92, 221n

Chicano movement, 72, 78, 98, 102, 129, 137, 142, 193–94; and League of Revolutionary Struggle, 38, 77, 84–5, 134–5, 160

Chinese Exclusion Act, 19, 39

Chinese Progressive Association (CPA), 77

College Readiness Program, 86

Commercial Club, 87

Communist Party, 10, 31, 76, 102, 134, 146

ConAgra, 130, 197

Congress of Industrial Organizations (CIO), 30

Console, Edward, 16, 41, 42, 49

Console, Kathryn, 18, 53, 155, 178

Console, Mort, 8–9, 48, 49, 50, 57, 62–65, 66, 107, 109–10, 122, 126, 132, 141, 154, 158–59, 160, 168, 172, 177–8, 192; and Richard King, 42, 50–51, 57–58, 93; strike preparations, 53–54, 59–61; and Watsonville Frozen Food Employers Association, 111; relations with media, 115, 163; and Wells Fargo Bank, 9, 54, 137, 155, 157–58, 169, 170, 174

Contreras, Anita, 1–3, 48, 145, 187–88

Contreras, Esperanza, 56, 62, 63, 113, 145, 182, 184–86, 188, 200

Convoy Dispatch, 98, 150

corporate campaign, 131–32, 137, 160

Corralejo, Maria, 173, 184, 188, 194

court injunction, 2, 68, 77, 112, 114, 115, 123, 176, 184, 214n *See also* restraining order

Crall, Robert, 110, 158–59
Crosetti, 95, 133, 141 152, 153, 178, 181; resistance to contract, 144–47; lockout, 152–53; plant closes, 195
Cruz Takash, Paule, 193–94
Curto, Bart, 121

Davis, R. G., 48
Dean Foods, 195
Decertification, xi, 3, 8, 9, 39, 149, 150, 154, 172, 210n, 222n
Dees, Joe, 125
Deindustrialization of America, The, 3, 5
Del Mar, 133, 139–140
Dellums, Ron 92
deportations, 22
deregulation of trucking industry, 3, 108
Díaz, Manuel, xiv, xv, 37, 71, 75, 77, 79, 81, 83, 84, 86, 89, 94–8, 102, 103–04, 113, 114
Díaz, Porfirio, 19
Díaz, Reina, 71–72, 78–79, 86, 103
Dick, Philip, xi
divestment, *see* Wells Fargo Bank
Dobbs, Farrell, 28–9

Economic Boycott Campaign, 139, 141, 142, 143–44, 156, 160, 169
Empacadora de Najarantes Azteca, 160
Employment Development Department (EDD), 100, 164; *see also* unemployment benefits
Ellis, Frank, 130
Ellis, Leon, 60, 64, 69, 92, 93, 105, 118, 120, 158, 164, 170, 176
Espinoza, Rafael, 86
evictions, 2, 99–101

Fahey, Joe, xii, 46–47, 51–52, 60, 67, 69, 83, 121, 123–24, 145, 148, 149, 153, 188, 192, 196; and Solidarity Day, 77–80, 83, 215n; Local 912 election, 93–96, 105; and Teamsters United 912, 117–18, 126–27; proposed NorCal contract, 179–81, 185
farm workers, 18, 31, 99, 102, 137
Farm Labor Organizing Committee (FLOC), 132, 221n
Fastiff, Wesley, 54; *see also* Littler, Mendelson, Fastiff, and Tichy
Federal Mediation and Conciliation Service, *see* Crall, Robert
Fitzsimmons, Frank, 32–34, 35
food bank, 68, 72, 88, 92, 99, 105, 117, 120, 130, 135, 142, 189
Food and Nutrition Service, 102
Food, Tobacco, and Agricultural Workers (FTA), 30–31
forklift, 18, 33, 64, 96
Frente Autentico del Trabajo, 197
frozen food industry, chapter 1, *passim;* 2, 8, 9, 41–42, 45, 48, 49, 50–1, 54, 56, 60, 61, 67, 67, 74, 109, 111, 121, 122, 132, 133, 134, 138, 146, 154, 161, 163, 164, 168, 191, 195, 196–97, 198

Gallegos, Frank, 98
García, Linda, 81, 122, 129
Garry, Charles, 86
general strike, 74, 133–34
Gill, David, 167–68, 177–78, 179–80, 181, 183, 185, 187, 189, 195, 225n
Gómez, Cruz, 76, 81, 101–03, 115, 129, 146, 148–49, 152, 181, 194
Gómez-Farias, 24
Gonzalez, Elena, 181

Gonzalez, Esther, 43, 58
Gould, Jay, 39
Gourley, David, 96
Gray, Lou, 141–42
Green, Hardy, 130
Green Giant, 49, 61, 133, 196
Gregg, Linda, 143
Greyhound, 3, 56
Guanajuato, 196
Guyette, Jim, 131, 191
Guzmán, Reyna, 88

Hansen, Con, 41
hardship fund, 82, 170–71
Harrison, Bennett, 3–4
health benefits, 42, 179–85,186, 189
Heim, Fred, 60, 66, 73, 92, 93
Hernández, Carlos, 72, 169
Hernández, Paula, 120
Highbarger, Arnold, 81, 164
Hobsbawm, Eric, xii
Hoffa, Jimmy, 27–30, 32–33, 108
homelessness, 100–01, 103, 151, 193
Hormel, 129–32, 146
hot cargo strikes, 147

Icahn, Carl, 142
Immigration and Naturalization Ser-
    vice (INS), 48–49, 102, 194
In Dubious Battle, 10
In These Times, 83–84, 97–98
Industrial Workers of the World
    (IWW), 34, 130
Ingersoll, Roy, 101
in-plant leadership, 81–83
International Brotherhood of Team-
    sters (IBT), see Teamsters
International Committee against Rac-
    ism (INCAR), 153
International Longshore and Ware-

house Union (ILWU), 30, 191
International Paper, 3, 56
International Socialists (IS), 33–34, 35,
    38, 39–40
Irapuarto, 197

J. P. Stevens, 131–132
Jackson, Rev. Jesse, 141, 146–47
Jalisco, 24, 25
James, Ralph and Estelle, 29
Jiménez, Emma, 43, 44, 47, 58, 99
Jiménez, Reyes, 95, 106
Johnson, Bob, xiii, 113, 182
Johnson-Reed Immigration Act, 21
Johnston, Michael, 36–38, 71, 72, 80,
    97–98, 142–43
Justice for Janitors, 197

Kelsay, Judge William, 62, 68
Kennedy, Robert, 27
Keynes, John Maynard, 6
King, Richard 41–45 passim, 46, 47, 49,
    66, 67–69, 73, 83, 85, 89, 92,
    93, 98, 110; and Console fam-
    ily, 42, 50–51, 53, 56, 59; 1985
    contract talks, 57–61 passim

LaBotz, Dan, 32, 199
Lackey, Bill, 113
Lagusman, Reina, 43
law enforcement, 62, 63–68 passim, 76,
    78–79, 84, 87, 92, 107, 112–16
    passim, 123–27 passim, 135,
    175–76, 184, 187
League of United Latin American
    Citizens (LULAC), 92
League of Revolutionary Struggle
    (LRS), xi, xii, xiii, 38–39, 72,
    73, 141, 194, 198–99; Solidar-
    ity Day, 76–77; and Strikers'

Committee, 83–84, 89–90; and Chicano movement, 95–98 passim; Local 912 election, 94, 95–98 passim; attitude toward Teamsters, 134–35, 160, 172

"leapfrog" strategy, 28, 30

Lendvai, J. C., 144, 153

Lerma, Lydia, 88, 99, 103, 142, 189, 200

Lerma, Santos, 200

Lessen, Sherry, 102

Lewis, David Levering, 195

Lichtenstein, Nelson, 4–5

Littler, Mendelson, Fastiff, and Tichy, 54–56, 115–16, 155

Local 912 *Weekly Bulletin,* 145, 162, 164

Loma Prieta earthquake, 193–94

Lomeli, Cuca, 25, 89, 179, 184, 186, 188, 192, 200

López, Jose, 47, 49, 51–52, 57, 60, 66, 71, 73, 74, 79, 91, 93–94, 103, 105, 114, 115, 169

López, Sergio, 48, 49, 50, 53, 56, 57, 59, 60, 63, 68, 89, 92, 116, 123, 136, 139, 140, 141, 152, 154, 156, 158, 161, 162, 169, 189, 192, 199; early union career, 44–45; Local 912 elections, 92–93, 94–95, 98, 105; Shaw settlement, 119–20; Teamsters United 912, 118, 126–27; Western Conference work team, 144; Crosetti contract, 146, 148–49; approaches David Gill, 168; relations with Joint Council 7, 170–71, 176–77; bank protests, 172–73; NorCal contract, 178–79, 183, 185, 189; on NAFTA, 197

Los Siete de la Raza, 86

lower strata workers, 85

Lynd, Staughton, 209n, 225n

Macias, Jose, 179

Mack, Chuck, 42, 59, 67–70, 92, 112, 121, 127, 139, 143, 147, 158–59, 170–71, 173, 174, 176–77

MacMillan, Dave, 102

maintenance workers and mechanics, 81, 83, 122–23, 184–85

Maltzman, Dick, 177, 183–84, 185

Martinelli, 15

Martínez, Margarita, 58–59, 99

Master Freight Agreement, 3, 28, 29, 33, 108

McCartin, Joseph, ix–x

McClellan Committee on Labor Racketeering, 27

McFerrin, Todd, 102, 194

McWilliams, Carey, 20

MEChA, 72, 92

Medina, Maribel, 65–66

Medina, Terry, 123, 176

Mendez, Delia, 65–66, 102

Mexican American Legal Defense and Education Fund (MALDEF), 192

Mexican American Political association (MAA) 129

Mexican debt crisis, 7, 8, 196

Mexican frozen food industry, 49, 133, 195, 196–96

Mexican immigration, 7, 8, 18–25 passim

Meza, Paul, 149

Michoacan, 2, 25

Miller, Barb, 129–30

Miller, Bud, 129–30

Molino, Bea, 129

Monkawa, David, 184–85

Moody, Kim, 7
Moore, David, 16–17
Morales, Armando, 25, 72, 81, 94–95
Moreno, Chavelo, 25, 42, 58, 88, 92,
  104, 124, 152, 169, 171, 192,
  196, 200; approach to leadership, 81–82; hardship fund, 82,
  161, 171; arrest, 175–76; debate
  over NorCal contract, 180
Murillo, Soccoro, 99, 100, 103, 112

Nader, Ralph, 33
National Association of Manufacturers
  (NAM), 136
National Labor Relations Act
  (NLRA), 5, 54, 136, 137
National Labor Relations Board
  (NLRB), 31, 54, 56, 110, 136,
  150, 152, 154, 160, 172
New West, 133, 140
Nixon, Richard M., 5
NorCal Freezers, 168, 175
NorCal Frozen Foods, 177, 178, 180,
  183–84, 195
North American Free Trade Agree-
  ment (NAFTA), 196–97
Northern California Strike Support
  Committee (NCSSC), 87, 88,
  103, 129, 135, 137, 170, 173, 184

O'Ban, Tom, 163
Obledo, Mario, 92
Operation Dixie, 5
over-the-road trucking, 27–28

packinghouse workers, 130–31
Paff, Ken, 37, 46, 47, 72
Panetta, Leon, 48–49, 102
Paramo, Margarita, 43, 59, 99, 175–76
Parra, Juan, 48–49, 56, 76, 135

pattern bargaining, 108–09, 131–32
People's Immigration Service, 102
People's Park, 45
People's Slate (La Planilla del Pueblo),
  94–96, 105–06
permanent replacements, ix, 54–56, 131
Phelps-Dodge, 3, 56
Posse Freight, 64
postwar accord, 4–7, 8
Presser, Jackie, 112, 121, 143, 158, 159,
  165, 176
Progressive Alliance, 4

raiding, 30–32
Ramírez, Fernando, 113, 162–63
Ramírez, Guillermina, 43, 72, 78, 79, 80,
  86, 87 99, 105, 106, 129, 200
Raza Sí, 72, 77
Raza Unida, 77, 86
Reagan, Ronald, 3, 45, 55
Reclamation Act, 20–21
redbaiting, 31, 84, 95, 126, 136
Reese, George, 157
restraining order, 62–64, 68
Reuther, Walter, 29
Richard Shaw, 49, 50, 51, 63, 64,
  80–81, 94, 107, 109, 113, 115,
  122; contract talks, 54–61;
  strike settlement, 110–12, 119,
  120–23
right to strike, ix, 54–56
Ríos, Jose, 86
Ríos, Oscar, 77–78, 79–81, 83,
  85–87, 89, 96–97, 98, 176, 192,
  193–94, 197–98
Rodríguez, Eddie, 144
Rogers, Ray, 131, 132
Roth, Philip, xi

Safeway, 160, 161, 163

San Jose Mercury News, xiii, 92, 99, 173
Santa Clara County Central Labor
    Council, 141
Santa Cruz Sentinel, xiii 100, 111–12,
    148, 155, 156, 161–63, 176
Santa Cruz Strike Support Committee
    76, 81, 103, 115, 134, 173
Schilling, Elizabeth, xiii, 61
Seafarers International Union, 41
secondary boycotts, 28, 136–37, 138, 172
Seize the Time, 72
Shubsda, Bishop, 110
Siegel, Dan 48, 135,
Silver, Jon, x, 102, 116, 125, 135, 209n,
    215n,
Socialist Workers Party (SWP), 28
Soldo, Ann, 101, 127
Solidarity Day, 66, 67, 76–80, 89
Steinbeck, John, 10, 15
Stop the Draft Week, 45
Strikers' Committee, 73–74, 80–83, 87,
    92, 117, 122, 161, 164–5, 170;
    and People's Slate, 91, 94–95;
    certification vote, 151–52, 154,
    NorCal contract struggle,
    178–182

Taber, Lawrence, 110
Taft-Hartley Act, 28, 31, 136–37, 173
Teamsters, International Brother-
    hood of (IBT), 2, 3, 9, 11, 25,
    Chapter 2 passim, 40, 50, 51,
    53, 74–75, 81, 108, 109, 111,
    117, 118, 132, 134, 136, 139,
    146, 164, 171, 172, 176, 181,
    189, 199; Economic Boycott
    Campaign, 136–37, 156; Las
    Vegas convention, 142–44; and
    Wells Fargo Bank, 157–160,
    165, 173–74

Teamsters Joint Council 7 (JC7), 42,
    54, 59, 67–70, 92, 107, 112,
    116, 121, 127, 135, 139, 148,
    170–71, 177, 179, 183, 184
Teamsters Local 36, 158
Teamsters Local 70, 69, 144
Teamsters Local 679, 41
Teamsters Local 890, 78, 192, 199
Teamsters Local 912, 8, 9, 12, 26,
    Chapter 3 passim, 64, 67, 81,
    83, 85, 88–89, 116, 118, 119,
    121, 124, 126, 144, 161, 162
    165, 169, 172, 196–97, 200;
    1985 contrqact talks, 56–61;
    Joint Council 7 report, 68–79;
    1985 local elections, chapter
    6 passim; imposition of wage
    standard, 139–41, 143, 147–49;
    certification vote, 150–155;
    talks with David Gill, 168–69;
    bank picketing, 172–74; Nor-
    Cal contract struggle, 179–89
Teamsters, Western Conference of
    (WCF), 41, 69, 107, 138–39,
    143–45, 148, 158, 184; and
    certification vote, 151–53
Teamsters for a Democratic Union
    (TDU), 60, 62, 72, 74, 89,
    117, 134, 159, 199; origins,
    33–35; and cannery workers,
    37–38, 72; history of Watson-
    ville chapter, 46–52 passim;
    Solidarity Day, 66–67, 76–79;
    and Strikers' Committee, 81,
    83 ; Local 912 elections, 91–98
    passim, 105–106
Teamsters United 912, 115, 118, 127
Teng, Shiree, 88–89, 103, 129, 135, 169,
    175, 181, 184, 221n
Termicold, 65

Torres, Alfonso, 94
Torres, Benjamin, 116
Torres, Eddie, 95
Torres, Enrique, 25–26, 95, 99, 116, 149
Torres, Esperanza, 25–26, 95, 99, 104,
        116, 149, 199
Treaty of Guadalupe-Hidalgo, 19, 38
Trine, Ron, 112, 114, 124, 125, 151,
        158, 163, 168
Trotskyism, 28, 34
Trujillo, Aurora, 63, 68, 80–81, 99, 117,
        122, 184, 186
trusteeship, 109, 142, 144, 177, 191
TWA strike, 142

US Steel, 6–7
unemployment benefits, 60, 100, 124,
        149, 161, 164
United Auto Workers (UAW), 3, 4, 29
United Cannery, Agricultural, Pack-
        inghouse and Allied Workers
        (UCAPAWA), see Food, Tobac-
        co, and Agricultural Workers
        (FTA)
United Farm Workers (UFW), 18, 26,
        35, 36, 43, 45, 69, 75–76, 78,
        132–33, 135, 137, 138, 141,
        142, 165, 198
United Food and Commercial Workers
        (UFCW) Local P-9, 11,
        129–132, 142, 191
United Foods, 196
United Steelworkers (USW), 3
Unity, xi, 90, 142–43, 160, 165

Vawter, Larry, 59, 63, 112, 124, 175
Verduzco, Smiley, 50, 59–60, 110, 120,
        162, 163, 172

Walsh, Bill, 67–68, 92, 110, 117, 127,
        130, 144, 164
Walsh, Joan, 97–98
warehouse fire, 114, 162
Watsonville Canning, 11, 12, 16, 17, 18,
        25–26, 40, 42, 49, 53, 56–58,
        59–63 passim, 65, 68, 80–81,
        82, 89, 94, 100, 107, 110–11,
        112, 113–14, 115, 119–123
        passim, 126, 131, 133, 138–149
        passim, 158, 159, 160, 161,
        167–68, 174–75, 178–79 181,
        183, 184; conditions in plant,
        43–44, 58–59, 64–65; Juan
        Parra case, 48–49; 1982 wage
        concessions, 50, 53, 54, 109;
        certification vote, 150–154,
        172; Sentinel expose, 161–163;
        and Wells Fargo Bank, 9, 54,
        154–157, 164–65, 174, 177
Watsonville City Council, 99, 100–03
        passim, 118, 127; 1989 elec-
        tions, 192–94
Watsonville Frozen Food Employers
        Association, 109, 111, 133
Watsonville High School, 25, 65–66,
        102, 129, 194
Watsonville on Strike, x, 125, 215n
Watsonville Register-Pajaronian, xiii, 1,
        59, 60, 61, 83, 100, 112, 114,
        115, 121, 126, 149, 157, 163,
        173, 175
Watsonville Strike Support Commit-
        tee, 76, 101, 102, 103, 116, 121,
        135, 145–46, 173, 194
Weinmeister, Arnie, 69–70, 143–44, 159
Weis, Skinny, 129
Wells Fargo Bank, 9, 54, 137–38,
        154–57, 165, 168, 169–70,
        172–74, 177–78
Western Conference of Teamsters

(WCT), see Teamsters, West-
    ern Conference of
Wynn, William, 131

Ybarra, Manuel, 81, 117
Ybarrolaza, Alex, 83, 95, 141, 153, 154,
    160–61, 164–65, 169–70; re-
    port to Joint Council 7, 67–70;
    Shaw contract, 107–110,
    119–121; boycott strategy,
    135–136, 137–39; at IBT
    convention, 143–44; Crosetti
    lockout, 148–49; bank divest-
    ment, 157–59

Zavella, Patricia, 24

About Haymarket Books

Haymarket Books is a nonprofit, progressive book distributor and publisher, a project of the Center for Economic Research and Social Change. We believe that activists need to take ideas, history, and politics into the many struggles for social justice today. Learning the lessons of past victories, as well as defeats, can arm a new generation of fighters for a better world. As Karl Marx said, "The philosophers have merely interpreted the world; the point, however, is to change it."

We take inspiration and courage from our namesakes, the Haymarket Martyrs, who gave their lives fighting for a better world. Their 1886 struggle for the eight-hour day, which gave us May Day, the international workers' holiday, reminds workers around the world that ordinary people can organize and struggle for their own liberation. These struggles continue today across the globe—struggles against oppression, exploitation, hunger, and poverty.

It was August Spies, one of the Martyrs targeted for being an immigrant and an anarchist, who predicted the battles being fought to this day. "If you think that by hanging us you can stamp out the labor movement," Spies told the judge, "then hang us. Here you will tread upon a spark, but here, and there, and behind you, and in front of you, and everywhere, the flames will blaze up. It is a subterranean fire. You cannot put it out. The ground is on fire upon which you stand."

We could not succeed in our publishing efforts without the generous financial support of our readers. Many people contribute to our project through the Haymarket Sustainers program, where donors receive free books in return for their monetary support. If you would like to be a part of this program, please contact us at info@haymarketbooks.org.

Shop our full catalog online at www.haymarketbooks.org or call 773-583-7884.

Fields of Resistance: The Struggle of Florida's Farmworkers for Justice
Silvia Giagnoni

The Future of Our Schools: Teachers Unions and Social Justice
Lois Weiner

*In Solidarity: Essays on Working-Class Organization
and Strategy in the United States*
Kim Moody

The Labor Wars: From the Molly Maguires to the Sit-Downs
Sidney Lens

Poor Workers' Unions: Rebuilding Labor from Below
completely revised and updated edition
Vanessa Tait, Afterwords by Bill Fletcher Jr. and Cristina Tzintzún

Rank and File: Personal Histories by Working-Class Organizers
Alice Lynd and Staughton Lynd

*Subterranean Fire: A History of Working-Class Radicalism
in the United States*
Sharon Smith

Also Available
from Haymarket Books

A Short History of the U.S. Working Class:
From Colonial Times to the Twenty-First Century
Paul Le Blanc

Autoworkers Under the Gun
Gregg Shotwell

Bananeras: Women Transforming the Banana Unions of Latin America
Dana Frank

Building Global Labor Solidarity
in a Time of Accelerating Globalization
Edited by Kim Scipes

China on Strike: Narratives of Workers' Resistance
Edited by Hao Ren, Eli Friedman, and Zhongjin Li

The Civil Wars in U.S. Labor: Birth of a New Workers' Movement
or Death Throes of the Old?
Steve Early

Detroit: I Do Mind Dying: A Study in Urban Revolution
Marvin Surkin and Dan Georgakas

Disposable Domestics:
Immigrant Women Workers in the Global Economy, second edition
Grace Chang, Foreword by Ai-jen Poo, Afterword by Alicia Garza

Doing History from the Bottom Up: On E.P. Thompson, Howard
Zinn, and Rebuilding the Labor Movement from Below
Staughton Lynd